GEONOMICS INSTITUTE FOR INTERNATIONAL ECONOMIC
ADVANCEMENT SERIES
Michael P. Claudon, Series Editor

Investing in Reform

Doing Business in a Changing Soviet Union

Edited by Michael P. Claudon
and Tamar L. Gutner

NEW YORK UNIVERSITY PRESS
New York and London

© 1991 by Geonomics Institute for International Economic Advancement
All rights reserved
Manufactured in the United States of America

Library of Congress Cataloging-in-Publication Data

Investing in reform : doing business in a changing Soviet Union
   / edited by Michael P. Claudon and Tamar L. Gutner.
        p.   cm. — (Geonomics Institute for International Economic
Advancement series)
   Includes index.
   ISBN 0-8147-1465-X
   1. Soviet Union—economic policy—1986—Congresses.
   2. Soviet Union—Foreign economic relations—Congresses.
   3. Investments, foreign—Soviet Union—Congresses.
   I. Claudon, Michael P.   II. Gutner, Tamar L.   III. Series.
   HC336.26.I565   1991
   332.6'73'0947—dc20   91-25090
                                                                  CIP

New York University Press books are printed on acid-free paper,
and their binding materials are chosen for strength and durability.

Contents

Acknowledgments

The seminar that produced this book was generously supported by Geonomics' corporate and seminar sponsors: The Dun & Bradstreet Corporation; Edward Aycoth Worldwide; Henry Kaufman & Company, Inc.; Holstein Corporation; Jones International, Inc.; New York Stock Exchange, Inc.; Scott-European Corporation; Sharpoint; and SAS (Scandinavian Airlines System).

We are especially grateful for an opportunity to work with a spirited, immensely purposeful, and particularly diverse group seminar participants. Their commitment and hard work contributed significantly to the seminar's concrete results. Those who contributed to this volume, all of whom completed their post-seminar rewriting and editing in an unheard of two months, deserve a special thank you from Geonomics.

The staff of the Geonomics Institute, including Nancy Ward, Elizabeth Leeds, George Bellerose, Ann Hoefle, and Melissa Dasakis, somehow made the Herculean task of organizing and executing the program seem effortless. I know the truth, and I thank them for their commitment and skill. Colleen Duncan's editorial and production assistance are also deeply appreciated. Her ability to transform a disorganized pile of edited manuscripts into a finished text is remarkable. I wish especially to recognize the immense contribution that Tamar L. Gutner made to the seminar, from conception through execution. Hers was a virtuoso performance in what was her baptism as Geonomics' research director.

Finally, Geonomics wishes to extend its heartfelt gratitude, and I offer my personal thanks, to Jenik Radon. Jenik is one of those special people whose boundless energy is matched only by his personal generosity. It was through Jenik's unrelenting effort that Geonomics was able to make its initial contacts in the Baltics and eventually to secure commitments to participate from the prime ministers of Estonia and Latvia, Edgar Savisaar and Ivars Godmanis, respectively.

Michael P. Claudon

Foreword

Today's Soviet Union is vastly different from the Soviet Union of just six years ago, possessing a far more accommodating environment for foreign trade and investment. Yet six years into perestroika, Western investors are confronted by more rather than less complexity. The turbulent uncertainty surrounding the Soviet Union's future political shape, coupled with the certainty that economic interdependence among its current republics will remain, greatly complicates strategy formulation. Whether investors will be operating within one large internal market or among fully independent, largely nonaffiliated, and even contentious states is difficult, if not impossible, to know. The "war of laws," in turn, makes it difficult for investors to know which laws will govern their businesses in the 1990s and beyond.

The Geonomics May 1991 seminar explored a variety of economic, legal, and investment-related perspectives on the state of Soviet reform and prospects for doing business in the changing Soviet landscape. This excellent collection of papers delivered at the seminar offers, individually and collectively, fresh perspectives on these issues. As such, the volume contributes to Geonomics' mission of devising workable and creative solutions to compelling economic problems.

The Geonomics Institute was formed in 1987 as a private, nonprofit, nonpartisan, globally oriented organization. Three years ago, we began focusing on one of the great challenges for the next decade, Soviet and Eastern European economic and political trans-

formation. While fully cognizant of the huge challenges and obstacles on the path ahead, Geonomics is getting results by working
with the people who will ultimately generate the needed changes.
Rather than studying and producing grandiose plans, Geonomics
is attacking specific problems using a pragmatic nuts-and-bolts approach, which builds on the successes and strengths of Western political and economic systems.

Geonomics' strategy of isolating and attacking specific problems from several angles helps to facilitate change from below and
to achieve measurable gains amid the myriad political, cultural,
and economic challenges associated with transforming the Soviet
Union and Eastern Europe into decentralized societies.

The Institute operates on three planes: our seminars challenge
small groups of top policymakers, business leaders, consultants,
lawyers, and scholars from East and West to identify key issues
and produce tangible, specific recommendations and action agen-
das; seminar issues, in turn, inspire in-depth workshops in which
smaller groups of experts develop detailed policy recommendations
and draft legislation relating to infrastructure development and
institution building; and, on the local level, we identify concrete
opportunities to foster change by designing and administering
self-sustaining, on-the-ground programs.

We welcome ideas and opinions for better achieving our goals.

Michael P. Claudon
President and Managing Director
Geonomics Institute

Introduction

Hopes for economic and political reform in the Soviet Union looked bleak in early 1991. President Mikhail Gorbachev's lurch to the right, the growing political struggle between the center and the republics, the military crackdown in the Baltics, and impending economic collapse increased uncertainty about the direction of reform, and indeed the political shape the Soviet state will assume. The shaky situation has prompted Western observers to focus increasing attention on the relationship between the center and the republics, and perhaps equally important, the relationships among the emerging assemblage of republics.

Pessimists say perestroika has failed, and disintegration and disunion are now the common terms used to describe the direction economic and political change are taking. Optimists say perestroika has given the republics more power by allowing the centralized structure to crumble. They think Gorbachev will stand up to conservative forces, and they foresee the speedy implementation of a union treaty that will transfer substantial power from Moscow to the republics that choose to be part of a reconstituted union.

In this time of flux, foreign investors are understandably skittish about the many risks of the Soviet market. The rise of conservatives such as Prime Minister Valentin Pavlov, who in early 1991 accused Western banks of plotting to overthrow the Soviet government, is menacing. The "war of laws" between the center and the republics makes it difficult for investors to know which laws govern, or, indeed, whether they are dealing with one market or fif-

teen separate markets. Local authorities, in turn, are asserting
themselves and seeking more power, making it increasingly difficult for investors to know at which government level, and with
whom, they must negotiate deals. Add to that the usual bureaucratic delays, red tape, difficulties repatriating profit, and other
well-known problems associated with the Soviet market, and it is
no surprise that many big Western companies are happier sitting
on the sidelines. Out of the almost 3,000 joint ventures established
by April 1991, only around one-third were operating.[1] Nonetheless, Western companies are keenly aware of the importance of
establishing a foothold in a potentially vast market of almost 300
million people. They know that whatever political shape the Soviet
Union takes, its current parts will remain economically interdependent for some time.

The Geonomics Institute convened an impressive mix of policymakers, business executives, lawyers, and scholars from East and
West in May 1991 to address trade and investment strategies in the
changing Soviet landscape. The seminar participants included the
prime ministers from the "breakaway" republics of Latvia and
Estonia; the executive vice-president of Vnesheconombank; the
chief economist of Deutsche Bank; the chairman of the U.S. headquarters of Yamaichi Securities; business executives involved in
setting up joint ventures in the Soviet Union; lawyers; and aca-
demicians whose views on the Soviet economy are widely published—in short, a group of people whose views and actions have
played a role in influencing thinking and events surrounding the
Soviet Union's transition. Gathering in Middlebury, Vermont,
the participants spent three days engaged in lively discussion and
heated debate before producing concrete policy recommendations.

One recurring debate pitted Western economists against Baltic
policymakers. In his keynote speech, Deutsche Bank's Norbert
Walter expressed his hope that under a new union treaty the ruble
would remain a common currency. The high degree of economic
interdependence among republics makes it meaningful to have
one currency, even if republics go their own way politically, he argued. Small currency areas, he said, "create barriers between regions, segment markets into very small pieces, and finally destroy
internal markets." Economist Gertrude E. Schroeder, in turn, argued that it is "economic folly" for individual republics to take steps

1. John Lloyd, "Joint Ventures Gleam Amid Economic Gloom," *Financial Times,*
April 26, 1991.

to fragment interlinked inter-republic markets, as they are now doing.

The response was immediate and strong. Latvian Prime Minister Ivars Godmanis countered by asking how the Soviet Union's dissimilar peoples could share anything, let alone a common currency. He and Estonian Prime Minister Edgar Savisaar acknowledged that their economies are inextricably linked to the Soviet Union; yet they also insisted that they can only prosper as politically independent countries.

Obviously, the number-one priority for the Baltic leaders is to achieve *de facto* political independence. The Baltic leaders see the establishment of free-market economic systems with ties to the West, independent of the collapsing Soviet system, as a major step in this direction. As a result, they have adopted their own economic reforms, from price hikes to foreign investment laws, as a means toward achieving economic sovereignty. For the Baltic states, the establishment of independent currencies and financial systems is as much a political statement as perceived economic necessity.

Is the Baltics' position unique? Perhaps in the sense that their struggle is for a *restoration* of independence following their forced entry into the Soviet Union in 1940, which most of the international community has never recognized *de jure.* Yet other republics have also declared their intention to leave the union. Georgians voted overwhelmingly for independence in their March 1991 referendum, and Georgian deputies declared formal independence the following month. Both Moldavia and Armenia joined Georgia and the Baltics in boycotting the March 1991 all-union referendum as well as the landmark meeting in April 1991 in which Gorbachev and the nine remaining republics agreed on a framework calling for the speedy adoption of a new union treaty, the adoption of a new Constitution, and all-union elections.

The Baltics, in fact, have set the stage for challenging the center's power. Republics likely to remain in a reconstituted union are clamoring for much greater autonomy, and indeed are taking steps toward achieving it. Russia, for example, has challenged union law in a number of important areas, from property to banking. The Ukraine, meanwhile, hopes it can develop a parallel currency that will eventually lead to the replacement of the ruble. Negotiations over a new union treaty are negotiations about the distribution of power between the center and the republics.

Another issue that repeatedly arose at the seminar concerned appropriate investment strategies for approaching the Soviet market. The seminar was entitled "Gateways to Trade and Investment in a Changing Soviet Landscape," reflecting the interest of many Geonomics members in exploring the concept of a "gateway," or strategic location for entering the Soviet market. Seminar participants agreed that the concept was useful but unsatisfactory as the sole focus of discussion, which broadened to look at the myriad other obstacles confronting potential investors. Group discussions on investment strategies explored steps republics could take to encourage direct foreign investment as well as criticized the lack of a level playing field from which Western companies could compete with each other for such investment. U.S. business leaders, in particular, felt that they had a disadvantageous position relative to their competitors due to the Jackson-Vanik Amendment's punitive tariffs, the meager U.S. Export-Import Bank credits available to cover U.S. exports to the Soviet Union, and the Soviets' lack of most-favored-nation (MFN) status.

This volume consists of the papers presented at the seminar, as well as the policy recommendations produced by all of its participants. The papers either reflect or provoked the many debates that took place. Part I presents different perspectives on the Soviet economy and the state of economic reform. Norbert Walter, in his keynote address in Chapter 1, paints a gloomy picture of the economy. Six years of perestroika have not resulted in economic growth and stability. Instead, we have seen a sharp decline in production hand in hand with a rise in money supply and the twin budget and current-account deficits. According to Walter, an important reason behind the economy's poor health is the inconsistency of Soviet reform efforts. He believes that the Kremlin is still seeking "a third way" between market and planned economies. Walter believes that the Soviet Union can only be reformed from the periphery, and that this periphery should have greater autonomy. However, as mentioned above, he argues strongly against any kind of separatism. The West, says Walter, should "help the Soviets help themselves" by transferring Western know-how and helping reintegrate the former Eastern bloc into the world economy.

Gertrude E. Schroeder in Chapter 2 looks in depth at economic relations among the Soviet republics. These relations are characterized by a tight web of interdependencies that grew out of centrally dictated policies of industrial development. According to Schroeder, whatever political relationships evolve among the republics, they will remain dependent on each others' markets for some time, whether they like it or not. In embarking on the daunting task of creating a market economy, it is in the republics' interest to be able to exchange their goods and services with their neighbors as freely as possible, she argues.

According to Vladimir Popov in Chapter 3, the Soviet Union missed an important opportunity to restructure its economy in the mid-1980s, because the economy's relative health then would have reduced the costs and pain of restructuring that now seem inevitable. Popov argues that a program slashing production quotas, replacing rationed supply with wholesale trade, and freeing prices would have quickly fueled the development of market forces. He discusses the negative consequences that arise as part of the restructuring process and recommends various policies to help counteract them. Popov is highly critical of the government's dithering over reform, especially since what he sees as its mismanagement of the economy has made the environment for reform that much more difficult. Whatever reform strategy is chosen, says Popov, the issues at stake now are how the costs will be distributed among people, republics, and regions, and to what extent people are willing to swallow the bitter medicine without strikes and unrest.

Eugene Uljanov in Chapter 4 discusses and reviews recent laws on banking, currency, and investment. He argues that these new laws are important steps toward a more decentralized, free market. For example, the reorganization of the Soviet banking system that resulted from laws adopted in late 1990 has separated the central bank, Gosbank, from newly established commercial banks and has allowed greater independence among formerly all-union financial institutions. New currency laws, in turn, allow foreigners to hold rubles within the Soviet Union, while increasing the ability of Soviet entities and individuals to hold and use hard currency. Uljanov believes that new investment laws, by protecting foreign and domestic investors and allowing 100 percent foreign ownership of business ventures in the Soviet Union, are "the starting point for a civil society managed largely on the basis of private contracts and their enforcement in public courts."

A major component of economic reform will no doubt be privatization. Given the fact that Eastern European nations are already embarking on an unprecedented attempt to transfer virtually their entire economies into private hands, the lessons they have learned may be of great value to the architects of privatization in the Soviet Union. In Chapter 5, Roger S. Leeds focuses on Eastern Europe's early privatization experiences, highlighting the issues that Soviet decisionmakers will be addressing. In addition to the more obvious needs—such as strong legal and regulatory frameworks and macroeconomic stability—Leeds stresses subtler political prerequisites as well. For example, he points out the fact that policymakers tend to underestimate the time it takes to privatize industries, which often inflates public expectations. And in light of growing disenchantment toward privatization in Eastern Europe, Leeds recommends that policymakers communicate with those who have a stake in the outcome of privatization, as well as specifically attempt to allay the fears of those who may be hurt in the process, such as workers who risk losing their jobs.

The papers in Part II critically assess three important aspects of the evolving legal landscape. Kaj Hobér in Chapter 6 examines recent trends in Soviet legislation relating to foreign trade and investment. Despite an outpouring of legislation, from decrees on joint ventures to the latest draft union treaty, Hobér argues that the power struggle between the center and the republics, and the resulting "war of laws," has created a legal vacuum. As a result, the impact of new legislation is likely to remain unclear until the power struggle is resolved. Hobér analyzes the constitutional crisis in the Soviet Union and examines steps being taken toward a new union treaty. Of critical importance, he says, is the need for the government to recognize the degree of decentralization that has already occurred. A union treaty can be a peace treaty among republics, Hobér argues. Unfortunately, the latest draft treaty, from March 1991, contains vague language that opens the door to continuing dispute.

The power struggles taking place in the Soviet Union are not just occurring between the republics and the center; various levels of local government, too, are becoming increasingly active in seeking greater control. Emily Silliman describes in Chapter 7 the complex structure of local governments in the Soviet Union and examines areas where they have a great deal of regulatory authority, such as in allocating land and housing, as well as taxation. Often, however, the lines of authority are unclear, which Silliman says has encouraged local governments to seek an increase in their power. The result has been an increasing degree of organizational confusion at every level of local government.

Peter B. Maggs argues in Chapter 8 that the Soviets must revamp their property-rights system in order to create the foundation for a working market economy and to attract significant foreign investment. Ownership rights, still uncertain, must be defined and protected. Maggs discusses many laws passed in the 1980s aimed at protecting enterprise rights, and he finds their enforcement mechanisms weak. Property rights will remain insecure, says Maggs, until strong judicial protection of these rights exists. Maggs adds that efficacious laws are themselves insufficient without other aspects of a market economy, such as a convertible ruble and free prices. Also essential to the creation of a new property-rights system is an end to the "war of laws" between republics and center, so that an effective system for registering ownership interest can exist. Maggs also recommends a revised tax system, mortgage and security registration, and more information about the law.

In Part III, Josef C. Brada, Ali M. Kutan, and Jenik Radon evaluate the "gateway" as a strategy for trade and investment in socialist economies. In Chapter 9, Brada and Kutan start from the perspective of the gateways themselves, by looking at the role Austria, Finland, and Hong Kong play as middlemen to East-West trade. In addition to sharing the characteristics of being small, highly developed, and highly dependent on international trade, these three countries also have unique "geopolitical assets" that make them attractive as halfway houses between East and West. There are many advantages to being a main link between Western business and the Soviet Union, Eastern Europe, and China. This specialized trade has created many jobs in banking, commerce, and trade, for example. However, being a gateway country also has costs. Brada and Kutan discuss the economic costs, such as the fact that the gateway countries' trading systems have been distorted to various degrees in order to accommodate the East's trading systems. They also look at political costs. For example, the political neutrality that has benefited Finland and Austria in their trade with the East has also hurt their ability to participate in European integration.

According to Jenik Radon in Chapter 10, the term "gateway" is the latest in a line of promotional jargon used by the East to attract foreign investment. Yet for businesses seeking access to the Soviet market, location is critical, and this often points toward establishing a base outside the Soviet Union, in a nearby strategic or competitive location. Radon argues that the Baltics are the premier gateway to the Soviet market for a variety of reasons, including geographical location, a well-educated population, and a positive environment for business. Radon points out that the Baltics are oriented toward the West and have embraced Western business practices, while at the same time they have a deep understanding of how the Soviet system works. He concludes by advising the Baltic nations to pursue a variety of strategies that enhance their gateway status, including the maintenance of a "sufficiently" open border with the Soviet Union, the establishment of a strong infrastructure and independent judicial and legal systems.

Part IV contains the findings and recommendations of the three working groups. In Chapter 11, the investment strategies working group tackles its area from two perspectives. First, it addresses the issue of what framework Soviet republics need to put into place in order to attract foreign investment. Soviet republics cannot create an environment for sustained Western investment until the power struggle between the center and the republics is resolved; basic laws on property ownership are established; a working financial system, which includes currency convertibility, is in place; and each republic is committed to introducing a coherent economic reform program. The group also looks at the most important factors Western companies must consider before moving into the Soviet market. Companies, for example, must decide where they want to be on the "risk-return frontier." The group advises companies who want to make quick profits to look elsewhere; a five- to ten-year period is seen as the minimum planning horizon for the Soviet market. In addition, the high cost of doing business in the Soviet Union may exclude small or even medium-sized companies unless they sell through an agent based in the country.

In Chapter 12, the working group addressing inter-republic economic relations recommends ways in which republics could optimize trade flows under two scenarios: a renewed federation and a confederation. Under the former, the group recommends that a democratically elected federal government's functions should include management of the communications and transportation infrastructure, the conduct of monetary policy, and the maintenance of an independent budget. Internal and external trade would be promoted through policies including the removal of price controls, the abolishment of mandatory state orders, and the introduction of laws that create free trade and encourage foreign investment. On the republic level, governments should have their own budgets and taxing authority, while promoting privatization and competition. Republics can also promote their exports and encourage private investment through special incentives.

Under a confederation, the republics would also take on the recommendations suggested for the center under the first scenario. The group also advises the republics to create a central body to manage agreed-upon functions, along with a method of sharing this body's costs. Trade flows can be promoted by capitalizing on the existing internal common market and external common tariff. The group recommends that the confederation adopt European Community legal codes and GATT trading rules.

In Chapter 13, the third working group recommends legal prerequisites for a market economy. Although full private ownership is a fundamental factor, the group realizes that private ownership of land remains a politically sticky issue in the Soviet Union. It therefore addresses the issue of long-term land leasing, which it finds acceptable, under an appropriate legal framework. Privatization plays a key role in the creation of a market economy. The working group recommends the privatization of farms and small businesses; industries made up of multiple enterprises; industries that enjoy an artificial monopoly; and industries that have a natural monopoly. The group advises strategic industries, such as nuclear arms plants, to remain under state control. The group notes that many encouraging laws supporting a market system are now in place, but it warns that progress made can be easily undone if the "war of laws" is not resolved.

For foreign investors, a recurring lesson to come out of the working groups, taken together, was best summed up by one participant, Ben Jaffray, who for many years guided the financial aspects of Cargill's Soviet and Eastern European operations: "Make sure that your investment plan is flexible. Identify potential 'escape routes' if something goes wrong. Above all, do not commit more resources than you can afford to lose in a worse-case scenario." There are immense business opportunities in this currently troubled land. The pioneers who enter this market today have an excellent chance to reap huge rewards early in the next century.

Michael P. Claudon
Tamar L. Gutner

Part I

Scoreboard on Economic Reform

1

The Soviet Union in the Trough: A Call to Action

Norbert Walter

The euphoria and rejoicing that greeted the revolutionary developments in Eastern Europe during 1989 are over. We now realize that the road to true democracy and the market economy will be long and hard. East-West trade relations have not received the boost originally expected. Instead, we see a collapse of that trade, particularly, a collapse of trade within the former economic region of Eastern Europe and between Eastern Europe and the Soviet Union. Is this surprising? I have to admit that I am surprised. I was hoping for a better outcome, and I believe that there were chances for a better outcome. But to a larger degree, I think we are not really capable of fully understanding the time needed for the readjustment and the complete overhaul of that system.

For us in the West, the goal must not simply be to turn political changes in East-West relations into economic opportunities. It must be much more. We ought to facilitate the reintegration of formerly isolated eastern economies into the world economy, which necessitates the creation, the establishment, and the transplant of institutions, structures, behavior, and attitudes.

This process is obviously difficult even for those countries in Central and Eastern Europe that have only been deprived for one generation of being a democracy and a market economy. It is much more difficult for a country such as the Soviet Union, which

This chapter is a lightly edited version of the keynote speech delivered at the Geonomics seminar in May 1991.

for three generations has followed a path that isolated itself from the rest of the world.

The present economic chaos in the Soviet Union and Eastern Europe can be explained in several ways. In Eastern Europe, I view the current difficulties in Czechoslovakia, Hungary, and Poland as the unavoidable fallout from the transition from planned to market economies. They are coping with the natural cost of adjustment. Poland is a case in point. The process toward democratization in Poland has been far reaching, and economic reforms have been quite abrupt and dramatic. Still, it is obvious that there are negative economic consequences, and I believe that the Poles know that they have not yet reached the trough. Certainly, however, Poland is a country that has good reason to be hopeful. There are positive expectations; the migration out of Poland has come to a complete stop despite the hardships. I believe it is obvious that a more courageous reform pays off even if it does not pay off as yet in terms of economic improvement.

The present economic chaos in the Soviet Union can be explained in various ways:

1. It is the unavoidable economic heritage of seventy years of communism.
2. It is the logical consequence of the negative side-effects of perestroika and glasnost.
3. It is the consequence of the lack of impetus for a stronger, more encompassing radical reform.

It is difficult to come up with a clear-cut answer. Nevertheless, one must be found. The pace of Soviet reforms and economic development will, to a great extent, dictate Western strategy. Until now, developments have been far from encouraging. Foreign business analysts and Soviet economic policymakers agree on the deplorable state of the economy. Six years of perestroika have changed the Soviet economy, but they have not brought stability or growth.

My personal impression from a visit in September 1990 is that the two sides, the old establishment and the radical reformers, are both blocking improvement. I share some understanding for both groups. Gosplan, the Soviet State Planning Committee, is incapable of understanding a market economy—they even want to plan it.

We in the West ridicule such an attitude, and we, of course, understand that it cannot work. On the other hand, I understand that many people do not fully share the views of the radical reformers. Throughout most of the Soviet Union, entrepreneurial spirit and experience do not exist, not even in the memory of the grandfathers. A market system is based on entrepreneurship. A market economy cannot be designed by Moscow. It can only come from the periphery, where there is more contact with entrepreneurs and sharper memories of that entrepreneurial history.

Meanwhile, problems are mounting and the economy hurtles toward complete chaos. Statistics on this decline are very good if they are about numbers and tons. They are next to worthless in talking about values such as a concept of net production or GNP. Therefore, I think it is not too important to discuss those numbers. It is obvious that production dropped last year in the industrial sector and is now falling at an even faster pace. The construction sector is in bad shape, and transportation, so very important for improvement of the economy, is in extremely bad shape.

At the same time, the money supply continues to swell. The Soviet budget deficit is increasing, a debt of something like 100 billion rubles, or a staggering 10 percent of GNP. The root of this gaping deficit is not additional investment expenditures but huge government outlays for military apparatus and subsidies. In light of the current situation, the prospects for a radical turnaround policy seem dim. In addition, the already meager supply of goods, even basic consumer goods, available to the Soviet population is shrinking from month to month. Consequently, we have higher personal incomes but a smaller supply of goods. The few goods that are available are often unneeded. They are bought anyway, because they are worth more than the steadily eroding ruble.

The government's currency reform, such as its move this winter to withdraw 50- and 100-ruble notes from circulation, was an attempt to come to grips with the problem. The price increases in April 1991 would have been a step in the right direction if they had not been accompanied by the creation of additional money. There is ample evidence of ongoing ruble printing, while simultaneously the production of goods is declining.

Soviet foreign trade is also in increasingly dire straits. During the last year, one would have hoped that increased oil prices would have helped to keep the current account of the Soviet Union in surplus, but the opposite occurred. The Soviet Union now has a current-account deficit that is adding to the foreign debt, and that, of course, is creating difficulties for the coming years. The recent IMF–OECD study indicates that the Soviet Union's 1990 current-account deficit was over US$10 billion (not including gold). Only three years ago, the country had a US$7 billion surplus.

The Soviets now must grapple with extensive debt-service obligations. Not only is the debt high, but repayment schedules are poorly structured. In short, the country's hard-currency earnings potential will be limited severely at a time when hard-currency reserves are at their lowest point in ten years. In theory, the January 1991 switch to world market prices and hard-currency payments for intra-Comecon trade constitutes a positive development for Soviet trade. However, it will have little immediate impact on the country's hard-currency situation. One reason is that Central and Eastern European countries have had surpluses in recent years and will initially try to finance their Soviet imports with these surpluses.

The most important source of hard currency, Soviet oil and natural gas deliveries to the West, decreased because of the poor shape of pipelines and production wells. At the same time, Soviet demand for imports, both consumer and industrial goods, is exceedingly high. However, the narrow, one-dimensional range of Soviet exports to the West, mainly oil and natural gas, makes it almost impossible to generate hard currency for these imports. The export of manufactured goods is not an alternative, because the quality of those products is not up to Western standards. At a moment when the government needs to prove that economic perestroika works and can improve the standard of living, it cannot afford additional imports.

What would remedy this situation? Western loans would certainly allow the Soviet Union to expand its level of imports. There is little leeway, however, to take such a step. The level of foreign debt has accelerated in the last few years and is now about US$70 billion. Since 1985, the country's debt ratio, the ratio of net foreign debt to annual foreign currency earnings, has worsened from 100 to 150 percent. A 200 percent ratio is considered dangerous. Our bank's assessment is that the debt-level ratio will reach 220 percent by the end of 1991. Even more alarming than those ratios are the repeated payment delays for Western exports. We had an intensification of that problem in 1990. Fresh loans, like the 5 billion DM loan from a group of German banks in 1990, which mainly went to cover overdue claims, were a temporary cure. Claims are overdue again. The result has been a considerable downgrading of the Soviet Union's credit rating by Deutsche Bank analysts and other observers.

It is very doubtful that the Soviet Union will be able to restore its once enviable credit rating anytime soon. Nonguaranteed bank loans to the Soviet Union total about US$35 billion. Today, it is obvious that commercial banks will no longer lend fresh money to the Soviet Union without government guarantees. I believe this will not change in the immediate future.

What would be an alternative? The best one would be direct investment from Western countries that creates the basis for long-term cooperation. But hopes of rapid increase in Western investment have gone unfulfilled, even though the Soviet Union began to open its market to joint ventures in 1987. Since then, the legal foundations for such ventures have been strengthened. As of the fall of 1990, 100 percent foreign-owned firms are permitted.

While there is an impressive number of registered joint ventures, about 2,500, only about 300 are working. Western investors face a host of problems in joint ventures: distorted price structures; suffocating bureaucratic regulations; collapsing infrastructure; and repatriation of profits. All in all, I believe that joint ventures have been much less significant as a catalyst for trade and interaction between the Soviet Union and the West than was originally anticipated.

What are the underlying reasons for the bad state of the Soviet economy? First, Soviet leaders have been indecisive and inconsistent in their reform efforts. For too long, Soviet leaders believed they could simply revamp the old structures. Only in 1990, the sixth year of perestroika, did the Soviet government finally publicly acknowledge the benefits of a market economy. Nonetheless, we still do not have a true acceptance of private property, free prices, and clearing markets as the most promising route to reform. Even today, Soviet economic policy oscillates between continued orthodox centralization and the liberal reform concepts of Stanislav Shatalin and other radical economists. Shatalin's 500-Day Plan was not accepted last summer, largely because Gosplan believes that the hardships involved in such a program are not politically or socially acceptable at this time. Similarly, whatever the merits of the Gorbachev plan announced in the fall of 1990, the plan fails to lay down the official stance on such fundamental issues as property rights and privatization. Experts agree that private property, including real estate, is an absolute prerequisite for successful economic reform.

Second, a credible political and legal system needed for a democratic system and market economy does not exist. The war of legislation between the center and the republics and among the republics themselves must be resolved if the outside world and the Soviet people are to have faith in their government. It is very important to have a functioning and accepted constitution. We have learned that in Germany as we try to integrate the two parts of the country.

We are lucky that the West German basic law, a model that has been tested for forty years, is accepted in the eastern part of the country. And we are lucky that this system is not a centralized system but a system where the federal states play an important role. I believe that when the allies helped us to develop our basic law in 1948 they wanted to weaken Germany by applying a noncentralist solution. Our federal states had an important say in our Constitution and that, in the end, has meant that we now have a more acceptable Constitution for modern times. Thus, the five eastern states could easily apply for and take over a legal system that has been tried for forty years. This is not an option open to other countries and certainly not to the Soviet Union. Without such a legal structure and consensus, however, all talks about private property or the right to contract are meaningless. We have learned in financial markets that it takes years and years to win the confidence of the investor. That is important to remember.

In essence, I believe that the Kremlin is still seeking a third way somewhere between a market system and a planned economy. I believe it is not helpful for the Soviet citizen or the outside world to support that policy. Instead of half-hearted attempts at currency reform, the Soviets should develop and implement a comprehensive plan to reform the country's monetary system. The freeing of prices, as painful as it undoubtedly will be, is the next logical step. Although, as I previously mentioned, some consumer prices were raised in April 1991, the prices of most products remain under government control. Prices thus continue to distort the realities of the market. Freeing prices will remain an ineffective effort, as long as Soviet production monopolies are not broken and markets are not opened to the West. But if citizens believe that a free market only means higher prices, they will not accept such a system.

Unfortunately, the price increase was not used to absorb the ruble overhang. Instead, a 300-billion-ruble fund was created to soften the impact of the price increase. The price hikes were also intended to stimulate production and increase the supply of goods. This has not yet materialized. This indecision and inertia has characterized the reform process. No wonder the population feels it has once again been duped.

Another very important and overlooked reform is the critical need for a modern infrastructure, particularly in transportation and communications. This almost criminal neglect of infrastructure will be, if it is not attacked, an insurmountable obstacle to progress. Waste is unbelievable in the energy sector, and production, especially oil production, is in extremely bad shape. Market pricing for energy is essential to reduce the excessive consumption of energy in the Soviet system.

Outside technical and financial help is essential. Permitting foreign ownership of energy facilities would encourage such help and would improve the production and distribution of energy. Similarly, the exploitation of new oil fields in the inaccessible northern areas will require enormous investments. Because the country's dilapidated financial system prevents the Soviets from attracting domestic capital, large-scale investment can only be financed by the West.

It is equally important to develop a financial system that is creditworthy. I think Lenin was right that one could destroy capitalism by destroying its money; vice versa, any hope of establishing a market economy depends on developing a creditworthy financial system. The optimum division of labor and resultant welfare gain are only possible if barter trade is overcome by a currency that is credible (price stability, convertibility), and a financial system that provides efficient (that is, cost effective) transactions and safety for the depositors.

There are discussions in several constituent republics between Soviet economists and central government officials about currency system reforms away from the center, and whether the ruble can become a convertible currency by an intelligent management of monetary affairs out of Moscow. It would be very helpful if, under a union treaty, the ruble remained the common currency of the Soviet Union. We in the West have learned that small currency areas create barriers between regions, segment markets into very small pieces, and ultimately destroy internal markets.

In the 1960s, it was modern to believe in floating exchange rates, because this would help insulate economies from the influences of foreign monetary authorities. I was brought up in that spirit. One of my first jobs at the Kiel Institute of World Economics in the early 1970s was to organize a worldwide platform for the introduction of floating exchange rates. We got floating exchange rates; we solved some of our problems, but we created more. It took us seven years in Europe to step back from that and to create what we now call the European Monetary System, which is a system of quasi-fixed exchange rates. Western Europe is now trying very hard to again become competitive in its financial markets by developing a European central bank and by developing a single European currency.

I understand that those republics discussing national and economic autonomy are also discussing monetary autonomy. But I would warn that monetary autonomy is a separate issue. The world economy is moving toward anchoring currencies, not toward truly independent currencies. Only as a last resort should republics consider stepping out of a currency union because that will split their internal market. In the past, we have learned that the hard way in the Western world.

In my view, a number of political causes also contributed to the dilapidated state of the Soviet economy. Chief among them are the increasingly nebulous power structures that reduce outside analysis to mere guesswork. Although the Communist Party officially renounced its constitutionally enshrined vanguard role in the Soviet Union, powerful forces inside the country are still actively resisting any change in the social order. This is particularly true in the military and large-scale industrial sector, where anti-reformers have become ever more vocal. As a result, Soviet politics have become increasingly polarized.

The problem does not end here. In the Soviet Union, reforms have come from the top and do not enjoy the popular support they have in Czechoslovakia or Poland. Hungary is the only exception; it has been moving toward democracy and a market system for a long time. Only very recently have organized strikes in the Soviet Union, primarily in the mining areas, begun to challenge the established power structures. Yet this grass-roots opposition appears only to reject the old regime without embracing a new, market-oriented system.

Let me now turn to the all-important issue of the republics, which are clamoring for independence and national sovereignty. One after another the republics have proclaimed their right to self-determination and the precedence of republican law over union law. The central government, in turn, has insisted that the integrity of the union is essential to economic recovery. But it is precisely the center's inability to stabilize the market and monetary system and the resulting free fall of the Soviet economy that have added fuel to the fires of the various independence movements. Moreover, in some cases rising tensions among different nationalities have erupted into civil war–like confrontations.

I am a strong believer that the Soviet Union can only be reformed from the periphery, that Soviet reform depends on the autonomy of the republics. However, if autonomy translates into separatism and greater economic barriers among the republics, then the Soviet Union's economic difficulties will only intensify. I strongly believe that it is in the self-interest of the Soviet people to keep the best of both worlds: harness the motivation and spirit behind the the autonomy movements while retaining the customs union, the internal market, and the currency union of the center. This may be asking for the impossible, but it is something worth talking about and trying.

I cannot fully evaluate the recent resurrection of a conservative-type government, but I do not believe it is as negative as some do. Let me speculate for a second. Could it be that Mikhail Gorbachev and Boris Yeltsin have agreed to have a conservative government carry out some of the nasty jobs in order to have a freer reign to do something more meaningful later? Is that too much of a conspir-

acy hypothesis? Consider that you would like to undertake a courageous, well-designed reform, but the people cannot understand that
even a well-prepared, well-thought-out reform translates into economic hardship for a number of years. Is it not better to have people upset with the conservatives so that later liberal reforms will be
more acceptable? I think there is still a chance that Yeltsin and
Gorbachev do understand the political process in the Soviet Union
better than outside analysts and are possibly still in command of
that rocky boat.

What should be the main elements of a union treaty? Defense,
foreign policy, currency, and the free-trade system should be established at the center. Fiscal policy, fiscal autonomy, and ethnic issues should be dealt with at the republic level. This should leave
room for autonomous republics to experiment with different models and learn from others. The recent agreement between Gorbachev and nine of the fifteen Soviet republics does devolve considerable economic and political autonomy to the republics and is a
step in the right direction, but its success as the basis of a future
union treaty is by no means guaranteed.

Whether the Soviet Union should adopt a "shock therapy" approach is as much a question of religion as it is economic analysis.
For example, the Polish government's effort to explain the implications of its economic reform plan to the people helped mobilize political support for reform. The Polish program has been relatively
successful in reducing inflation and establishing realistic prices.
although the success of the reform is currently threatened by a continuing decline of production due to an almost complete collapse of
Poland's trade ties to the Soviet Union.

On the other hand, the Hungarian step-by-step alternative has
also worked well. They have had price reform, but they do not
have the full convertibility of the forint. Foreign investment is increasing, and they are privatizing at least as fast as Poland. So,
there is an alternative model that seems to work as well.

I believe, however, that shock therapy is a better approach in
the Soviet Union. A more gradual approach will prolong the ago-
ny of transformation considerably. Even with significant reform, I
doubt that the Soviet economy will grow much in the future.
Imports will decline, further reducing the incentive for Western
firms to do business with the Soviet Union. This would be particu-

larly untimely, because the Soviets are hoping to increase trade with the West as intra-Comecon trade declines.

What then are the prospects for trade with the Soviets? We are talking about a market of 300 million consumers, which is 40 million more than in the United States. To evaluate the Soviet Union's tremendous potential for trade expansion, it is useful to look at its percentage of world trade. For example, the Soviet Union's share of world trade in 1989, about 3.5 percent, was only one-fourth the United States' share. Trade with the Soviet Union represents only about 1 percent of the total trade of Western industrialized countries. Even Western Germany, which has comparatively strong trade relations with the Soviets, only conducts 1.5 to 2 percent of its trade with the Soviet Union. If the Soviets want a bigger share of the world market, they must first create the necessary preconditions: stabilize the internal political situation; create market conditions; and guarantee foreign access to reliable legal structures. Whereas foreign trade took a backseat to domestic production under the planned economy, it will become an integral part of economic development once the Soviets fully subscribe to the principles of an open market. If foreign trade is to flourish in the long run, the Soviet Union must substantially expand its export capabilities. For the moment, this obviously means that it will continue to rely on the export of raw materials and energy to pay for the needed industrial imports. Aside from oil and natural gas, the Soviet Union has a long list of valuable raw materials to offer, ranging from iron ore, copper, and chrome to silver and gold. If the economic and political obstacles are overcome, the Soviet Union could well expand its position as one of the world's leading suppliers of raw materials.

By itself, however, this is not enough. There are recognizable limits to the expansion of raw-material exports. In the last few years, the industrialized countries have begun extensive energy conservation, as well as substitution and recycling programs, which have significantly reduced their consumption of oil and other important raw materials. In other words, the West has reduced the percentage of raw materials per unit of production.

It is therefore vital that the Soviets devise a versatile export strategy. That means, above all, diversifying its exports to include high-quality and high-value-added products. The impact of such a strategy on overall trade is demonstrated by the experience in those developing countries that pursued this strategy. South Korea, for example, saw its volume of exports jump by five to six times from what it was fifteen years ago, and the value of its exports multiply by twelve over the same period. This increase occurred despite the fact that South Korea has virtually no natural resources of its own. In Poland and Hungary, the liberalization of foreign trade, together with private initiative, has helped quickly resuscitate the export sector.

The Soviet Union obviously still has a long way to go before it can export much more than oil and natural gas. If the country is to become a valuable trading partner, we in the West must be prepared to actively support and participate in the process. In short, we have to help the Soviets help themselves. We must do our share to help them exploit their raw-material sources, modernize their production base, and create an infrastructure capable of fostering industrial growth. The single most important thing we can do is to engage in a rapid and comprehensive transfer of know-how—especially management expertise. Initial cooperation efforts should focus on converting Soviet military factories to nonmilitary lines of production. We should also help them turn the results of their basic research into marketable products.

What does the Soviet Union's trade potential mean for the neighboring countries? What does it mean for specific countries? One of the papers at this seminar discusses the role of three gateways: Finland, Austria, and Hong Kong. Gateways have political and economic costs and benefits. Finland has strong ties with the Baltics but is economically dependent on Soviet energy. This economic dependence affects its political autonomy. Germany, another possible gateway, has particular interests and responsibilities. But it is difficult for Germany to be very outspoken on some Soviet political issues when there are still 350,000 Soviet soldiers on German soil. Gateways are interesting concepts and are very important for trade and business, but gateway countries are not the political platform the West should utilize to develop strategies to help the Soviet Union. Negotiating with the Soviet Union should be done at the European Community level, not at the national level. The European Community must decide how it can help develop Central and Eastern Europe and its main economic center, the

Soviet Union. Western Europeans should also form a strong al-
liance in formulating strategies to support those countries that have
adopted Western values, democracy, and an open, free market.
Americans should not stay on the sidelines during this process.
We cannot continue the policies of the past. This is not the
time for balance-of-payments loans. Balance-of-payments loans
have never worked in the past, and they have helped possibly to
create the Soviet Union's current problems. The renegotiation of
Soviet debt is not a meaningful policy, even if the Soviet government becomes less conservative. What we need are relationships
that intensify the transfer of technical know-how. We ought to
bring about those capital transfers that automatically bring with
them technical know-how and managerial training. Initial cooperative efforts should focus on converting Soviet military factories to
nonmilitary lines of production. We should also help them turn
their excellent basic research into marketable products.

As I noted earlier, financial credibility takes years to develop.
Eastern Europe and the Soviet Union, however, cannot wait years
for development assistance. We now have an historic opportunity
and cannot wait to see what happens in five years time. Equity capital will not flow East if there are not Western government guarantees. In light of the Soviets' considerable foreign debt, fresh
money will initially have to come almost exclusively from public
sources, such as individual Western governments, the International Monetary Fund (IMF), the World Bank, and the new
European Bank for Reconstruction and Development (EBRD). We
need those government funds because of the lack of a credible
Eastern system. This Western help should be conditional upon
macro- and micro-policies that promote change. Funding should
be used for improving infrastructure, and it should be supervised.

The former head of the Deutsche Bank, Alfred Herrhausen,
argued before he was assassinated that national banks for reconstruction and development should be created. He suggested, for example, that the Poles should have their own Polish bank for reconstruction and development. During the postwar period in Germany, a similar German institution was established with U.S.
Marshall Fund help. This institution provided conditional seed
money, a substitute for equity capital, to establish new firms.

For the time being, the second-best solution is the EBRD and other multilateral institutions, which can provide the necessary funds, assistance, and supervision to get the ball rolling. In the long run, however, it is imperative that the private sector does its share in providing funds for the restructuring and modernization of the Soviet economy.

In the future, successful cooperation requires that the West builds new relationships with new trading partners in the Soviet Union. Increased decentralization of the economic decisionmaking process means increased autonomy for individual production centers and greater leeway in foreign trade. Western partners will therefore have to deal with a whole new set of trade contacts. After so many years of dealing with just a few central government officials, this new approach will complicate trade in the short run. But decentralization will ultimately enhance efficiency on both sides, because it eliminates the middleman.

Finally, if we want our business with the Soviets to flourish, we will have to adapt to the changing political realities in the country. This entails, first and foremost, recognizing that individual republics are important trading partners and treating them as such. The West can only hamper the economic reform process by ignoring internal developments in the Soviet Union. If we refuse to deal directly with the republics, the West may unwittingly support anachronistic centralist structures.

Future cooperation will likely take place at the regional level. Each Soviet republic is unique and will require its own development program. In fact, there are enormous differences among republics in economic development, natural resources, industrial capacity, and infrastructure. This, of course, complicates risk assessment by the West. Until now, merely dealing with the individual countries of Eastern Europe has represented a significant level of risk. Now the risks in the Soviet Union must be calculated for all fifteen republics individually.

We should not exaggerate the importance of the initial level of cooperation. We must first get to know the Soviets and build common experiences. Our goal must be to proceed step by step to achieve greater cooperation. Because trade among highly developed economies is generally paramount, the West can only benefit from a structurally and technologically revamped Soviet Union.

Increased economic cooperation, especially with the Soviet

Union, also has an added political dimension. For decades, politics provided little impetus for economic relations between East and West. In fact, it was the other way around. Economic interests ensured that the East-West dialogue never broke off completely, especially in times when the political climate was particularly frosty.

The deideologization of Soviet foreign policy has freed East-West economic cooperation from the constraints of day-to-day politics. We have before us a window of opportunity. Moreover, the Soviet government has expressed its intent to make cooperation with the West a pillar of its new economic policy. This new attitude is particularly evident in the Soviet Union's efforts to improve its cooperation with Western multilateral institutions. Who could have imagined even three years ago that the Soviets would willingly submit to a group study by the IMF, the World Bank, the Organisation for Economic Co-operation and Development (OECD), and the EBRD. And who would have thought it possible that the Soviets would not only provide current data on their economic problems—excluding, of course, information on gold and foreign reserves—but would also accept the results of that study without the usual ideological rhetoric.

For our part, we in the West bear responsibility for creating a solid foundation for economic cooperation. Granted, the task is not an easy one. On the one hand, given the prevailing uncertainties, we must ensure that our economic and particularly financial aid does not end up propping up outdated political structures and thus obstructing economic reform. On the other hand, in view of the progress made to date, slight as it may be, Western governments must dispense with bureaucratic hang-ups and lend support to the reform process in the Soviet Union—if not by extending untied loans, then by providing technical advice. At a minimum, we must keep our markets open to Soviet exports.

Only if we succeed in putting the Soviet economy on a sound footing and improving the standard of living of the average Soviet citizen will legitimate and lasting political structures be able to take hold. But if people feel there is no light at the end of the tunnel, growing economic despair could easily lead to widespread disillusionment and bitterness. As a result, internal upheaval could erupt into civil war in the Soviet Union, and hostilities could ultimately spill beyond its borders. In such a scenario, millions of

Eastern Europeans may flock to the West in search of a new and better life. Nothing would be more dangerous than if the early successes of reform in the other Eastern European countries relegates the Soviet problem to the sidelines.

This is time for action. We must act as the West, not as separate nation states. It is obvious that Europe plays a particularly important political role in this process. It is equally obvious that capital-rich countries like Japan, with its need for natural resources, ought to be part of the process. And it is equally obvious that the United States must be involved, especially in defense policies. Détente does offer the possibility of peace dividends for both East and West. The more isolated the Soviet Union becomes from the world economy, the harder it will be for the government to justify its reform policies. We cannot allow the situation to deteriorate to that point. In my view, both the public and the private sectors in the West have a golden opportunity: If we work hard enough, we can prove the superiority of the market economy in the very cradle of socialism.

2

Economic Relations Among the Soviet Republics

Gertrude E. Schroeder

INTRODUCTION

Since the inception of central planning, the Soviet government has pursued a general policy of promoting economic development, especially industrial development in all of its constituent republics. The pace has been quite uneven among the republics, however, and implementation of the general development strategy has been carried out with the explicit objective of promoting the interests of the Soviet Union as a whole as defined by the central government in Moscow. The production structures that have evolved in each republic, while reflecting its natural resource endowment, have been heavily influenced by particular facets of Soviet development strategy.[1] In general, central policy has sought to promote specialization rather than diversity within republic economies. Thus, cotton growing in Central Asia was vigorously promoted at the expense of food crops, and industrial development there was focused on the primary processing of cotton rather than on the production of final products. In the Ukraine, industrial development has been oriented toward the extractive industries and the manufacture of intermediate products. In Azerbaidzhan, machinery production has been geared to the needs of the petroleum industries there. All republics have been affected by the central planners' penchant for gigantomania and for concentration of production of one or an-

1. For a good discussion of Soviet development policies and their consequences, see Dellenbrant (1986).

19

other important product in one or two plants. With the heavy priority given to industrial investment over the years in each republic, industrial capacities have been created that are geared to serve the needs of the other republics and to a lesser extent to serve foreign (largely CMEA) exports that the Moscow planners deemed necessary to pay for needed imports.

As a result of such policies made in Moscow, but based in part on geographic factors, an intricate network of inter-republican economic dependencies has evolved over the years. Each republic has become heavily dependent on other republics to supply essential raw materials and final manufactures and also to provide markets for its own products. Each republic has become heavily involved in the "all-union market" or the "national economic complex," as Gorbachev likes to put it. For many republics, the degree of involvement has been growing in recent decades. The extent and pattern of these trade dependencies are deeply imbedded in a distorted structure of production (relative to comparable Western countries) that is the legacy of central planning and Soviet development strategy.

INTER-REPUBLIC TRADE

A full picture of the importance of inter-republic economic relations to the economy of a republic is best seen in complete input/output tables and related trade flows for each republic. The Soviet Union has never published complete input/output tables either for the Soviet Union as a whole or for the individual republics.[2] The fragmentary tables that have been made available pertain to material production and trade flows and thus omit the services. With the push for independence in the Baltics and the drive for economic sovereignty elsewhere during 1988–1990, the Soviet State Committee for Statistics (Goskomstat) has released an unprecedented amount of data on the balance of trade and trade flows among the republics, as well as on their role in foreign trade. Because the data are necessarily expressed in domestic ruble

---

2. From the incomplete data made available, James Gillula (1979, 1982) has put together partial input/output tables for the republics in 1966 and 1972.

prices, the inter-republican trade data are affected by the well-known distortions in Soviet prices, which have tended to under-value raw materials and energy relative to final manufactures. For this reason, the net trade balances shown for the republics have become the subject of acrimonious arguments about "who feeds whom?" The crux of the pricing problem is as follows. As a matter of policy, prices of raw materials and machinery have had low domestic prices relative to the prices of consumer goods. This general pattern holds for both domestic and foreign trade. Hence, the particular products in which a republic has specialized will greatly influence its balance of trade, and charges of "unfair" prices can readily be hurled back and forth.

Nonetheless, these prices are those in which trade among the republics has been transacted and recorded. Moreover, the ruble values of both imports and exports reflect underlying real flows of physical products among the republics and with the outside world. When related to other magnitudes (value of production and of consumption) expressed in these same domestic prices, the data on the values of imports and exports will reflect the extent of the dependencies that have developed, dependencies that should come as no surprise to anyone. Value data can be supplemented by data expressed in physical units (tons, number of units).

Probably the most revealing set of data depicting overall economic interdependencies among the republics relates the values of exports and imports to the values of total republic production and consumption (supply), respectively. Table 2-1 shows these trade data expressed as percentages of the totals in 1988. The data relate to commodity (material) production. As one would expect, the large republics (the RSFSR, the Ukraine, Kazakhstan) are the least trade dependent: in 1988, imports (both domestic and foreign) provided 15 to 19 percent of total supply, and exports took 12 to 16 percent of the total production in these republics. In the other republics, imports provided 22 percent (Uzbekistan, Azerbaidzhan) to 31 percent (Armenia) of total supply, and exports took 19 percent (Kirghizia) to 27 percent (Belorussia) of total production. Because these data relate to total trade, one needs to know the relative proportions of foreign and domestic trade in the total trade of individual republics. These percentage shares are shown in Table 2-2 for 1988. In all republics except the RSFSR and the Ukraine, domestic trade ac-

Table 2-1. Shares of Imports and Exports in Republican
Supply and Production, 1988

	Share of Imports in Total Supply	Share of Exports in Total Production
Baltics		
Lithuania	27	22
Latvia	27	24
Estonia	29	24
Transcaucasia		
Georgia	28	26
Azerbaidzhan	22	26
Armenia	31	26
Central Asia		
Uzbekistan	22	20
Kirghizia	26	19
Tadzhikistan	27	20
Turkmenia	24	22
Core Republics		
RSFSR	15	12
Ukraine	17	16
Belorussia	25	27
Kazakhstan	19	12
Moldavia	28	25

Source: Narodnoe khoziaistvo SSSR v 1989 godu, Moscow, Finansy i statistika, 1990, 635.
Data include both inter-republican and foreign trade and are based on ruble values
in domestic prices.

Table 2-2. Shares of Domestic and Foreign Trade
in Total Trade Turnover, 1988

	Imports		Exports		Total Turnover	
	D[a]	F[b]	D	F	D	F
Baltics						
Lithuania	83	17	91	9	87	13
Latvia	82	18	92	8	87	13
Estonia	81	19	90	10	85	15
Transcaucasia						
Georgia	80	20	93	7	87	13
Azerbaidzhan	75	25	94	6	88	12
Armenia	82	18	98	2	89	11
Central Asia						
Uzbekistan	86	14	85	15	85	15
Kirghizia	80	20	98	2	87	13
Tadzhikistan	87	13	86	14	86	14
Turkmenia	79	21	92	8	89	11
Core Republics						
RSFSR	51	49	68	32	57	43
Ukraine	73	27	85	15	79	21
Belorussia	79	21	93	7	86	14
Kazakhstan	84	16	91	9	86	14
Moldavia	82	18	95	5	88	12

a. D = Domestic.
b. F = Foreign.
Source: Percentages were calculated from ruble values in domestic prices given in
Vestnik statistiki, no. 3, 1990, 36.

counted for at least 85 percent of total trade. For all republics but two, the shares of domestic sales in total exports exceeded the shares of domestic deliveries in total imports. Domestic sales accounted for at least 90 percent of total exports in eleven republics. Overall, the five core republics accounted for some three-fourths of total domestic trade and nine-tenths of all foreign trade.

Recently released data for 1988 allow us to examine the branch structure of each republic's total exports to other republics.[3] Except for Kazakhstan and Uzbekistan, industry provides 93 percent or more of the total exports of each republic. Within industry, the distribution of exports among branches differs substantially among the republics, reflecting as it does the particular pattern of industrial development that has evolved in each one. In all republics of the Baltics, Transcaucasia, and Central Asia, and also in Moldavia, the light and food-processing industries account for over 40 percent of their total industrial exports; the shares range from 42 percent in Lithuania to 66 percent in Georgia, but the share was only 13 percent for the RSFSR. Machinery products accounted for over 30 percent of the total industrial exports in six republics. Fuels provided sizable shares in the major energy-producing republics—the RSFSR, Kazakhstan, Azerbaidzhan, and Turkmenia. Metallurgical products were important in the export structures in Kazakhstan, the Ukraine, and Tadzhikistan. Chemical products figured importantly in the industrial exports of the RSFSR, Belorussia, and Kazakhstan. The picture for imports is similarly diverse, and similar considerations determine their structures. The industrial sector accounts for the vast bulk of imports in each republic, with machinery having the largest share in most cases.

To obtain a complete picture of the web of economic relationships among the republics, one needs data showing for each republic the amount and type of trade that it conducts with each other republic. Although Goskomstat periodically compiles such data as part of the compilation of input/output tables for the republics, the data have never been published. Only fragmentary information is available. Judging from the relative size of total trade flows, one would suppose that the RSFSR would be by far the largest trading partner for all of the other republics. Such was the case for Estonia

3. *Vestnik statistiki*, no. 3, 1990, 39–53.

in 1982, for example, when the RSFSR accounted for 54 percent of total imports and 58 percent of exports (Kukk 1988). The other Baltic republics accounted for 9 percent and 11 percent, respectively. The situation was similar for Lithuania.[4]

REPUBLICAN TRADE IN CONSUMER GOODS

Table 2-3 presents data for each republic showing the contribution of imports and exports of consumer goods to total republican supply and total republican production, respectively. Percentage shares are shown separately for three groups of goods—food, products of light industry, and all others, mainly consumer durables. The data relate to total trade, but inter-republican trade accounted for the vast bulk of both imports and exports for all republics. All of the republics obtain significant shares of their supply of consumer goods from imports, although the shares differ widely. In 1988, they ranged from 17 percent in the Ukraine to 66 percent in Turkmenia. Overall, the Central Asian and Transcaucasian republics, along with Kazakhstan, are the most dependent on imports, and the Ukraine is the least so. For the most part, these generalizations hold true for all three classes of consumer goods. With regard to food supplies, these data tend to overstate a republic's overall dependence on outside sources, because the data relate to products that are sold through the various state supply networks; they do not take account of food produced and consumed in kind within a republic, nor do they include food sold in collective farm markets. On the other hand, the data omit alcoholic beverages, which some republics evidently import in sizable quantities.

Exports of consumer goods account for significant shares of consumer goods production in all republics. In 1988, their shares in total production ranged from 11 percent in the RSFSR to 49 percent in Georgia. Overall, the shares are largest in the Baltics and Transcaucasia, along with Moldavia. For the Baltics and Moldavia, Georgia and Azerbaidzhan, these large shares are found in all three groups of consumer goods; for the other republics, the shares differ markedly among the groups, reflecting particularities in the

---

4. *Sovetskaia Litva*, October 25, 1989.

production patterns in the republic. Alcoholic beverages also figure importantly in the exports of the major producers of such products.

Overall, seven republics were net importers of consumer goods in 1988, and eight republics were net exporters. Eight republics were net importers of food products, and twelve were net importers of nonfood consumer goods. Six republics were net importers of both types of goods (the RSFSR, Kazakhstan, Azerbaidzhan, and all of Central Asia except Kirghizia). Belorussia and the three Baltic republics were net exporters of both types.

Goskomstat has recently published some information on the sources of supply of nonfood consumer goods in the republics in 1989.[5] According to these data, the three Baltic republics obtained 50 to 60 percent of total supplies of such products from their own production. Comparable shares were 45 to 46 percent in the three Transcaucasian republics, 21 to 50 percent in the four Central Asian republics, and 42 (Kazakhstan) to 76 percent (the RSFSR) in the remaining republics.

ENERGY AND RAW-MATERIALS INTERDEPENDENCIES

According to recently released data for 1988, only four republics were self-sufficient in fuels and energy overall—the RSFSR, Kazakhstan, Azerbaidzhan, and Turkmenia.[6] Imports provided more than half of the total requirements in six republics and from 28 to 42 percent in the rest. Belorussia, Moldavia, and Latvia imported 90 percent or more of their energy. For seven of the eleven energy-importing republics, their dependence on imports has been rising; for example, the Ukraine and Uzbekistan, which were self-sufficient in energy in 1970, imported 42 percent and 28 percent of their total requirements, respectively, in 1988.

Within this pattern of overall energy dependencies, each republic is both an importer and an exporter of various kinds of fuels and energy. Table 2-4 presents data on the shares of imports and exports in the total energy supply and the total use for each republic in 1975 and 1985. These data, expressed in standard fuel equiva-

---

5. Goskomstat, *Statisticheskiy press-byulleten'*, no. 2, 1991, 9.
6. Goskomstat, *Press-vypusk*, no. 394, September 1989, 5.

lents, show the sizable role that inter-republic exchanges of energy play in the economies of all republics. In 1985, the Baltics imported four-fifths of their total supply, but exports also accounted for over half of their total use. They were net energy importers, as were the Transcaucasian republics as a group, whereas Central Asia and the core republics were net exporters overall. Owing largely to natural endowments, there were large variations among the republics in each group. The volume of inter-republican exchanges of fuels and energy appears to have increased between 1975 and 1985. In 1988, exports of fuels and electricity to other republics valued in domestic prices accounted for 11 percent of Turkmenia's industrial exports, 19 percent for Kazakhstan, and 18 percent for Azerbaidzhan. They accounted for 11 to 12 percent in Lithuania, Uzbekistan, and the RSFSR. For the rest of the republics, the shares ranged from 2 to 8 percent.

Goskomstat has published detailed data for the republics on trade and supply of a number of key raw materials in physical units in 1985.[7] The Baltics imported all of their coal, oil, and gas from the RSFSR, Belorussia, and the Ukraine. They were net exporters of electricity overall; in 1985, 49 percent of exports and 75 percent of imports were exchanged within the region. They also had to import nearly all of their requirements for rolled ferrous metals and raw materials for light industry, as well as substantial shares of timber and lumber. The Transcaucasian republics imported almost all of their coal and oil, all of it from the RSFSR, the Ukraine, and Kazakhstan. The Transcaucasian republics were net importers of gas, but 36 percent of total imports and 97 percent of total exports were exchanged among themselves. They were also small net importers of electricity in 1985, with 75 percent of imports and 83 percent of exports representing intra-regional exchanges. These three republics imported from 47 to 100 percent of their requirements for rolled ferrous metals and from 65 to 100 percent of their needs for timber and lumber. Although the three republics taken together were net exporters of cotton and wool raw materials for light in-

7. The physical data on trade and supply of energy and raw materials for heavy industry in 1985 are given in *Material'no-tekhnicheskoe obespechenie narodnogo khoziaistva SSSR*, Moscow, Finansy i statistiki, 1988, 144–71. Data on key raw materials for light industry are published in *Vestnik statistiki*, no. 4, 1990, 53–60.

Table 2-3. Shares of Imports and Exports in Republican Supply and Production of Consumer Goods, 1988

	Share of Imports in Total Supply				Share of Exports in Total Production			
	Total	Food Products	Light Industry Products	All Others	Total	Food Products	Light Industry Products	All Others
Baltics								
Lithuania	23	14	23	32	39	38	39	43
Latvia	22	12	32	23	36	31	39	39
Estonia	29	22	26	42	47	41	52	49
Transcaucasia								
Georgia	44	49	35	50	49	66	42	31
Azerbaitzhan	44	45	40	46	38	36	40	40
Armenia	35	50	33	29	40	17	64	11
Central Asia								
Uzbekistan	41	33	31	63	19	20	14	25
Kirghizia	42	25	44	60	30	28	24	41
Tadzhikistan	42	36	32	91	33	18	26	90
Turkmenia	66	58	90	90	33	47	18	22
Core Republics								
RSFSR	21	24	12	13	11	6	14	15
Ukraine	17	5	25	24	18	22	9	17
Belorussia	22	15	20	31	33	27	30	44
Kazakhstan	39	20	46	58	12	14	13	6
Moldavia	31	14	30	45	39	51	33	30

Sources: Percentage shares were calculated from data giving ruble values in domestic retail (purchasers) prices. Alcoholic beverages are excluded from all data. Trade data include foreign trade. *Narodnoe Khoziaistvo. SSSR v 1989 godu,* Moscow, Finansy i statistika, 1990, 406. *Vestnik statistki,* no. 4, 1990, 53–60. Shares in totals for food products are somewhat overstated, because the trade data apparently include fresh produce, whereas the production data do not.

Table 2-4. Role of Imports and Exports in Fuel and Energy Supplies

	Share of Imports in Total Supply		Share of Exports in Total Use		Net Imports as Shares in Total Supply	
	1975	1985	1975	1985	1975	1985
Baltics	80	81	54	54	26	27
Lithuania	93	88	45	48	48	40
Latvia	89	91	67	69	22	22
Estonia	33	37	31	19	2	18
Transcaucasia	56	52	44	29	12	23
Georgia	86	80	33	39	53	41
Azerbaidzhan	87	80	2	8	49	72
Armenia	39	34	55	38	-16	-4
Central Asia	38	44	71	66	-33	-22
Uzbekistan	59	69	68	61	-9	8
Kirghizia	61	61	25	24	36	37
Tadzhikistan	62	55	18	21	44	34
Turkmenia	3	5	87	84	-84	-79
Core Republics	22	27	30	38	-8	-11
RSFSR	14	10	27	33	-13	-23
Ukraine	32	58	31	37	1	21
Belorussia	78	95	58	74	20	21
Kazakhstan	26	31	43	41	-17	-10
Moldavia	93	92	30	22	63	70

a. Shares were calculated from data on fuel-energy balances in standard fuel equiv-alents. The data include foreign trade.

Source: Goskomstat, *Material'no-tekhnicheskoe obespechenie narodnogo khoziaistva SSSR statisticheskiy sbornik*, Moscow, 1988, 66-75.

dustry (in 1988), both Armenia and Georgia imported substantial amounts of cotton fiber.

All four Central Asian republics were net importers of coal in 1985, with 68 percent of exports and 29 percent of imports being intra-regional exchanges. Three republics were net importers of oil, with 17 percent of the group's imports and 86 percent of its exports reflecting intra-regional trade. Two republics were net importers of gas, and 37 percent of imports and 51 percent of exports reflected intra-regional trade. All four republics were net exporters of electricity, but they imported and exported electricity mainly among themselves. The region imported almost all of its rolled ferrous metals and timber, but it was a large net exporter of cotton. The core republics taken as a region were self-sufficient in coal, oil, gas, and electricity. Virtually all of these products that were not produced within a republic were imported from others in the region. The RSFSR and the Ukraine produced three-quarters of their requirements for rolled ferrous metals, whereas the others imported most of their supplies, probably almost entirely from the rest of the group. With regard to timber and lumber, the RSFSR and Belorussia were largely self-sufficient, and the others evidently had their needs satisfied within the region. All core republics except Kazakhstan were substantial net importers of raw materials for light industry in 1988.

Recently published data for nine products in physical units for 1989 indicate that the patterns of import dependencies have been quite stable.[8] The new data, however, add several products to the list and provide information about the shares of exports in total production in the republics. Most republics depend heavily on one another for meeting their needs for paper, cardboard, fertilizer, tires, and synthetic resins and plastics. These products also figure heavily in the exports of many of the republics. The Ukraine, for example, exported 67 percent of the tires that it produced, and Lithuania exported 88 percent of its cardboard and 69 percent of its paper. Even the RSFSR exported 33 percent of its tire production and 25–26 percent of its paper and cardboard production.

---

8. Goskomstat, *Statisticheskiy press-byulleten'*, no. 2, 1991, 47–57.

SOME RECENT DEVELOPMENTS

While the overall magnitudes and patterns of dependencies probably were not much altered, the events of 1989 and 1990 have had important consequences for inter-republic economic relationships. The persistent deterioration in consumer markets throughout the Soviet Union, coupled with the burgeoning movement for republic economic sovereignty, spawned numerous manifestations of regional autarky and a consequent weakening of inter-republican trade ties. Without providing full data, a Goskomstat official suggests that the importance of inter-regional trade in the production and consumption of individual republics declined in 1989 and 1990.[9] He reports that in 1989, despite increases in production, many republics reduced their deliveries to other republics of food products by substantial percentages (for example, a 25 percent cut in meat exports by Lithuania and an 11 percent reduction in exports of dairy products by Estonia). The situation worsened in 1990. Goskomstat reported actual reductions in inter-republic deliveries for a number of nonfood consumer goods.[10] From data for the first ten months of 1990, it appears that plans for inter-republic deliveries were not met for many consumer goods by much wider margins than the shortfalls in the corresponding plans for production. The curtailment of inter-republic trade in other products, notably in raw materials, no doubt contributed to the decline in national income and industrial production that occurred in the Soviet Union as a whole and in most of the republics in 1990.

As the economic situation worsened, particularly in the last half of 1990, the republics, as well as many administrative units within the republics, adopted a variety of measures to "protect" their local populations. These actions took a variety of forms: barter swaps between republics on an increasing scale; bans on exports of specified products; refusal to honor contracts; attempts to set up customs barriers; rationing schemes that sought to limit purchases of consumer goods to local residents; and demanding "extortionary" terms for signing new contracts. Moreover, tourism, which pro-

---

9. *Soyuz*, no. 52, 1990, 12–13.
10. Goskomstat, *Statisticheskii press-byulleten'*, no. 2, 1991, 9–12.

vides considerable revenues to some republics, clearly was reduced in both years as a result of such protectionist policies, an upsurge in ethnic strife, and increased tensions between the center and the periphery.

The upsurge in regional autarky that occurred in 1990 played out in an arena of unprecedented republic assertiveness in political-economic affairs that was a hallmark of that year. By the end of the year, Lithuania had declared its independence, and Estonia, Latvia, Georgia, and Armenia had announced intentions to move toward it. All republics issued declarations of sovereignty during the year. These declarations differ considerably in specificity and in other ways among republics, but most declarations call for independent currencies, banking, and budgetary systems, and for the right to set up customs arrangements, conduct foreign trade, and establish pricing policies. These declarations have been supplemented by a flurry of bilateral economic treaties and agreements among the republics. By the end of March 1991, the RSFSR and the Ukraine had signed such agreements with all other republics. Belorussia and Tadzhikistan had agreements with all but two republics, and the rest, except for Georgia, had signed accords with at least half of the other republics. Some republics have signed economic agreements with individual oblasts or cities within another republic (for example, Estonia's agreement with Leningrad).[11]

The inter-republic agreements evidently vary widely in content and specificity, but most of them contain a pledge to retain existing contractual trade relationships through 1991. Some of them are of long duration (for example, the economic treaty between the Ukraine and Lithuania for 1991–1995).[12] Several agreements declare the intent to maintain a "common economic space" for trade between them. While noting the importance of encouraging inter-enterprise contacts between republics, most of the agreements have a strong state-to-state orientation. For example, the pact between Lithuania and the RSFSR signed in August 1990 calls for a supplementary protocol to be signed by the RSFSR State Committee for Material-Technical Supply and the Lithuanian State Committee for Economics and the Ministry of Material Resources.[13] It seems,

11. *Sovetskaia Estoniia*, September 21, 1990.
12. *Pravda Ukrainy*, December 9, 1990.
13. *Ekho Litvy*, August 17, 1990. See also *Sovetskaia Estoniia*, December 7, 1990.

however, that this plethora of bilateral agreements has only added to enterprise managers' problems in obtaining raw materials and supplies.[14]

In addition to these bilateral agreements, two multilateral agreements have been made in what might be viewed as embryonic steps toward regional common markets. The first such agreement was that among the three Baltic republics signed in April 1990, and scheduled to run through the year 2000.[15] This accord explicitly states the intent to create a "Baltic Market" affected "primarily within the framework of direct ties among independent enterprises and organizations and other legal entities." The agreement calls for working out detailed protocols for cooperation and integration in fourteen specified areas. The accord states the intent to create a Financial Foundation and an Investment Bank for the Baltic states. A somewhat less explicit accord was signed in late June 1990 by the four Central Asian republics and Kazakhstan.[16] The document is entitled "Agreement on Economic, Scientific-Technical and Cultural Cooperation" and lasts through 1995. It provides for maintenance of existing economic ties at the 1990 level through 1991. A Coordinating Council is to be set up to implement the agreement.

Meanwhile, the central government has been taking actions to preserve the union and its existing large internal common market. In many speeches Gorbachev has extolled the mutual advantages for all republics of being part of the "all-union market." In April 1990, the Supreme Soviet adopted the law entitled "On the Fundamentals of Economic Relations Between the USSR and the Union and Autonomous Republics," which spelled out an unprecedented delegation of authority to the republics over their economies.[17] Article 4 deals with the all-union market, which is to be based on the "independence of enterprises . . . carrying out their economic activity in an environment of competition and equal rights for all forms of ownership, taking into account the anti-monopoly and other legislation on the market." The law forbids the republics to discriminate against one another in trade or

14. TASS, Moscow, March 4, 1991; *Izvestiia*, March 6, 1991.
15. *Ekho Litvy*, April 17, 1990.
16. *Sovetskaia Kirghiziia*, June 26, 1990.
17. *Izvestiia*, April 17, 1990.

to erect barriers to inter-republican commerce (except by mutual agreement). It also sanctions the making of treaties and agreements among republics, an option that they quickly seized, as we have seen.

Following a parade of economic reform programs in late 1989 and in 1990 that failed either in implementation or in enactment, the Supreme Soviet in October 1990 adopted the so-called Presidential Plan entitled "Basic Guidelines for Stabilization of the Economy and Transition to a Market Economy," which constitutes the present operational program for economic reform at the national level.[18] Based on the stated premise that "the choice of switching to a market has been made," this program states further, "Economic relations between sovereign republics are built on the basis of recognition of republics' state sovereignty and equality and at the same time on the integrity of the Union as a federation, on the understanding that the enterprise is the basis of the economy and the state's task is to create the most favorable conditions for its activity." The document specifies the areas of authority to be delegated by the republics to the federal government for the purpose of enabling them to establish a "single Union-wide market."

Having been given legislative sanction to implement economic stabilization measures by presidential decree, Gorbachev issued three of them in September, October, and December 1990 that concern inter-enterprise and inter-republican economic ties.[19] These decrees were intended to halt the slide in production and the growing disorganization that was taking place as a result, at least in part, of the rise of economic protectionism and autarky among republics and regions. The first decree ordered all state enterprises to maintain existing contractual ties at the 1990 level through 1991. The second decree introduced as of January 1, 1991, the new and much higher industrial wholesale prices to be used in finalizing contractual deliveries in 1991. When these measures seemed to be inadequate, Gorbachev issued the third decree in mid-December ordering a speedy completion of contracts for 1991 and invalidating in 1991 "decisions of Union departments and republics and local bodies that lead to the disruption of economic ties

18. *Izvestiia*, October 27, 1990.
19. *Pravda*, September 28, 1990; *Izvestiia*, October 5 and December 15, 1990.

for deliveries of products, direct barter between regions and enterprises, and bans on sending products to other regions." Finally, a
presidential decree issued in early January 1991 embodied an
agreement reached among the republics with the central government to reintroduce for 1991 state orders (compulsory deliveries) by
farms of food products to be delivered to state stocks.[20]

CONCLUSIONS

Over many decades, the Soviet Union's fifteen union republics have
developed within the framework of a large common internal
market. The regional specializations that have evolved as a consequence of centrally dictated policies have produced the present intricate network of economic and trading relationships among the
republics. For each republic, imports from the rest of them account
for large shares of the supply of goods within the republic, and exports to other republics take large shares of each republic's industrial production. In short, economic interdependencies have been
formed that are absolutely critical to the economic health of each
individual republic and of the Union as a whole. These are economic facts of life that each sovereignty-seeking republic must take
into account. Many, if not all, of the republics would seem to be
natural trading partners for one another, based merely on considerations of contiguity of territory. Moreover, these economic interdependencies not only stem from natural endowments, but also are
deeply imbedded in the production patterns and the capital stocks
in each region. In some cases (for example, cotton in Central
Asia), agricultural product specializations have been created in the
service of national goals of autarky for the country as a whole.
These patterns cannot be altered in a major way in the near term.
But to a much greater extent, industrial production specializations
and plant capacities have been built up to serve the needs of other
republics in the Soviet internal market. The size, design, and
product specializations of thousands of individual plants are geared
to that market. Moreover, the industrial labor force in each republic has been trained and deployed to the same end. The existing

20. *Pravda*, January 11, 1991.

stocks of physical and human capital are those that necessarily must be used to produce the goods and services in each republic in the near term. To alter the composition and quality of those huge stocks is bound to take many decades and massive new investments.

To obtain some perspective, we need to look beyond the dreadful macro-muddle that exists at present in all republics; it will have to be resolved somehow sooner rather than later through so-called economic stabilization programs of some kind, be they mandated from the center or worked out in each "sovereign" republic. As of now, both the center and all of the republics are committed to move to create some species of a market economy. The task of building market institutions and creating a competitive market environment with free prices is going to be gargantuan for every republic, whether it is a member of a federated union or a confederated union or remains outside such a structure. These Herculean tasks of building market institutions must be accomplished, so that the required restructuring of production and of the human and physical capital stocks can take place in accord with market signals, including those from international markets.

In the meantime, economic life must proceed. In the short run, the republics cannot get along without each other's market. Moreover, they now are locked into a common transportation and communications network. If they are to prosper in the longer term, they need to be able to exchange their products and services in the largest unfettered "economic space" possible, whether this end is achieved through union treaty, multilateral accords, or state-to-state agreements. To fragment this space, as now seems to be happening, is to commit economic folly. In sum, however the relationships among the Soviet Union's present constituent republics are to be restructured, it is critically important to the economic welfare of each and every one that the process be carried out with amity. Whether economic rationality can prevail over political and ethnic passions remains to be seen. The latest draft of the union treaty, which the republics are now considering, assigns the task of "creating conditions for the development of the unionwide market" to the central government.[21] But the treaty also lists as one of the areas of joint responsibility of the central and republican

21. *Izvestiia*, March 9, 1991.

governments that of promoting "the functioning of a single unionwide market."

REFERENCES

Dellenbrant, Jan Ake. 1986. *The Soviet Regional Dilemma.* Armonk, N.Y.: M. E. Sharpe.

Gillula, James W. 1979. "The Interdependence of Soviet Republics." *Soviet Economy in a Time of Change* 1, 618–55. Joint Economic Committee, U.S. Congress.

———. 1982. The Reconstructed Input-Output Tables for Eight Soviet Republics. Report No. 19. Foreign Economic Committee, U.S. Bureau of the Census, December.

Kukk, K. 1988. *Economic Relations of the Estonian SSR.* (In Estonian.) Tallinn.

3

Soviet Economic Reforms: Missed Opportunities and Remaining Hopes

Vladimir Popov

It is easy to be smart post factum, after decisions have already been made. The Soviet Union's many shortages do not include a lack of opinion on what the leadership should have done in the first years of perestroika. Yet, to be fair, it is necessary to confess that several years ago a group of economists suggested a package of measures that still has not been implemented (see, for instance, Shmelev 1987, 1988; Selunin 1988; G. Popov 1988). These proposals were a sort of plan for national economic revival that resembled the program put forward in September 1990 by a group of economists headed by Stanislav Shatalin. Unlike Shatalin's 500-Day Plan, the earlier proposals, though widely discussed, were not elaborated in the form of a concrete policy document. However, many of these ideas constituted the core of the Shatalin Plan. If these ideas had been adopted in 1987–1988, the Soviet economy would probably be much better off now. This was a chance to proceed with economic restructuring at a low cost, without major economic sacrifices, that is, without considerable reduction of living standards. It was a chance that, to a considerable extent, we have missed.

A BLUEPRINT FOR RADICAL ECONOMIC RESTRUCTURING

The whole plan was based on the fact that the economic heritage of the Brezhnev era was, probably unexpectedly, not all that bad. More than that, in comparison to today's economic situation it

looked really impressive: the government budget deficit and international indebtedness were considerably lower than they are
now; the consumer market was much closer to equilibrium; and
consumer prices were rising more slowly than they are today. In
fact, the government budget deficit increased from less than 20 billion rubles in 1985 to 100 billion in 1988 and remained at this
level in 1989 and 1990. The Soviet Union's net hard-currency international indebtedness increased from US$16 billion in 1985 to
US$43 billion in 1990. The delayed consumer demand,[1] calculated
as the difference between the growth of personal disposable income
and the growth of retail sales of consumer goods and services, increased from 60 billion rubles in 1984 to 165 billion in 1989, that
is, from less than 20 percent to 40 percent of retail sales. It probably reached 50 percent of retail sales before the April 1991 price increase update.

Using this favorable heritage, it would have been possible at
that time to make a transition to an efficient market economy
quickly and painlessly, provided that three major sets of reforms
were implemented decisively and simultaneously, in a package.

First, the old administrative system of centralized planning
had to be destroyed to create room for the operation of market
forces. The idea was to drastically reduce obligatory state orders for
enterprises (that is, to cut mandatory production quotas to less than
50 percent of productive capacity) and eventually to place these state
orders on a voluntary, competitive basis; to replace the system of rationed supply with wholesale trade; and to deregulate prices, let-
ting them fluctuate freely, thus balancing supply and demand.
This implied that industrial departments and regional authorities
would be deprived of a major part of their economic power, that
peasants would be allowed to quit collective and state farms with
land and means of production, and that state enterprises would in
fact be treated in the same manner as cooperatives. Radical
economists recommended that these reforms be implemented
quickly in order to make the transition period as short as possible.

---

1. The delayed consumer demand, or the monetary overhang, is the excess savings made by households because they cannot buy goods in shortage. It shows how
much of their savings consumers are willing to spend if goods become available at
the same low prices at which the government eventually sells them (not at market
clearing prices).

A gradual, step-by-step reform strategy might be expensive and dangerous, because distortions, costs, and social tensions are inevitable during the period when the old economic mechanism is no longer working and the new one is not yet working.

Second, there were proposals to create mechanisms of market regulation. Markets that are going to be created tomorrow, stated some radical economists, will inevitably be highly monopolized in most industries (except, probably, for agriculture and services). This implies that there would be a slump in production, price increases, bankruptcies, and a rise in unemployment. Besides, structural shifts in the emerging market economy would be associated with the necessity for many workers to change jobs and occupations, with rising inequalities in income distribution.

To minimize the costs of transition to a market economy, it was suggested that the Soviet Union adopt special measures and policies aimed at neutralizing the negative consequences of an emerging market: antitrust legislation and competition policy; a system of retraining of employees and labor force policy; strong social policy (unemployment insurance, low-income family allowances, pensions, indexation of fixed incomes, taxation); and monetary and fiscal policies (pumping out excess money from circulation, establishing a normal central bank and independent commercial banks, and designing a set of macroeconomic policies).

Third, because every major restructuring is accompanied not only by benefits but by costs (and costs, unfortunately, come first, while benefits come later), it was necessary to be prepared to meet these costs of transition. Because economic restructuring (reallocation of resources) would certainly be associated with recession— that is, with the temporary reduction of output due to the conversion of production (from defense to nondefense goods, from investment to consumer goods)—it would be necessary to raise funds in order to support living standards and investment in some crucial areas during the economic downturn. In the Soviet case, "perestroika costs" were associated with the need to liquidate the monetary overhang; to establish an equilibrium in the markets, especially the consumer goods market, without substantial price increases; to raise expenditure for welfare programs; to increase investment in education, medical care, and housing; and to increase investment in order to replace capital stock, which in some industries was physically worn out (for example, in railways, energy, and steel). Funds could be raised in a variety of ways: internal borrowings; privatization—the selling or leasing of some tangible assets of government property, such as state-owned apartments, land, equipment, and plants; reduction of military expenditure; regaining budget revenues from sales of vodka by stopping the anti-alcohol campaign started in 1985; and international borrowings and foreign direct investment. While proposing the use of all these methods, some radical economists were most enthusiastic about borrowings abroad. This issue finally became the major topic of discussion.

Those who advocated foreign borrowings used the following logic. Soviet net international indebtedness in hard currency was relatively low (US$26–27 billion in 1987–1988) and gold reserves were large (up to US$25–30 billion). In addition, there were large credits in rubles to developing countries, which, if the ruble were to become convertible, might be partly used to repay Soviet debt to the West (or which might be sold in the secondary market for, say, US$10–20 billion). In this scenario, the Soviet Union would have been able to borrow an extra several tens of billions of dollars in hard currency and use it to import consumer goods to saturate the market. Some economists estimated that these funds would have been sufficient to survive the transition period without a reduction in the living standards of major groups of the Soviet populace. Also, external borrowings and foreign direct investment seemed to be attractive ways to raise funds because they allow the possibility of increasing consumption without major cuts in investment. All the other ways of raising funds, by contrast, were associated solely with the redistribution of national income. Internal borrowings or sales of state assets to the public would have been a good means of eliminating the monetary overhang by transferring forced savings into voluntary savings. Strictly speaking, however, these would have been inappropriate for counterbalancing the expected reduction of living standards, due to the slump in production that should have been caused by restructuring.

After five years or so, there would have been a possibility of repaying debt, as the new market economy that emerged after the transition period would have been much more efficient than the old, centrally planned one. In fact, in the mid-1980s, nearly 20 percent of Soviet national income was spent on defense, another 30 percent on investment in fixed capital and inventories, and just 50 percent on consumption, while corresponding data for the United States were 7 percent, 6 percent, and 87 percent, respectively. The structure of Soviet GNP is quite similar: 35 percent is devoted to investment, 10 to 15 percent to defense expenditure, and only half of GNP is left for consumption, compared to 75 percent in the United States (see Table 3-1). Tremendous excess investment was caused by losses resulting from the very nature of a system of overwhelming centralized planning—a very low capacity utilization rate and extremely large inventories. The origins and the magnitude of these losses have been discussed in detail elsewhere (Shmelev and V. Popov 1989, 183–84; V. Popov 1990, 55–73), and no doubt these losses were indicative of the striking inefficiency of central planning in general and the Soviet economy in particular. This was the evidence of a very low coefficient of useful work of the whole economic system, as a 1-ruble increase of national income resulted in only 0.5-ruble growth of consumption, while in market economies this ratio is normally somewhere between 1:0.7 and 1:0.9. This should have been regarded as a clear indication that we lived much worse than we worked (in contrast to Deputy Prime Minister Leonid Abalkin, who once claimed that "we live no worse than we work"). As Gavriil Popov once put it, our economy resembles a car that just consumes gas but does not move.

At the same time, the size of the losses embodied in the centrally planned economy was the appropriate indicator of the magnitude of the economic restructuring that was going to occur during the transition to a market economy. Assuming minimal changes, that is, that the share of net investment in national income would be cut, say, in half, from 30 to 15 percent (and this would still be quite a lot for a market economy), while the share of military expenditure would be reduced from 20 to 10 percent (which would also be higher than in any Western country), there would still be a need to convert 25 percent (10 percent + 15 percent) of the national economy from the production of defense and investment goods and services to the production of consumer goods and to residential construction. In other words, at least 25 percent of Soviet employees would have to change their jobs and/or occupations. I stress *at least*, because this estimate does not take into account inevitable restructuring inside the consumer sector itself due, say, to the elimination of subsidies, as well as the need for restructuring associated with the opening up of the Soviet economy to international competition.

There was, however, another way to look at an extremely high share of investment and defense expenditure in national income. Not only was the situation a sign of the inefficiency of the Soviet economy and an indicator of the magnitude of needed restructuring, it was also a vast potential reserve for the improvement of economic performance. If the losses associated with excess inventories and idle production capacities could have been reduced to the level of those in an average market economy, there would have been ample reason to believe that economic efficiency would increase considerably due to better resource allocation. Together with envisaged cuts in military expenditure, this was supposed to provide us with the necessary funds to repay the debt. Likewise, if radical reform in agriculture (returning the land to peasants) had been implemented several years ago, a considerable increase in food production would reduce or even stop food imports, thus saving several billion dollars annually to service international indebtedness.

Needless to say, there was no sense in proceeding with foreign borrowing without simultaneous decisive measures to implement radical changes. If the new market economy was not created during the transition period, the old system probably would have swallowed all foreign credits without any increase in output, much as it did in the 1970s when it "ate up" petro-dollars (increased revenues from oil and gas exports, which were then used to buy grain). In other words, the whole program, consisting of these sets of measures, was designed to be implemented in a package. If that had really been done, it would have been by far the best and most elegant scenario of perestroika—a sort of anesthetic surgery, an easy way of restructuring, allowing full compensation for the negative economic and social consequences of reforms with the help of foreign borrowings until the time when perestroika would begin to pay for itself.

This scenario failed to materialize. Radical reforms were never carried out—partly because the government itself chose the strategy of gradual, step-by-step reforms, and partly because of bu-

Table 3-1. Gross National Expenditure by Component,
% of Total, 1989

	Soviet Official Data	Soviet Alternative Estimates	U.S.
Personal Expenditure on Consumer Goods and Services	48.1	40 – 45	66.3
Government Expenditure on Goods and Services (without Capital Outlays)	20.8	20 – 25	15.9
Nondefense	12.7	5 – 10	9.8
Defense	8.1	10 – 15	6.1
Gross Capital Investment	31.1	35	19.4
Net Exports and Statistical Discrepancy	–	-5 – +5	-1.6

Sources: Goskomstat; CIA; U.S. Department of Commerce.

reaucratic resistance, which impeded the implementation of even those reform-related laws and regulations that were approved by the Supreme Soviet and the government.

One way or another, the transition to a market economy was delayed to an indefinite future. At the same time, virtually nothing was done to create appropriate mechanisms of market regulation. Only in 1989 did the government recognize the necessity of designing laws on competition, banking, and employment and begin the work of elaborating specific policies in these areas. Laws on these activities were adopted in 1990–1991. What was probably worst of all, the government in these years (1985–1990) decided to finance an increasing budget deficit by printing money. This move created terrible shortages of everything and nearly destroyed the consumer market, replacing it more and more by a system of rationed supply.

Regarding foreign borrowing, the government publicly declared its unwillingness to increase its debts, pointing out that the international investment position of the Soviet Union was already bad. No comments were made about the proposal by economists such as Nikolai Shmelev to use gold reserves as collateral (in fact, there are still no official data on Soviet gold reserves). The net international indebtedness of the Soviet Union in hard currency increased in 1985–1988 from US$16 to US$27 billion, but this was largely the result of dollar depreciation. (Roughly half of the Soviet debt is denominated in Western European currencies and in Japanese yen).

The net indebtedness nearly doubled in 1989–1990, this time because of increased borrowing, but the credits were used mostly to meet the current balance-of-payments requirements rather than to pay the costs of restructuring, as there was simply no major restructuring going on. As the Soviet debt-service ratio grew and political instability increased, the Soviet credit rating deteriorated. Soviet debt was already trading at a discount in the secondary market in 1990, while credit arrears increased to several billion dollars. Private banks stopped lending money to the Soviet government without state guarantees.

Eventually, the government found itself in 1989 in a position where major economic reforms had not yet been started, while economic conditions had seriously deteriorated. The government budget deficit had increased considerably, as had the government internal and external debt. Monetary overhang became huge, and inflation accelerated. The partial dismantling of the old system of administrative planning resulted in distortions and the weakening of work discipline, so production virtually ceased to grow and living standards fell. For 1989, Goskomstat (the State Committee for Statistics) reported a 1.7 percent increase in real industrial output, but due to the poor price indexes used in these calculations, it probably meant that there was no growth at all. For example, of 144 of the most important industrial products that are constantly monitored by Goskomstat, the physical volume of output of sixty-two products was lower than in the previous year.[2] This corresponds with CIA and DIA estimates that there was no growth in Soviet industry in 1989. For the first half of 1990, even Goskomstat reported a decrease of 0.7 percent in industrial output; and a 2 percent reduction in GNP and a 4 percent reduction in national income was reported for 1990 (CIA/DIA 1990, 30; Goskomstat reports).

The government proposed in May 1990 to increase consumer goods prices starting from 1991. This was another major mistake, as people began to hoard goods immediately, expecting price rises, and the consumer market collapsed. Virtually everything from noodles to groats to cigarettes disappeared from the shelves during the summer of 1990.

OPTIONS FOR ECONOMIC REFORMS IN 1990

By September 1990, the options for financing the economic restructuring and, more broadly, for transforming the Soviet economy into a market-type one, materialized into two distinctly different programs put forward by radicals (democrats) and conservatives (bureaucrats). The first program was prepared by a group of economists, headed by Shatalin and created by the joint decision of Mikhail Gorbachev and Boris Yeltsin. The second program was designed by the government and in fact was just a modified version of the government program that failed to get the support of the Supreme Soviet in May 1990.

2. *Kommunist,* N2, 1990, 27.

The Shatalin Plan was by and large a real plan for radical
market-type reforms, based on a blueprint described earlier. It envisaged decisive measures for financial stabilization (for example,
privatization of state enterprises, internal borrowing, and sales of
state apartments and gold reserves); rapid dismantling of central
planning (elimination of obligatory production quotas together
with the rationed supply system and deregulation of prices); truly
radical agrarian reform; creation of the appropriate "market infrastructure" (a new banking system, antitrust legislation and competition policy, social security net); and borrowing abroad (also,
asking for financial assistance from the West to support the program) and other ways of obtaining foreign currency to finance the
costs of transition.

Most important, the Shatalin Plan was supported by most, if not
all, the republics. It envisaged considerable decentralization of
economic power and thus provided a real chance to preserve the all-
union monetary system, to keep the ruble as a single currency for
all the republics, and to avoid the disintegration of the emerging
Soviet market, through the setting of republican and regional currencies and other barriers to trade.

The government (Prime Minister Nikolai Ryzhkov) program,
prepared by September 1990, was more radical than the previous
version submitted in May on the issue of privatization,[3] but nevertheless it was still based on an old approach to price reform, that is,
administrative manipulations with prices and compensation instead of deregulation of prices. In other words, the Ryzhkov program still did not envisage the creation of a market-type economy,
because there can be no market with fixed prices. By the time this
plan appeared, the government recognized that the economy was
already rapidly sliding into a recession. By Ryzhkov's estimate, if
no measures were taken, industrial output and national income
would decrease in 1991 by 15 percent and investment in material
production by 35 percent.

---

3. The Council of Ministers took a liberal stance toward privatization between
May and September 1990. During this period, it issued decrees allowing private
businesses with up to 25 to 200 employees and transformation of state enterprises
into joint-stock companies. This attitude toward privatization was reflected in the
September program.

The immediate implementation of the Shatalin Plan (scheduled in the program itself for October 1, 1990) was definitely the preferable option, allowing for rapid, shock-therapy treatment of the economy on the basis of consensus among republics. It was thus possible to avoid a painful and costly collapse of the command economy and to ensure that the rules for restructuring would not be changed constantly, misleading enterprises and individuals, but rather would be set from the very beginning, facilitating economic agents to elaborate and pursue an adjustment strategy.

This is not to say that there were no costs associated with the Shatalin Plan. In fact, one must take with extreme caution the predictions of the program itself: a temporary (unspecified in quantitative terms) reduction of output during the first 400 days; an increase in unemployment from 6 million in 1990 to 12 million by the end of 1991 (a rise in unemployment from 4 to 8 percent); and a stabilization of living standards during the transition period.[4] This was just wishful thinking. Government estimates that the implementation of the Shatalin Plan could lead to 30 percent or more reduction in living standards might be closer to reality.[5] Nevertheless, there is no doubt that costs associated with the Shatalin-type restructuring would have been lower than in the case of the implementation of the Ryzhkov plan of step-by-step reforms.

Unfortunately, the Shatalin Plan was not carried out. Although Gorbachev lent his support to the plan early on, he later backed a combination of both the Shatalin and Ryzhkov plans. Eventually this new presidential plan, liberal in essence and very vague and general in form, was approved by the Supreme Soviet in October 1990. This plan forced the republics to abandon the idea of economic compromise and to seek their own ways out independently. Russia and many other republics stated their intentions to pursue 500-Day (or similar) plans, no matter what the central government chose. The Ukraine introduced in the beginning of November 1990 a sort of republican consumer money: 70 percent of workers' wages and salaries are now paid not only in rubles but also in coupons, which must be used together with rubles when

4. "Contseptsiya i Programma," *Perekhod k Rynky*, 1990, 132. Working Group created by a joint decision of Mikhail Gorbachev and Boris Yeltsin.
5. For a discussion of this issue, see Hewett (1990, 161–62).

purchasing consumer goods. Other republics and regions started to take similar steps, so that the balkanization of the Soviet economy received additional stimulus. Finally, in the beginning of November 1990, the same economists that worked on the 500-Day Plan, including Shatalin himself, came up with an open statement that their own program was no longer feasible. Republican governments, they said, no longer believed in the idea of economic union and common market managed by the central authorities; they now relied on protectionist policies, while the all-union government increased wholesale prices instead of promoting financial stabilization, thus doing everything to stimulate economic separatism of the republics.

By the end of 1990, it looked very much like the Shatalin Plan was buried, and there was no more hope for joint and coordinated efforts by the republics and central authorities to ensure radical market-type reforms. Still, there was some chance for the second-best option: gradual transition to the market carried out by presidential decrees without a major clash between central, republican, and regional authorities. This scenario implied that either republican governments would hold back their demands for greater economic independence, or the central authorities would somehow ensure that different regions and republics would not pursue the strategy of economic separatism. A gradual transition period was definitely more expensive than "shock therapy" in terms of restructuring costs, but this may well have been a preferable option, as it avoided the burden of regional disintegration. But more radical-minded republican governments and regional authorities were not willing to support the less radical economic program of the president. The chances that this second-best option would be adopted grew worse and worse as time passed, and the republics one by one opted for full economic independence to ensure that they had enough power to implement radical reforms.

Finally, the third option, economic disintegration of the Union, involved the highest costs for citizens. Economic disintegration would result in the emergence of many different markets separated by their own currencies, customs duties, and other trade barriers, as the republics and smaller regional units proceeded with their own distinct reform programs. The costs of this scenario were obvious: the central government, republics and regional authorities would have been engaged in a disastrous fight over the distribution of economic power, a fight that would absorb the time, effort, and energy that otherwise would have been invested in the implementation of much-needed reforms. Introducing separate currencies and tariff and nontariff trade barriers would cause an expensive restructuring of existing inter-regional trade flows. Prospects for Western financial assistance, direct investment and credits would have become more uncertain.

As can be seen in Table 3-2, for all the republics, with the exception of Russia, trade with the rest of the Soviet Union is absolutely essential. Exports and imports, respectively, amount to 25 percent or more of the republics' GNPs (for eleven republics the indicator is over 34 percent, for six over 45 percent). Most republics (ten out of fifteen) have negative balances in inter-republican trade in Soviet domestic prices, and all republics, except Belorussia and Azerbaidzhan, import more than they export (including trade with foreign countries). The shift to world prices is likely to result in deteriorating trade balances in nine republics (Belorussia, the Baltics, the Caucasian republics, Moldova [formerly Moldavia], and Uzbekistan) and to improve trade balances in six (mostly for Russia, but also for Kazakhstan, the Ukraine, and the Central Asian republics, except Uzbekistan). For the six republics that currently want to secede (the Baltics, Armenia, Georgia, and Moldova), the total trade deficit in world prices ranges from 13 to 30 percent of GNP—far more than the independent states can sustain.

The disintegration of the all-union market through the introduction of trade barriers and separate republican currencies (third scenario) was likely to cause a restructuring of the magnitude of 10 to 20 percent of GNP for the Soviet Union as a whole and an even greater one for smaller republics. When added to the burden of restructuring resulting from the transition to a market-based economy, inevitable for all the republics (that is, conversion of the construction and heavy and defense industries to the production of consumer goods and residential construction), the total cost might have been as high as 50 percent of GNP for some republics. It was hard to imagine how these costs would be shared, given the high degree of social and national tensions that existed even before the restructuring started.

By the end of 1990, events were definitely developing along the lines of the third scenario, because Gorbachev was not willing or able to accept the ultimatum of the democratic bloc (to change the government and to accept the Shatalin Plan), while the democrats were not prepared to compromise with Gorbachev by supporting his program of gradual reform. The paradox of the situation was that the democrats (that is, the republican and regional authorities highly influenced by the democrats), pushing strongly in favor of the first option, in reality speeded up the development along the lines of the third, most painful, scenario.

RECENT DEVELOPMENTS

The new political developments in late 1990–early 1991 created a completely different environment for economic perestroika. After liberals were replaced by conservatives in the key government positions in December 1990–January 1991, after the censorship in the media was tightened, and after the military started an open fight against republican authorities in the Baltics and began patrolling major cities, it became apparent that a recent shift to the right in Soviet politics should be regarded as something more serious than just a temporary episode. What this recent shift actually means is that the army (together with the KGB and military-industrial complex) tried to establish itself as a major acting force in Soviet politics, making it clear it will not hesitate to use force to prevent the disintegration of the Union.

Unfortunately, those analysts that used to say it was unreasonable to expect a country such as the Soviet Union, with no firm democratic traditions, to make a smooth transition from totalitarian state to parliamentarianism proved to be right. Nevertheless, the conservative renaissance in politics does not mean that the economic reform process is over or that market-oriented restructuring will come to an end.

It would certainly be wrong to argue that an authoritarian rather than democratic political rule may be preferable and/or inevitable for the period of transition from the administrative-command economy to a market-based one. First, democracy and political freedoms are of high value by themselves, not just as a

Table 3-2. Trade Flows and Trade Balances for the Republics, 1988, as a Percentage of GNP

| Republic | Trade Flows[a] | | Trade Balance | | | |
	D^b	F^c	D	F	Total 1[d]	Total 2[e]
USSR	21.11	8.27	-0.01	-5.76	-5.78	0.21
RSFSR	12.92	9.37	0.05	-6.28	-6.23	5.76
Ukraine	26.90	7.14	2.55	-4.61	-2.05	-2.04
Belorussia	44.56	7.39	11.14	-5.42	5.72	-5.78
Lithuania	47.26	7.21	-6.56	-5.83	-12.39	-29.97
Latvia	46.85	7.21	-1.03	-6.18	-7.21	-13.39
Estonia	50.11	8.79	-5.27	-7.03	-12.31	-22.86
Armenia	47.85	5.84	-4.23	-9.70	-13.92	-17.40
Georgia	37.88	5.90	1.98	-6.15	-4.17	-13.43
Azerbaidzhan	35.38	5.95	13.89	-6.61	7.28	-3.31
Kazakhstan	29.48	4.69	-14.47	-5.09	-19.56	-17.69
Uzbekistan	34.10	5.62	-5.78	-0.59	-6.37	-8.71
Turkmenia	37.58	4.60	-1.53	-3.07	-4.60	0.00
Kirghizia	39.65	5.98	-7.21	-10.24	-17.45	-15.86
Tadzhikistan	37.70	6.01	-15.32	-2.10	-17.42	-16.52
Moldavia	45.88	6.37	-1.87	-7.86	-9.74	-24.34

a. (Exports + Imports):(2 x GNP), at domestic prices, assuming the same GNP/NMP ratios for the republics as for the Soviet Union as a whole. Domestic Trade is trade with the rest of the Union. Foreign Trade is trade with the rest of the world.
b. D = Domestic.
c. F = Foreign.
d. Total 1 = Total in domestic prices.
e. Total 2 = Total in world prices.
Source: Stabilization, Liberalization and Devolution: Assessment of the Economic Situation and Reform Process in the Soviet Union. Report prepared by the Commission of the European Communities. December 1990. Data are derived from official Soviet statistics.

framework for implementing economic reforms. Second, it is possible to develop political democracy during the transition period, given that appropriate policies are pursued. Third, democratization, leading to the emergence of the new centers of political power, may well be the precondition for overcoming the resistance of existing bureaucratic structures in order to push forward economic reforms.

On the other hand, it would be wrong to conclude that market-type reforms may not be carried out under an authoritarian regime. In fact, this has been proven by the recent experience of such countries as Turkey, South Korea, and Chile. As far as the current Soviet situation is concerned, it seems rather obvious that the profound economic and political changes initiated by Gorbachev, and, even more important, the tremendous shift in public consciousness that occurred during the glasnost period, are now irreversible. It is hard to imagine how the Soviet Union can return to the system that existed prior to 1985.

Gorbachev, who compromised with conservatives, should be regarded mostly as a tragic figure, a politician trying to avoid greater sacrifices by agreeing to smaller ones. Leaving emotions aside, one should admit that Gorbachev now is a constraint for the military and other conservatives. Likewise, if he resigns, as demanded by the radicals, it is possible that he would be replaced by a less influential politician who would be easily manipulated by conservatives. However, the new team of politicians promoted to high government positions does not seem to be radical or reform-minded—they are primarily state bureaucrats strongly associated with and responsible for the government policies in recent years, politices that, needless to say, were not radical enough and involved a great deal of mismanagement.

In fact, the first major economic measures of the new leadership do not look encouraging. The January 1991 presidential decree giving the KGB the right to enter any business enterprise (including joint ventures) and carry out on-the-spot audits of accounts, stocks, and cash, as well as the confiscatory monetary reform, does not contribute at all to the transition to a market economy. In addition, the April 2, 1991, price reform, which boosted prices of consumer goods over 60 percent on average while raising wages and pensions, was in fact the old government program of price increases rejected by the Supreme Soviet in May 1990. It was not designed to carry out the transition to a market economy, because it did not envisage major price deregulation, and it was not even the best way to deal with the monetary overhang in the framework of a centrally planned economy. According to preliminary estimates, price increases will improve the situation in the consumer market only temporarily, and by the end of 1991 the monetary overhang will start to accumulate again, which means that new price increases are inevitable in the near future.

Nevertheless, monetary and price reforms certainly contribute to elimination of the monetary overhang and thus make it easier for the government to proceed with price deregulation and other market-type reforms. The issue at stake therefore, is whether the government will be willing to take advantage of these opportunities.

A recent fortunate development is that the republics and the center seem to have started to move toward a compromise. On April 23, an agreement (the "nine-plus-one" agreement) was signed by nine republics (Russia, the Ukraine, Belorussia, Kazakhstan, Azerbaidzhan, and four Central Asian republics) and Gorbachev. The document that was published envisaged the signing of a new union treaty among nine republics; the adoption of a new Constitution based on a new union treaty by the Congress of People's Deputies no later than six months after a union treaty is signed; the elections of new power bodies, provided by the treaty and the Constitution; most-favored-nation treatment for the republics signing the union treaty; cancellation of the 5 percent (presidential) sales tax introduced in early 1991 for consumer goods and services of everyday demand, lowering some consumer goods and services prices and tariffs; income indexation; and a joint call to stop strikes, civil disobedience, and calls to overthrow existing lawfully elected state power bodies.

Some newspapers reported there was another unpublished agreement in which Gorbachev in fact promised to respect fully republican legislation and not to interfere in republican affairs. There were also reports of a new accord on the issue of the distribution of tax revenues between the center and the republics.

Whatever the case, mutual polemics after the accord stopped, and Yeltsin started to call Gorbachev an ally. In April, nearly all

of the Russian mining industry—half the Soviet total—was transferred from the jusrisdiction of the center to that of the Russian
government, and Yeltsin persuaded the miners to end the strike.

CONCLUSION

In the first years of perestroika, when the initial economic
conditions for restructuring (monetary overhang, government
budget deficit, and external indebtedness) were not bad at all,
there was evidently a real opportunity to pay for the costs of economic reforms by increasing imports of consumer goods. This
could be financed without any assistance from abroad, through
normal commercial borrowings in international financial markets, using gold reserves as collateral. There was a real opportunity
to pay back these credits in five to seven years, after perestroika began to pay for itself. Unfortunately, this opportunity was missed, as
the Soviet government failed to implement radical market-type reforms while borrowing abroad without any definite plan, just to
meet current balance-of-payments requirements. As a result, by
1989, as economic conditions deteriorated and foreign indebtedness increased, it was no longer possible to pay the inevitable costs
of restructuring just by normal borrowings, without any Western
assistance.

It also looks as if another chance to ensure a smooth transition
to a market economy in the Soviet Union was missed in 1990,
when the Soviet government failed to approve the Shatalin Plan
and to ask for assistance, while the Western countries failed to offer the Soviet Union an assistance package for such collateral as a
commitment to radical economic reform and an agreement
among republics to implement it. It may be argued that if this
package was put together by Western governments and international organizations and offered to the Soviet Union in exchange
for a commitment to the radical market-type reform, it could have
become a major factor in Soviet internal politics, leaving much less
chance for the conservative restoration that occurred in late 1990
and early 1991.

Recent conservative developments in Soviet politics do not necessarily mean that all Western assistance to the Soviet Union

should be cancelled and that new aid should not be considered. For the West, the single most important channel of influencing the course of events in the Soviet Union is still the assistance package. Leaving the door open for the negotiations about this package, the West may have better opportunities for encouraging democratic and market-oriented reforms in the Soviet Union.

It may be reasonable, therefore, to consider the project of putting together a "perestroika assistance package," announcing that it would be available for the Soviet Union on certain political and economic conditions, such as: (1) no human rights violations; (2) commitment of the government and parliament to the radical market-type reforms; and (3) a union treaty agreement between republics and the central government on the distribution of economic powers and on economic and monetary union. It is quite likely that this kind of joint proposal, worked out by the major Western countries, the European Community, the International Monetary Fund, the World Bank, and the European Bank for Reconstruction and Development, may lead to a sort of national debate in the Soviet Union that will stimulate democratic and market-oriented reforms.

The issue of financial assistance to the Soviet Union is going to be discussed this year in any case. Soviet financial requirements (current-account deficit + debt amortization) are projected for 1991 at a level of up to US$27 billion, with only US$17 billion promised by Western governments. The other US$10 or more billion is a financing gap that may well require debt rescheduling.[6]

One way or another, there are still different scenarios for market-type reforms, none of which, however, ensures a low-cost transition to a market economy. The issues at stake are different now. For how long and how much people will have to tighten their belts? In what way will the costs of perestroika be distributed among different social groups, republics, and regions? And will people be willing to accept these sacrifices without strikes and unrest? It is necessary to admit that by now, after five years of perestroika, the opportunities for painlessly restructuring the Soviet economy are lost once and for all, and Soviet citizens, who have al-

6. See the joint study by the IMF, IBRD, OECD, and EBRD, *The Economy of the USSR*, a study undertaken in response to a request by the Houston summit. Summary of Recommendations, December 1990, 16.

ready experienced a slow erosion of their living standards, are now facing an inevitable considerable reduction of real incomes. The slump in output and real incomes, as previously noted, may be as deep as 25 to 30 percent, and the unemployment rate may reach as much as 15 to 20 percent. Regions of depression may emerge, most likely in areas where heavy industry dominates, such as the Donbass coal mining region in the Southern Ukraine, the Urals, and Leningrad.

Over the next one to two years, perhaps the highest national priority will be to survive the looming economic difficulties without social and national unrest. We must get used to the idea that drastic cuts in real incomes in the upcoming years are inevitable, and that now we can only attenuate the blow, but not dodge it. Again, it is common knowledge that losses are much harder to share than profits: when material difficulties increase, people are apt to show their worst qualities. Will the Soviet Union avoid an excessive escalation of social demand, an increase in the number of strikes that reduce real incomes, and other developments that could turn the entire process into a chain reaction? Also, can we all— radicals and conservatives, Jews and Russians, members of cooperatives and trade unions—agree in a civilized manner on our common respective expenditures?

We shall exercise enough self-control, I hope, to pass the now inescapable time of economic hardship without panic and/or violence. There is nothing we can do now, for without tightening our belts we would fail to establish an efficient market economy. Life goes on, and so does perestroika. In the past, things were at times even worse, so let us be patient in overriding the trials we face now and do our best to hasten our movement to a full-fledged market economy, to which there is no alternative anyway.

REFERENCES

CIA/DIA. 1990. "The Soviet Economy Stumbles Badly in 1989." A paper presented by the CIA and DIA to the Joint Economic Committee, U.S. Congress, May.
Hewett, Ed A. 1990. "The New Soviet Plan." *Foreign Affairs.* Winter.

Popov, Gavriil. 1988. "Tseli i Mechanism." *Znamya.* July, 168–74.

Popov, Vladimir. 1990. "Perestroika and the Demand for Capital." In Michael P. Claudon and Josef C. Brada, eds. *Reforming the Ruble: Monetary Aspects of Perestroika.* New York: New York University Press.

Selunin, V. 1988. "Glubokaya Reforma ili Revansh Burokratii?" *Znamya.* July, 155–67.

Shmelev, Nikolai. 1987. "Avancy i Dolgy." *Noviy Mir.* July 1987, 142–58.

———. 1988. "Noviye Trevogy." *Noviy Mir.* April, 160–75.

Shmelev, Nikolai, and Vladimir Popov. 1989. *The Turning Point: Revitalizing the Soviet Economy.* New York: Doubleday.

4

The Latest Developments in the Foreign Currency Practices and Regulations of the Soviet Union

Eugene Uljanov

The Soviet Union today is in the midst of an historic attempt to transform its economic system. Under the leadership of President Mikhail Gorbachev, the Soviet Union has made tremendous strides in dismantling the old, administrative-command economy. However, investors wishing to take advantage of opportunities in the Soviet Union are still confronted by an enormously difficult business environment. Difficulties include the lack of a strong, Western-oriented legal framework for property ownership and transfer; the lack of a local stock market for facilitating ownership transfers and the intermediation of capital resources; the underdevelopment of Soviet disclosure and accounting standards; the inconvertibility of the ruble; and the general shortage of foreign exchange.

Nonetheless, while the Shatalin 500-Day Plan and other high-profile plans for reform have been grabbing the headlines, there has been a slow but steady movement toward the resolution of many of the above problems. Specifically, during early 1991, the Supreme Soviet passed a number of critical laws related to banking, currency, and investment. Chief among them were: the USSR Law on the USSR State Bank;[1] the Decree on Implementation of the USSR Law on the USSR Law on the USSR State Bank;[2] the USSR

The views expressed in this paper are those of the author and do not necessarily reflect any official Soviet interpretation.

1. *Izvestiia*, December 18, 1990.
2. Ibid.

Law on Banks and Banking Activity;[3] the Law of the USSR on Currency Regulations;[4] and the Fundamentals of Legislation on Investment in the USSR.[5]

The paper will discuss and review the most critical aspects of the above legislation, as well as some general points about the overall banking, currency, and investment situation in the Soviet Union.

THE CURRENT SOVIET BANKING SITUATION

The Role of the Bank for Foreign Economic Affairs of the Soviet Union

The Bank for Foreign Economic Affairs of the Soviet Union (BFEA) occupies a critical place in the financial system of the Soviet Union. It is involved in the financing of foreign trade and investment projects, the transfer of payments across the border, the extension of hard-currency credit to domestic and foreign borrowers, the trading of precious metals and currencies, and a number of other activities. (A fuller description of these activities can be found in Appendix 4-A.)

Until the end of 1987, the Soviet Bank for Foreign Economic Affairs was organized as a joint-stock company. Seventy percent of its shares were owned by Gosbank, the State Bank of the USSR, the ministries of finance, and foreign trade. The remaining 30 percent of the shares were held by various foreign trade organizations (FTOs).

On July 17, 1987, Decree No. 821 of the Soviet Council of Ministers and the Communist Party of the Soviet Union Central Committee reorganized the Soviet banking system. Gosbank became a central bank, and five specialized banks were established. One of those specialized banks, Vneshtorgbank, was also given an expanded role and renamed the Bank for Foreign Economic Affairs of the USSR (Vnesheconombank, or BFEA).

---

3. Ibid.
4. *Izvestiia*, March 15, 1990
5. *Izvestiia*, December 16, 1990.

Pursuant to the decree and effective from January 1, 1988, the Soviet government settled the claims of Vneshtorgbank's shareholders, and the value of Vneshtorgbank's stock and reserve capital was effectively converted into BFEA's statutory capital and reserve fund. BFEA assumed all of Vneshtorgbank's assets, rights, and powers, and it assumed full responsibility for all Vneshtorgbank's liabilities and obligations.

Among the powers and responsibilities specifically given to BFEA by Decree No. 821 were:

1. carrying out all international settlements and all foreign currency banking operations of the Soviet Union;
2. granting foreign currency loans to domestic clients and operating in international markets; and
3. exercising control over and monitoring the execution of the country's Consolidated Foreign Exchange Plan. (Under this plan, BFEA, on behalf of the Soviet government, monitors all hard-currency debits and credits and works to ensure that adequate amounts of foreign exchange are available to meet the country's balance-of-payments needs.)

Subsequently, BFEA was also given the further, important responsibility of licensing all foreign borrowing by all domestic entities, that is, deciding which domestic entities can borrow abroad (Decree No. 203, March 7, 1989).

In December 1990, the Supreme Soviet adopted several new banking laws: the USSR Law on the USSR State Bank, the Decree on Implementation of the USSR Law on the USSR Law on the USSR State Bank, and the USSR Law on Banks and Banking Activity. According to these laws, the five specialized banks were reconstituted, and they must now begin to operate increasingly on a commercial basis. Several of these banks are now attempting to transform themselves into joint-stock companies. Because joint-stock companies have greater independence from the government, it is hoped that this status will allow the banks to operate in a more profitable and economically rational manner. In addition to all operations previously stipulated in its statutes and all new operations received while acting as a commercial bank, BFEA was also given several specific "agent of state" functions. These included:

1. borrowing on the international capital markets on behalf of the Soviet government;
2. servicing existing debt obligations; and
3. managing, in its own name, the foreign exchange reserves of the country under the guidelines set by Gosbank.

BFEA's activities, as well as the activities of all other commercial banks (including both the four other ex-"specialized" banks and all newly formed banks) are supervised by Gosbank. Gosbank applies supervisory standards such as capital adequacy ratios, liquidity guidelines, and single borrower exposure limits. Gosbank's standards are based on the current international practice and the recommendations of the Basle Committee on Banking Supervision.

In accordance with BFEA's statutes, the Bank possesses its own assets and may invest in the share capital of its affiliates, participate in joint ventures and national organizations in the Soviet Union, and establish branches and representative offices in the Soviet Union and abroad. The Bank is a juridical person under the laws of the Soviet Union and does not enjoy immunity from any suit, action, or proceeding, or from execution of a judgment or attachment (whether in aid of execution, before judgment or otherwise). Its capital is described in its statutes (Article 12) as "statutory capital" which may not be reduced without amending the Bank's statutes. BFEA may be sued in the event of any default on its obligations, and judgments obtained against the Bank in foreign courts of law will be enforced by the courts of the Soviet Union in accordance with Soviet laws.

BFEA's obligations do not carry the explicit guarantee of the Soviet government. In fact, the statutes of the Bank (Article 55) expressly provide that the Soviet government "is not liable for the obligations of the Bank." All industrial, commercial, and financial organizations in the Soviet Union are now expected to be self-financing and liable for their own obligations, and this too is provided for in the Bank's statutes (Article 18). Conversely, the Bank is not responsible for the obligations, external or domestic, of government organizations (for example, FTOs) that may be transacted through the Bank, but are not expressly guaranteed by the Bank (Article 55).

The Wider Commercial Banking Market

In accordance with the December 1990 laws on banking, the Soviet banking system is undergoing a reorganization. In its most basic form (as noted above), the change breaks up the banking system into two tiers: the first is the supervisory level, that is, Gosbank and the central banks of the republics, and the second is a commercial level, that is, all other banks.

The activities of Gosbank and the republican central banks are aimed at supporting the stability of the national currency of the Soviet Union; implementing national policies in the field of money supply and domestic credit, settlements, and foreign exchange operations; protecting the interests of banking clients; and facilitating the development of the national economy and its integration into the world market.

Gosbank and the republican central banks of the reserve system are money-issuing authorities. They act as lenders of last resort for commercial banks, organize interbank settlements, service the public debt of the Soviet Union and the republics, carry out operations in the securities and foreign exchange markets, and manage gold and foreign exchange reserves of the Soviet Union. The highest body of management of the reserve system is the Central Council of Gosbank, comprising the chairman, first deputy chairman, and ten other members representing the republics.

Gosbank does not interfere in the day-to-day business of the commercial banks but supervises their activities and performance, by way of issuing licenses for domestic and external operations, establishing minimum capital and risk requirements, setting capital, liquidity, and reserve ratios, and establishing basic accounting principles.

Under the December 1990 Union Law, only the Union Gosbank is authorized to issue currency. But under various republic laws, the republican central banks claim the right to issue, or otherwise independently control, currency issuance. Since the April 1991 "nine-plus-one" agreement between Gorbachev and representatives of the republics, the currency issue seems to be headed for a more centralized status whereby the republics work together through the Union Gosbank to control the issuance of currency.

The commercial banks represent an important new part of the banking system. In many ways, the recent banking laws are bringing order to the process of banking decentralization that began in early 1988 with the establishment of the new joint venture laws. Because banking can be described as a normal, albeit specialized, feature of business, many individuals and enterprises took advantage of the law on cooperatives to form banks. Because these activities were not proscribed under existing Soviet law, the new banking enterprises were allowed to operate in the periphery of the Soviet financial system.

In addition to the earlier formation of the bank cooperatives, a number of formerly all-union financial institutions, such as the local offices of BFEA in the Baltic republics, used the new atmosphere to create more independent financial operations. This independence is evident in such matters as the Baltic central banks' ability to manage their own currency auctions, bypassing the more centralized system formerly operated by BFEA in Moscow, and now operated by Gosbank in Moscow (please see below). The Baltic foreign exchange auctions were even sanctioned under a 1990 agreement with Union authorities. The thrust of the recent banking reform laws will more fully sanction the operation of these newly formed banks, bringing them into the center of the Soviet financial system and providing a framework for their safe and appropriate regulation.

Founded on principles of competition and self-sufficiency, commercial banks represent the most radical aspect of the reorganization of the banking system. By authorizing the establishment of a new tier of banks, competition for customer business is encouraged. These banks do not exert the economic control inherent in a system where credit allocation decisions are made centrally. These banks receive no financial support from the government and are expected to be self-financing. They are free to decide both the type and volume of business they wish to undertake, as well as the commercial terms on which it is transacted. Their business is based upon a commercial assessment of risk and profitability and is not influenced by government planning.

As of the end of April 1991, more than 2,000 commercial banks were registered with Gosbank. The minimum capital requirement set by Gosbank for the establishment of a commercial bank is

5 million rubles. Although the commercial banks are permitted to establish branches and affiliates throughout the Soviet Union, their activities are still mainly confined to their local areas of operation. A National Association of Commercial Banks was established in April 1989 to coordinate the activities of and provide practical assistance to the commercial banks and represent them in various Soviet and international organizations. By early 1991, about 160 Soviet commercial banks had become members of the Association. Since March 1, 1991, thirty of the above commercial banks have received licenses from Gosbank to conduct foreign currency operations. For all practical purposes, however, BFEA remains the major Soviet operator on the international currency and capital markets, the biggest creditor in terms of foreign currency loans granted to domestic borrowers, and it holds a predominant part of all the foreign exchange funds of Soviet companies in the form of current and term accounts. Thus, the Bank maintains the *de facto* position of the specialized foreign exchange bank of the country.

CURRENCY REGULATIONS AND OPERATIONS

Regulations and practices regarding the use of foreign exchange in Soviet business operations have changed significantly over the last few years. The most recent pronouncement on this subject is the March 1, 1991, Law of the USSR on Currency Regulation (hereafter, the Currency Law).

Ruble Operations

According to the Currency Law, nonresidents, which can include both companies and individuals, can hold Soviet currency acquired legally. Without special permission from Gosbank, however, this currency cannot be exported from the country. Additionally, nonresidents for foreign exchange purposes can open and maintain ruble accounts at any of the duly licensed banking institutions (see below). Terms and conditions of these accounts are currently being established by Gosbank.

The recent Currency Law (as well as the above-noted banking laws) is also significant because it affirmed the role of the ruble in domestic Soviet transactions. Previously, most hard-currency dealings on Soviet territory had been illegal. The affirmation of the importance of the ruble was designed to promote its domestic use. Consequently, foreign exchange (with several exceptions) can only be used inside the Soviet Union with the permission of the Ministry of Foreign Economic Relations.

The ruble must now be accepted "without limit" in the payment of any domestic claims and obligations.[6] As a result, and in keeping with the previous laws, Soviet entities and citizens do not always have the immediate right to invoice foreign clients in hard currency without first receiving special permission from Gosbank. Under recent clarifications issued by Gosbank, foreign entities resident for exchange purposes in the Soviet Union can be invoiced for certain services related to foreign trade.[7]

Hard-Currency Operations

A second feature of the Currency Law concerns the ability of Soviet entities and individuals to hold and use hard currency. Previously, Soviet individuals and institutions that were able to demonstrate that hard currency was acquired legally could maintain accounts at BFEA. The current Currency Law widens the right of Soviet enterprises and foreign joint ventures to maintain hard-currency accounts at any authorized Soviet bank as long as the banks have specific permission from Gosbank. During 1991, the holdings of Soviet enterprises and joint ventures with less than 30 percent of foreign participation, are subject to the mandatory sale to the state of 40 percent of all revenue earned from the export of goods and services, as well as other reporting requirements. This change is significant because it substantially widens the role of commercial banking operations in the Soviet Union, and it provides Western business operations a choice of partners when considering where to place their funds.

6. Op cit., Article 2, Sections 1 and 2.
7. "On the Regulation of Foreign Currency Operations on the Territory of the USSR," *Ekonomika i Zhizn*, no. 22, May 1991.

A third feature of the Currency Law is that it replaces the previous system of foreign exchange auctions rates with a new exchange system. The new auction system that opened on April 9, 1991, is designed as a preliminary step toward convertibility. The idea is to channel more and more hard-currency transfers by companies into this market-based mechanism. This system differs from BFEA's previous "exchange" system in that Gosbank works more like a currency specialist attempting to match buyers and sellers. (The Gosbank auction system also requires that the purchaser of foreign exchange have a valid import contract indicating where the currency will be used. BFEA's previous exchange system had no such requirement.) Within several weeks of this opening, a reported US$2 million in hard currency was changing hands at each session. At the end of April 1991, the most recent rate was 36.3 rubles to the dollar. The auctions are managed by Gosbank and are located within Gosbank offices in Moscow. Approximately twenty banks and financial institutions are authorized to bid and offer at the new auctions. These banks or firms must receive licenses and purchase a seat from Gosbank. All other companies and enterprises have to trade through them. The new auction mechanism is designed to be a major outlet for the acquisition of dollars by Soviet or other enterprises. There are, however, restrictions on how this money can be utilized once it is acquired. Specifically, Soviet enterprises must demonstrate that the cash acquired at the auction will be spent on the import of hard-currency items and not be recycled for speculative purposes.

The Union-Republic Currency Committee

A fourth feature of the March Currency Law is that it provides a solid legal basis for the establishment and operation of the Union-Republic Currency Committee, stating that, henceforth, the Union Republic Currency Committee is the ". . . central State executive body for the management of the USSR currency resources."[8] As many are aware, this Committee was first established by presidential decree in November 1990. It was primarily formed to

---

8. Article 7, Section 2.

manage the non-BFEA foreign debt run up by the various FTOs. The 40 percent of hard-currency earnings surrendered by the enterprises (also announced in November 1990) was earmarked for collection and disbursement by this committee. It should also be noted that the March Currency Law widened the scope of this tax to include joint ventures with less than 30 percent foreign participation.

Constituently, the Union-Republic Currency Committee is an ad hoc committee chaired by the Soviet prime minister. The republic prime ministers also are represented on this committee. BFEA is primarily involved in its capacity as agent of state, with its most significant functions being technical and managerial. Except for those matters that are in the bounds of BFEA's own statutes, its involvement with the Committee is one of a subordinate role.

INVESTMENT LEGISLATION

The recently passed Fundamentals of Legislation on Investment in the USSR (the Fundamentals . . . of Investment), was designed to provide the basis for the protection of the rights of both foreign and domestic investors, and of the general population of the Soviet Union. It concentrates both on the protection of invested capital and the people affected by these investments. In this sense, the investment law is also concerned with the overall ecological and social environment. The Fundamentals . . . of Investment was not designed to answer every concern of every investor but to provide the framework from which a more coherent legal regime can develop. It was also meant to serve as an extension and amplification of President Gorbachev's October 1990 Decree on Foreign Investment in the Soviet Union. Neither the decree nor the Fundamentals . . . of Investment, however, have removed the prohibition on private ownership of land and natural resources.

In the October investment decree, the Soviet Union allowed for the first time 100 percent foreign ownership of business ventures. The decree gave foreigners the right to acquire shares in existing Soviet enterprises and to obtain, independently or together with a Soviet partner, "rights to the use of land." The more recent Fundamentals . . . of Investment extended these rights to guarantee all persons the general right to carry out investment activity and to use and transfer these investments as they see fit, within the overall confines of Soviet law. The Fundamentals . . . of Investment also specifically guarantees "protection of investments regardless of the forms of ownership, including foreign investments." It further states: "Investments cannot be nationalized without compensation, and no measures can be taken which are equal to nationalization or requisition without compensation."[9] Significantly, the recent investment legislation includes language guaranteeing investors compensation if their rights of investment are violated by government organs. The Fundamentals . . . of Investment also specifically establishes "agreements" between the parties to an investment as the governing document for the investors' relationship. This is the starting point for a civil society managed largely on the basis of private contracts and their enforcement in public courts.

CONCLUSIONS

Over the last several years, the Soviet banking system and the ability of Western and local concerns to transact business in hard currency and invest in the Soviet Union has been undergoing significant change. The latest round of legislation represents a major step toward the rationalization of the economic and financial order. While the legislation still may need to be amended, or new laws may need to be passed, the trend is clearly toward a freer and more open market approach to finance.

Recent statistics on the operation of foreign joint ventures in the Soviet Union seem to reveal a fairly high rate of growth, especially in the service and high-technology area. This recent growth is testament to the fact that the business climate in the Soviet Union, due to changes like those described above, is improving.

---

9. Article 23, Section 2.

APPENDIX 4-A: TYPES OF BUSINESS CONDUCTED BY BFEA

As the successor to Vneshtorgbank, one of the Bank's principal functions continues to be the financing of the Soviet Union's foreign trade. The Bank does, however, also act as a universal financial institution providing a full range of banking services.

In terms of day-to-day business, BFEA accepts and places deposits with foreign banks and other international financial institutions, maintains correspondent accounts, and opens current and term accounts in rubles and foreign currencies for domestic and nonresident customers.

The Bank provides project and trade finance to domestic enterprises, operates bank accounts for foreign currency loans granted to entities in the Soviet Union, and performs other related services. The Bank grants loans in foreign currencies to Soviet foreign trade organizations and other entities engaged in foreign trade. Apart from the traditional sources of funding, the Bank uses the Euro-commercial paper markets, as well as banker's acceptance facilities.

The Bank extends credit facilities of all maturities to customers within the Soviet Union. The terms and conditions of the loans denominated in rubles and in foreign currencies are determined by the Bank itself. The Bank grants credits in rubles and foreign currencies against security, in the form of pledges, guarantees, securities, or other forms of collateral in accordance with legislation in the Soviet Union and international banking practices.

International payment transactions executed by the Bank include letters of credit, bill collections, and transfers. In 1989, the Bank became a member of the Society for Worldwide and Inter-Bank Financial Transfers (S.W.I.F.T.). The Bank also supports the obligations of importers in the Soviet Union by guaranteeing and/or discounting promissory notes and accepting bills of exchange.

The Bank buys and sells foreign currencies to effect international settlements and to facilitate the extension of credits in foreign currencies to Soviet importers and exporters. The Bank also trades foreign exchange for its own account and on behalf of customers.

The Bank trades in gold, silver, and platinum and is also authorized to trade in other precious metals. It also deals in foreign government and public bonds, as well as in new financial instruments such as options and futures, interest rate swaps, and currency swaps.

The Bank's source of funds includes balances on current accounts and deposits, in rubles and foreign currencies, from Soviet and foreign banks and other international organizations, as well as from private customers. The Bank is free to set the rates of interest on current and deposit accounts in rubles and foreign currencies both for Soviet residents and nonresidents, and in rubles for nonresidents as well as the other terms and conditions governing the accounts and deposits in rubles and foreign currencies.

The Bank is active on the international capital markets, where it raises long- and medium-term funds for its own purposes, and it also raises funds on behalf of customers in the form of loans and public bond issues.

In the retail sector, the Bank is striving to improve client services by introducing new payment instruments for issuance and acceptance on Soviet territory. In 1988, the Bank obtained licenses to issue EuroCard-Mastercard and Visa credit cards and to sell Eurocheques. It also issues traveler's checks denominated in rubles and foreign currencies. In addition, the Bank provides custodial, cashier, and other related banking services to customers in the Soviet Union.

5

Privatization in Eastern Europe: Early Impressions

Roger S. Leeds

Reality has set in across the breadth of Eastern Europe.[1] Notwithstanding the euphoria that accompanied the scent of new-found political freedom and the perceived opportunities for financial gain, there is now painful recognition that each country is beset by an array of problems that are daunting by any historical standard. Aside from the inevitable domestic tension that results from attempts at sweeping political reform, each country in its own way faces two tightly interwoven economic challenges: achieving a reasonable degree of macroeconomic stability and creating a market economy, starting from scratch. Directly related to these two broad goals, a quantum leap is needed in the productivity and efficiency of the tens of thousands of enterprises currently owned and operated by the state. These gains, it is widely believed, will be achieved only if the private sector emerges as the predominant force in shaping the Eastern European economies after communism. Privatization is one important element of this effort to develop the private sector.

The author gratefully acknowledges the valuable assistance of Patricia Mickens.

1. The standard caveat applies about the difficulty of generalizing about a region consisting of seven countries (Albania, Bulgaria, Czechoslovakia, Hungary, Poland, Romania, and Yugoslavia), each with a distinctive history and culture. Moreover, at present these nations are at different points on the economic and political spectrum, with some far more advanced than others. The common denominator, of course, is that each has begun to dismantle the political and economic structures that were erected forty-odd years ago, and the transition is underway toward political pluralism and market-based economies.

The Soviet Union will soon embark along a similar path. The debate already is underway on how the transition should be designed and orchestrated, with little question that the ultimate goal is to abandon the centrally planned command economy in favor of a system that is driven primarily by market forces. By focusing on the early experience of the Eastern European nations with privatization, this essay aims to highlight many of the issues that Soviet decisionmakers must address in the months ahead—such as crafting a legal system for private ownership, designing strategies for the rapid sale of thousands of state-owned enterprises, surmounting human resource constraints, and contending with privatization skeptics. Although the privatization program in the Soviet Union will inevitably differ in some respects from what is presently occurring in Eastern Europe, the following pages demonstrate that there also is a striking resemblance between the two experiences. Possibly, the lessons gleaned from this early period in Eastern Europe will provide direction to the privatization architects in the Soviet republics.

Over the years, governments have adopted different interpretations of the term privatization depending on national sensitivities about the appropriate balance between the state and the private sector. Here, the term refers simply to the transfer of ownership and/or operating control of an enterprise from the state to the private sector. This is a broad interpretation, it should be noted, that includes enterprises operated commercially by professional managers, without a change in ownership. Leases, for example, fit into this category, as do management contracts and a variety of other mechanisms that allow the private sector to operate public services without actually owning them.[2]

Although the purposes of privatization may vary,[3] in virtually every case the overriding objective is to enhance enterprise efficiency. In Eastern Europe, where state enterprises account for 65 percent to 90 percent of national output, attainment of these effi-

2. In the United States, it is becoming commonplace for municipal governments to contract with private firms to operate such diverse services as waste disposal, prisons, library management, and even municipal golf courses.

3. Frequent mention is made, for example, of reducing public-sector deficits, broadening share ownership and developing capital markets, encouraging employee share ownership, and reducing the crowding out of private-sector participation in key productive activities.

ciency gains is fundamental to the achievement of the other important economic goals—macroeconomic stability and the creation of a market economy.

Privatization, of course, is only one way to improve enterprise efficiency. Where markets are competitive and enterprises are permitted to operate along commercial lines, free of political interference and subject to bankruptcy when they fail to perform, the differences between public and private ownership should become less significant. There is, however, a mounting body of empirical evidence that private firms are more likely to thrive than their state-owned counterparts—they are less vulnerable to political meddling in commercial decisions (for example, hiring, pricing), they are subject to the so-called hard budget constraint that imposes discipline on financial decisionmaking, and they are less likely to be subsidized and protected in other subtle ways that undermine the competitive forces found in open markets. It is also increasingly evident that owners who have their own capital at risk are likely to behave differently than those who will neither gain nor lose financially as a direct result of enterprise performance. Echoing a refrain commonly heard in Eastern Europe, Czechoslovakian President Vaclav Havel highlighted one of the fundamental shortcomings of ownership in a socialist economy: "The company allegedly belongs to everyone, but in reality it belongs to no one. . . . People lose—and this is the worst of all—any contact whatsoever with the meaning of their work" (Havel 1990, 17). This, in turn, has proven to be disastrous for productivity and efficiency.

Implementing privatization is extremely difficult and time-consuming under the best of conditions.[4] In Eastern Europe the climate could hardly be less favorable. Each country is suffering through a deep recession, with output declining in 1990 by an average of about 11 percent. Inflation ranged from 10 percent in Czechoslovakia to almost 600 percent in Poland, and there may be more than four million unemployed workers in the region before

---

4. Medium- and large-sized enterprises are considerably more difficult to privatize than small ones. In Poland, for example, an estimated 60,000 small shops were leased or sold to the private sector in 1990 and the first half of 1991. In contrast, eight months of preparation were required to sell five medium-sized enterprises using the technique of initial public offering.

the end of 1991.[5] During the first quarter of 1991, in the aftermath of the collapse of Comecon, trade between the Eastern European nations and the Soviet Union plunged to about 10 percent of the volume for the corresponding period a year earlier, with no significant increase in sales to the West. This is the bleak reality confronting the privatization planners in Eastern Europe. There is little to suggest that conditions in the Soviet Union are any better, and, in fact, they are considerably worse.[6]

PRIVATIZATION: WHY EASTERN EUROPE IS DIFFERENT

In Eastern Europe, as undoubtedly will be confirmed in the Soviet Union in the coming months, the task of privatizing thousands of state-owned enterprises has proven to be unimaginably more difficult than anything attempted elsewhere—in the Third World or industrialized countries. The first question to address is why.

Numbers

The dominance of state enterprise in Eastern Europe manifests itself in sheer numbers that are staggering in comparison to countries elsewhere that have implemented privatization programs. With up to 90 percent of productive capacity and employment controlled by the state, the magnitude of the transition process is unprecedented. For example, in Poland there were more than 8,700 medium- and large-sized state-owned enterprises at the end of 1990, 2,000 in Hungary, and 2,500 in Czechoslovakia.[7] No matter

---

5. *International Herald Tribune,* May 4, 1991, 4.

6. In the first quarter of 1991, Soviet GNP registered an 8 percent decline compared to a year earlier, foreign trade was off by 33 percent, investment declined by 16 percent, labor productivity in the state sector was down 9 percent, and national income fell 10 percent. Furthermore, the budget deficit has already reached 26.9 billion rubles for the first quarter of 1991 against the planned ceiling of 26.7 billion for the current year (*IMF Morning Press,* April 19, 1991, and *Wall Street Journal,* April 22, 1991).

7. The numbers are even more overwhelming in the Soviet Union. An early 1991 estimate placed 92 percent of all productive capacity in state hands, including more than 47,000 state-owned industrial enterprises and 800,000 entities in trade and services (Nellis 1991, 1).

what type of innovative formulas are created to accelerate the pace of privatization, sooner or later each of these enterprises must be subjected to some level of appraisal and valuation. And unless chaos and massive fraud are permitted to reign, this privatization process must be effectively administered and monitored by some public authority. These tasks require levels of skilled manpower that roughly correlate with the volume of enterprises eligible for privatization. The numbers in Eastern Europe suggest a work load of massive proportion.

The Enterprises

The difficulties that distinguish privatization in Eastern Europe from other parts of the world are not simply numeric. If most of these enterprises were attractive to prospective investors, the task would be considerably less formidable. But, they are not. Vast numbers are unprofitable, over-indebted, riddled with excess employment, poorly managed, and burdened with outdated, run-down plants and equipment. The result, not surprisingly, is that many are unable to operate competitively in a market economy. Many are valueless to prospective investors; others have negative value.[8]

These enterprise conditions on such a large scale pose unprecedented challenges to the most seasoned and creative minds in the privatization business. Painful tradeoffs abound. For example, should the unprofitable enterprise be liquidated, which would aggravate an already serious unemployment problem? Should privatization be delayed until value can be enhanced through enterprise restructuring? Or should the company be sold immediately, at any price, to expedite the transfer to private control? For the medium- and large-sized enterprises, the political, financial, and economic stakes are so high that questions such as these must be answered on a case-by-case basis. This, in turn, suggests a protracted process that cannot be completed quickly.

---

8. Enterprise indebtedness exceeds the book value of the company's assets.

BUILDING A FOUNDATION FOR
SUCCESSFUL PRIVATIZATION

Legal Framework

Progress in virtually every Eastern European country has been thwarted by the absence of a legal framework that clarifies how and under what circumstances property and other assets can be transferred from the state to private investors, and how corporations will behave once privatized. Debate also has raged on how to define the legal rights of the previous owners of property seized by the state. In Czechoslovakia, for example, a fierce parliamentary debate was waged for six months to determine an equitable formula for providing restitution to owners of property seized by the Communists between 1948 and 1989.[9] The legislatures in Poland, Hungary, and some of the Yugoslav republics continue to agonize over the same question of how to compensate pre-Communist owners.[10]

Once the sanctity of private ownership has been legally established and the rights of previous owners clarified, the privatization architects in Eastern Europe must address a host of other legal issues. Investor protection, for example, must be legally safeguarded; a legal code established to govern corporate behavior; copyright protection and bankruptcy laws created; and there must be a privatization law that defines the procedures for valuing and transferring state-owned assets to first-time private investors. Before it is reasonable to expect prospective investors—domestic and foreign—to risk their capital in these ventures, these measures must be taken.

---

9. The Czechoslovak Federal Assembly passed two laws establishing the legal basis for the return of properties expropriated during this time period. The first, passed in October 1990, concerns the return of approximately 70,000 smaller businesses and properties seized by the Communists between 1955 and 1961. The second, the Law on Extrajudicial Rehabilitation, is intended to govern the return of the majority of larger expropriated businesses. Controversy surrounded this second law because of disputes over who should be eligible to receive compensation and which properties should be included. See Obrman (1991, 12–13).

10. In the Soviet Union, the more fundamental debate over the legitimacy of private ownership of property has yet to be fully resolved. Legal clarification of this, it would seem, is an absolute prerequisite to any serious progress toward implementation of a privatization program.

Perceptions of Ownership

It is no wonder that after almost forty-five years of state dominance, accompanied by a skillfully orchestrated public campaign against the evils of private ownership, East Europeans are confused, ambivalent and, in some cases, suspicious of the privatization movement. Whereas a fairly widespread and growing consensus exists that the state-dominated economic system must be dismantled and replaced by something resembling Western-style capitalism, the details and character of this transition are the cause of sustained debate. Although some are unabashed advocates of free markets and capitalism, many are skeptical. They recognize that the old system is bankrupt and radical change is needed. But, these doubters have a deep-rooted commitment to egalitarianism and associate profit seeking with unethical practices, greed, excessive consumption, and, most importantly, the opening of vast chasms between rich and poor.[11] Paradoxically, even though they seek far-reaching change, there is resistance to forsaking many of the costly entitlements that are associated with socialism, such as subsidized housing, free health care, and education, and extended paid maternity leave.

Nowhere is this ambivalence more manifest than in discussions about who should be the future owners of privatized enterprises. In some countries, such as Yugoslavia, Poland, and Hungary, the workers and managers of many state-owned enterprises claim that they are the legitimate owners by virtue of their long years of toil and commitment. The workers in these countries traditionally have been responsible for enterprise management, and they strongly believe that ownership should be transferred to them at little or no cost. Opponents claim that the enterprises are the property of the state and the public at large. All citizens, according to this point of view, should have the opportunity to benefit from privatization. In Czechoslovakia, for example, the government advocates mass share distribution that would place a significant portion of enterprise shares in the hands of all citizens

11. These problems are amplified in the Soviet Union, where "the search for economic reforms can be expected to begin under the constraint of preserving economic security and the egalitarian basis," as explained by Hewett (1988, 93).

at virtually no cost.[12]

There is also the separate but equally sensitive issue of foreign ownership. In April 1991 the Hungarian government announced a list of enterprises that would not be privatized. The roster included such sectors as oil exploration, electricity generation and distribution, the national airline, arms manufacturing, and telecommunications.[13] The list reflected official anxiety over losing control of the so-called commanding heights of the economy to foreign interests.

Few dispute the need for large-scale direct foreign investment given the shortages of domestic savings in some countries, modern technology, management know-how, and marketing outlets. A major role for foreign investors is the only way to overcome these shortfalls if privatization is to proceed at an acceptable pace. But there is much debate, once again, on the specifics. How, for example, should foreign investors be taxed and what policies should govern profit remittance? Are there certain strategic industries, as the Hungarian example suggests, where foreign investment should be prohibited or limited? Should separate regulatory frameworks be established, as in Czechoslovakia, to distinguish permissible foreign investment behavior in small enterprises from large ones? Without exception, Eastern Europe decisionmakers are painfully torn between their recognition that direct foreign investment is essential to the future competitiveness of key sectors, and fear that foreign domination could have unacceptably high political and economic costs. Decisions on these issues will profoundly influence the balance between foreign and domestic ownership.

The pace and direction of privatization in Eastern Europe have been closely linked to government views on ownership, and no less can be expected in the Soviet Union. Each country must carefully weigh the tradeoffs among (1) massive give-aways to the domestic populace, (2) long delays in privatization implementation, until domestic savings rates increase, and (3) large-scale participa-

12. According to Czechoslovak authorities, all adult citizens are eligible to receive 2,000 "investment points" for Kr 1000, which is equivalent to approximately one-third of one month's average salary.

13. *Hungarian Financial Review* 2, no. 7, April 15–30, 1991, 1. No doubt, in time the list will be revised. But, like most of their Eastern European counterparts, the government sent a clear signal that private ownership will have its limits.

tion by foreign investors. These options are not mutually exclusive, and unpalatable as they may be, the privatization climate in the region will necessitate the need for compromise and the acceptance of second-best solutions.

Macroeconomic Stability

Another ingredient for successful privatization, particularly on the scale of Eastern Europe's endeavor, is macroeconomic stability. And again, the degree of difficulty sets the Eastern European nations and the Soviet Union apart from other countries. The vexing dilemma for each country is how to create this stability without triggering a protracted economic tailspin that undermines efforts to attract private sources of capital to the privatization program. Poland's so-called shock therapy (Sachs and Lipton 1990, 75–147), and associated rapid macroeconomic adjustments, is a case in point. In 1990, virtually overnight, price controls were lifted, subsidies and other protective measures were abolished, and controls were slapped on wages. As expected, inflation soared, industrial production in state-owned enterprises plummeted 25 percent, and GNP declined by 12 percent. At the same time, unemployment rose from zero to 7.5 percent in the nonagricultural labor force, and 5.5 percent in the overall economy, real wages dropped by some 30 percent, and consumption by 16 percent (Jackson 1991, 53).

A year later, in mid-1991, recovery appeared to be underway, and private-sector output had begun to play an increasingly important role. Despite the poor overall economic performance in 1990, for example, output in the private sector increased at an annual rate of 17 percent, at the same time output in the state and cooperative sectors plummeted by 21 percent (Fallenbuchl 1991, 15). The data suggest that though Poland has paid a staggering price for its harsh economic reforms, some real progress was made.

The rest of Eastern Europe is struggling through a period of adjustment similar to Poland's; and in the Soviet Union the process has hardly begun. The predicament for policymakers could hardly be more challenging. Efforts to stabilize the macroeconomic environment temporarily set back privatization programs by undermining the climate for new investment. The level of domestic private savings is contracting, regulatory frameworks are in flux, traditional trading relationships have been decimated, and international creditworthiness is declining at a rapid pace.[14] Thus, at a time when the highest national priority is to attract new investment on a massive scale, deteriorating macroeconomic conditions and economic and political uncertainty are thwarting this aim.

Institutional Infrastructure

Privatization also requires an institutional support system. This is taken for granted in the Western industrialized countries, where capital markets intermediate between savers, investors, and borrowers; banking systems provide financing for sizable transactions; and accounting firms validate the accuracy of financial information, an essential prerequisite for enterprise valuation. This network of institutions comprises what is commonly known as the private-sector infrastructure, which can significantly accelerate the pace of privatization implementation. Absent in Eastern Europe for more than two generations, these institutions are beginning to reemerge. But the process is slow and painstaking, which in turn will retard progress on the privatization front.

The Human Factor

Finally, there is the intangible but enormously significant human dimension. For privatization and other market-oriented reforms to succeed on a large scale, possibly the most difficult tasks will be to gradually change attitudes and values toward work, enhance technical skill levels, and improve approaches to management. As noted by Hungarian economist János Kornai, "What is needed is

14. The 1990 aggregate borrowing in Bulgaria, Czechoslovakia, Hungary, Poland, and Romania actually declined by US$1.42 billion, and BIS reporting banks reduced their outstanding claims on Eastern Europe by US$6.8 billion (-7%) during the first nine months of 1990 (BIS 1991, 17–28). The speed and extent of the contraction have been so dramatic that, as a recent OECD report claimed: "the international financial community, observing the rising level of debt, higher borrowing and the uncertainties inherent in the process of moving towards market economies, has completely changed its views of the region's creditworthiness" (OECD 1991, 15).

not only a revolutionary change in institutions, but also one in thinking. New sets of values will replace the old ones imprinted on many generations by the old regime" (Kornai 1990, 20). Productivity will improve only as fast as changes occur at this human level.

Unlike other countries, the void of a private sector for over forty years in Eastern Europe took a toll on attitudes about the work place. Although massive injections of technical training will play a significant role, even more important will be the challenge of reviving a work ethic that placed parts of Eastern Europe among the most competitive in the world during the prewar period. The early signs suggest that in time this tradition will resurface and rebuild the competitive potential of the region.

OTHER EARLY OBSERVATIONS

Setting Realistic Targets

In virtually every country where privatization is high on the public policy agenda there has been an unfailing tendency to underestimate the time required for implementation. This, in turn, spurs political leaders to make announcements that raise public expectations to unrealistic heights. President Corazon Aquino promised publicly in October 1987 that she would privatize Philippine Airlines in sixty days; three and a half years later, and after many abortive attempts to sell the flagship carrier, the public continues to wait. In March of 1990 in Brazil, newly elected President Fernando Collor confidently predicted that he would sell US$10 billion of state-owned assets in the first year of his administration; more than a year later, the ambitious program has only just begun. And in the Soviet Union, the ink was barely dry on Stanislav Shatalin's highly publicized 500-Day Plan for market reform before it became obvious that the timeframe was grossly unrealistic and there was no political consensus to forge ahead with market-oriented economic reforms.

These examples are not unique. Rather, they represent the norm. Political leaders are prone to misjudge the consequences of their public statements, failing to recognize that each privatization transaction is complex, monopolizes the time of scarce skilled manpower, encounters numerous unforeseen obstacles, and takes many months, if not years, to complete. The compulsion to make promises that will garner public support is understandable, if misguided and unrealistic. Privatization is first and foremost a political process, one that can only succeed if the leadership mobilizes public opinion in support of the government's goals. With economic conditions deteriorating in Eastern Europe at a rapid rate, the temptation to offer innovative solutions that will reap quick results is most compelling. The problem is compounded because the true believers have a sense that their nations are passing through a fleeting moment in history; a window of opportunity has opened to transform these economies and it must be seized quickly before the opponents of change regain the upper hand.[15] The sense of urgency is also understandable because of the political imperative in these emerging, still-vulnerable democracies to mobilize public support for change.

Nonetheless, government leaders must resist this temptation to overpromise. The early signs suggest that the lesson is not being heeded in Eastern Europe. In January 1990, the Polish government announced that 150 firms would be privatized by public share offering in the first year; only five had been sold a year later. Czechoslovakia announced its intention to auction off at least 130,000 small businesses during 1991, but only a few hundred had been sold by mid-year. And in Hungary, the widely publicized First Privatization Program, directing the State Property Agency to divest of twenty relatively attractive large state enterprises, was well behind schedule almost from its inception. The Managing Director of SPA announced in September 1990 that many public sales would be completed by mid-1991; by that time only one transaction had been completed. Unaware of the enormous complexity that surrounds the privatization process, political leaders in Eastern Europe share the tendency of their counterparts elsewhere in the world to inflate public expectations and then struggle lamely to explain what went wrong. The problem, as Czechoslovak Finance

---

15. Again, the similarities among the current thinking of many leaders in the Soviet Union is striking, particularly widespread fears that the nomenklatura will recapture control and reap windfall gains from privatization.

Minister Vaclav Klaus explained, is akin to his young son playing chess: "He foresees some steps, but not the end of the game."

Educating the Public

In July 1990 the Polish Sejm, or parliament, was the first Eastern European legislature to pass a comprehensive, large-scale privatization law amidst considerable fanfare. Out of 370 legislators, 328 voted in favor of the new law (Fallenbuchl 1991, 11). Less than a year later, a high-ranking official in the Polish government revealed that an estimated 60 percent of the parliament members now were disenchanted with privatization, and he predicted that many of them could not be expected to support the government's program for much longer. He claimed, "they simply do not understand what is at stake."[16]

At a different level, the manager of a large state enterprise in Slovenia emphatically advocated that his firm be privatized as quickly as possible. When queried about how it should be carried out, however, he was unable to respond with a single concrete suggestion.[17]

These anecdotes are indicative of one of the great ironies surrounding privatization. In the abstract it receives widespread support; but when public discussion turns to the details of implementation, the consensus quickly breaks down and critics emerge from various quarters. For example, according to its adversaries, privatization will:

1. sell the "family silver";
2. sell assets too cheaply;
3. allow too much foreign control;
4. lead to higher unemployment and/or lower wages;
5. result in diminished concern for environmental and job safety; and
6. be based on corrupt, behind-the-scenes deals;
7. result in higher consumer prices and reduced service;

16. Off-the-record conversation with the author.
17. Ibid.

8. increase disparities in wealth; and
9. simply transfer ownership to the old guard.

Immersed in the mechanics of privatization implementation, privatization planners frequently overlook some of the more subtle and subjective aspects of their work, such as communicating effectively with those who have a stake in the outcome. Even the most creative financial engineering will be for naught if care is not taken to allay the concerns of those who perceive that the transaction could have adverse consequences for their welfare—workers and managers who may fear for their job security, the nomenklatura who risks the loss of special privileges, and the public, worried that privatization will be accompanied by price liberalization. A professionally competent team must ensure that the concerns of these constituencies are not overlooked.

Privatization Techniques

There is no single model or formula for privatization success. Country circumstances and the characteristics of individual enterprises and markets will dictate the appropriate and acceptable method of privatization. So will the desired pace of implementation. Initial public offerings may be relevant for some of the more competitive enterprises, while private placements make more sense for the less well-known and profitable enterprises. Some companies may be ready for privatization immediately; a more sensible option for others might be a commercialization phase that provides time for restructuring the enterprise and enhancing its value prior to sale. Employee buy-outs are a widely used technique in some parts of Yugoslavia, while the Polish and Czechoslovak preference is to allocate only a minority proportion of the shares for the workers. Enterprises that are expected to compete in domestic markets will be treated differently from monopolies.

One of the most important demarcations influencing privatization technique is enterprise size. Larger companies are technically more complex in terms of audit, appraisal, valuation, and the determination of financing requirements. They also are more likely to be in a strategic sector, such as telecommunications or public transport, where the regulatory and political consequences of privatization must be carefully studied. The likelihood of foreign participation in the transaction is much greater with large enterprises than with small ones, and the repercussions of large employee layoffs must be carefully weighed. Due to factors such as these, the larger enterprises invariably require more time and labor.

In recognition of the significant distinctions between large- and small-scale privatization, a number of Eastern European countries have designed separate privatization programs that take into account size differentials. Czechoslovakia went so far as to write separate laws defining different procedures for each type. The procedures for privatizing the medium- and large-scale enterprises are considerably more elaborate, reflecting the complexity and sensitivity of many of these transactions (for example, treatment of displaced employees, permissible foreign participation, and government review of valuation). In contrast, the law simplifies the process for small enterprises, in order to permit rapid divestment.[18] Poland and Hungary also have adopted totally separate sets of procedures for small enterprises that are designed to accelerate the ownership transfer.

Another factor that heavily influences privatization technique, particularly in Eastern Europe, is the political and economic imperative to speed up the process. The combination of an extraordinarily large number of privatization candidates and low domestic savings levels has led many decisionmakers to conclude that conventional methods will not suffice. Polish Minister of Ownership Changes Janusz Lewandowski explained the dilemma: "In one year, we sold five companies. That is five out of 8,000. It is very slow, very time-consuming. It would take 100 years to privatize Poland at the speed of 1990."[19]

This view that the pace must be quickened has incited many countries in the region to consider various nontraditional methods

18. The "small" privatization law, passed by the Federal Assembly on October 25, 1990, directed the sale of over 130,000 small state-owned businesses, mainly small stores, restaurants, and workshops, in a two-phased auction. During the first round, only Czechoslovak citizens are eligible to participate, in order to ensure that wealthier foreigners do not capture the most prized assets. In the second round, scheduled for early 1992, the restrictions against foreign participation will be dropped (Obrman 1991, 13).

19. *Washington Post*, February 2, 1991.

of wholesaling the privatization process. Czechoslovakia has adopted a program of distributing vouchers exchangeable for shares in individual large enterprises to all adult citizens. Poland, also motivated by a desire to accelerate the implementation process, is studying a slightly different approach that would permit the government to distribute 30 percent of the shares of hundreds of large enterprises. As in Czechoslovakia, the shares would be free and all adult citizens would be eligible. Romania too has settled upon 30 percent free distribution, although some of the mechanics differ.

Promises of free share distribution, of course, are politically attractive. The appeal is particularly alluring in Eastern Europe, where the egalitarian ethic remains strong, and these programs appear to offer a quick fix to the seemingly intractable problem of sluggish implementation. But it is far from certain that they will succeed. Each of these programs is complicated and none has been tested in the market place. They will create an enormous administrative burden on government staff, who already are severely overextended. Furthermore, these programs do not directly benefit the enterprises by bringing new capital to the process, nor do they generate any revenue for the financially strapped governments. Critics also point out that the rapid distribution of a small number of shares to the entire population is not likely to contribute to the achievement of privatization's ultimate objective—the enhancement of enterprise efficiency.

Valuation and Asset Pricing

The ultimate task of any privatization assignment is for the seller and buyer to agree on price. The first step in the process is for the seller to determine a range of acceptable values that serve as the basis for negotiations with prospective investors. This requires a rigorous analysis of the enterprise and the environment in which it operates, and then a determination of how the assets should be configured and valued to attract desirable investors.

In Eastern Europe, as undoubtedly will be the case in the Soviet Union, it is virtually impossible to conduct this valuation exercise in a manner acceptable to most investors. At the Lenin shipyards in Gdansk, for example, the prospective American investor followed conventional practice by requesting an audit and valuation. When two internationally reputable accounting firms arrived independently at widely different values, the investor lost confidence in the process and withdrew from the transaction.

Valuation normally begins with a close examination of historical operating costs and sales revenues, which serves as the basis for projecting the future performance of the enterprise. But in Eastern Europe, one result of the transition from centrally planned to market-based economic systems is that prices are changing rapidly and dramatically as they begin to adjust to the newly freed forces of supply and demand. Consequently, historical cost data, based on artificially controlled prices, is rendered almost meaningless, and forecasting future values becomes an awesome task for even the most accomplished financial analyst.

The problem of "getting the price right" is also more complicated in countries where capital markets are undeveloped or nonexistent. And again, the availability and accuracy of data about the enterprises are vital. The lifeblood of pricing decisions is timely and reliable information—financial and operating data that describe historical and projected enterprise performance, stock market information (for example, trading volume and share price movements), and exogenous factors that are likely to affect share prices (for example, interest rates). Unfortunately, in Eastern Europe information that meets these standards is in short supply, making it difficult for the public to make investment decisions with confidence.

The valuators also must contend with the temptation to undervalue in order to boost investor demand. The limited supply of capital for investment provides one explanation for this practice. Another is the previously noted urge of political leaders to demonstrate quick results—low prices generate demand. And a third is the political gain that comes from offering easy profits to large segments of the electorate. Decisionmakers in both industrialized (for example, the United Kingdom and France) and developing (for example, Jamaica, Malaysia, Turkey, and Chile) nations have the propensity to set share prices at a level that virtually guarantees oversubscription, which leads to windfall gains for investors as soon as the shares open for trading in the secondary market. The shares of British Telecom, for example, were massively oversubscribed when first issued in 1984, causing the price to jump to a 90 percent premium on the first day of trading; similarly, the share price of the National Commercial Bank of Jamaica stock increased 67 percent on day one; and in Hungary, share prices of that country's travel agency, Ibusz, tripled once it floated on the Vienna Stock Exchange (Young 1990, 7).

These problems are not insurmountable, and conditions are likely to gradually improve. The quality of financial information and reporting already has shown progress as accounting standards become defined and Western financial institutions establish a local presence and begin transferring their knowledge and skill. There also has been a rapid proliferation of technical training programs that focus on valuation techniques, accounting, and financial analysis. And, after forty-five years of dormancy, stock markets are reappearing and can be expected to expand gradually and develop as the privatization movement creates a growing supply of new public issues. Witness, for example, the April 1991 opening of the Warsaw Stock Exchange, where the first publicly traded securities are the shares of the five privatized companies sold in an initial public offering. These early signals suggest that these technical issues can be systematically addressed and resolved.

Overcoming the Human Resource Constraint

The frustration level of decisionmakers across the breadth of Eastern Europe reaches its highest pitch when they discuss the acute shortage of skilled manpower with the capability to undertake the technical tasks that are essential to privatization success: auditors and accountants who can verify and construct financial statements that will be credible to international investors; industry specialists who can assess the operational restructuring needs of enterprises that have degenerated to sub-standard levels of competitiveness; financial analysts who can construct complex financial models and value enterprises using a variety of techniques; economists who can assess the costs and benefits of, for example, liquidating a large enterprise that has long been a drain on the public treasury; and attorneys who can assist in the writing of legislation and industry-specific regulatory frameworks that will withstand the test of time. Given the strong commitment that most Eastern European countries have traditionally demonstrated to education and technical training, this human resource constraint will eventually be surmounted. Until then, however, there will be an uncomfortably high level of dependence on foreign sources of expertise. The challenge for governments in the region will be to carefully define results-oriented tasks for these foreign specialists, carefully select them on the basis of competitive bidding, and then systematically monitor their performance. Whenever possible, it should be insisted that local personnel be used to supplement the teams of foreign experts, in order to gradually upgrade domestic technical skill capabilities.

CONCLUSION

No current or historical precedent compares to the complexity of the privatization task in Eastern Europe. The challenge both confounds and excites all who have a significant role to play in the process—the policymakers responsible for shaping the framework that will govern the pace and direction of privatization, domestic and foreign private entrepreneurs and investors who must decide whether and how to risk their capital, and the array of public and private institutions from abroad that are sources of financial and technical assistance, which is essential in one form or another if success on any level is to be achieved. Each country in Eastern Europe will proceed along the privatization path in its own way and at its own pace, but in the same, unmistakable direction.

The political transformation that has swept across the region occurred at an extraordinary pace. Economic change, however, will take longer, particularly as it requires the virtual creation of a private sector. Although the inclination to move quickly is understandable, circumstances suggest that it simply is not possible or desirable to make speed the guiding principle of implementation. To be sure, measures can be initiated to accelerate the process, and the intricate network of constraints can be systematically attacked and gradually eliminated. But given the reality of the Eastern European economies and the labor-intensive nature of executing so many transactions, there should be no illusions that the necessary ownership and productivity changes will occur overnight. János Kornai has advised that "step-by-step changes are characteristic of the private sector. It is impossible to institute private property by calvary attack. Embourgeoisement is a lengthy historical process" (Kornai 1990, 54). Everyone involved must remember this.

We have learned over the decades that development is as concerned with human values and attitudes as it is with policy adjustments and capital infusions. One of the great unknowns in Eastern Europe is whether workers and managers will respond as enthusiastically and quickly to the new economic realities as they did to the political changes that swept across the region. It was easy to embrace the concepts of political freedom and pluralism, and the public's enthusiastic response was predictable. More difficult to gauge, however, is how these same supporters of political liberalization will respond to radical changes in a working environment that places new and more stringent demands on them—such as greater worker accountability and intensified competition.

In time, we will learn the answer to this question. But it is already abundantly clear that, unlike many countries around the world that are pursuing privatization in a half-hearted fashion, Eastern European nations have an important advantage: they possess an unmistakably genuine political will to forge ahead. They want to move as quickly as possible toward a market economy, and privatization is viewed as an essential component of the strategy. There is a fierce determination and a contagious enthusiasm that pervades the offices and corridors of every privatization ministry in the region, and in the end these qualities may be decisive. Dr. Marko Simoneti, head of the Slovenia Privatization Agency, spoke for his colleagues across Eastern Europe when he explained: "There are no conditions for privatization in our country, but we must and we will succeed."[20] In the final analysis, it is this level of commitment and perseverance that may prove to be Eastern Europe's most valuable asset in the quest for privatization success.

20. Conversation with the author.

REFERENCES

BIS. 1991. *International Banking and Financial Market Developments.* Basle, February.

Fallenbuchl, Zbigniew M. 1991. "The New Government and Privatization." *Report on Eastern Europe.* March 22.

Havel, Vaclav. 1990. *Disturbing the Peace.* New York: Alfred A. Knopf.

Hewett, Ed A. 1988. *Reforming the Soviet Economy: Equality versus Efficiency.* Washington, D.C.: Brookings Institution.

Jackson, Marvin. 1990. "The Economic Situation in Eastern Europe in 1990." *Report on Eastern Europe.* January 4.

Kornai, János. 1990. *The Road to a Free Economy.* New York: Norton.

Nellis, John. 1991. "Improving the Performance of Soviet Enterprise." Mimeo. Washington, D.C.: World Bank, January.

Obrman, Jan. 1991. "Two Landmark Bills on Privatization Approved." *Report on Eastern Europe.* March 15.

OECD. 1991. *Financial Market Trends,* no. 48. Paris, February.

Sachs, Jeffrey, and David Lipton. 1990. "Creating a Market Economy in Eastern Europe: The Case of Poland." *Brookings Papers on Economic Activity* 1. Washington, D.C.: Brookings Institution.

Young, S. David. 1990. "Business Valuation and the Privatization Process in Eastern Europe: Challenges, Issues, and Solutions." Mimeo. December.

Part II

Legal Regulation of the Economy:
Managing Conflicting Interests

6

Recent Trends in Foreign Trade and Investment

Kaj Hobér

I. INTRODUCTION

On January 13, 1987, after several months of discussion and speculation in the press, the USSR Council of Ministers adopted a decree concerning the establishment of joint ventures in the Soviet Union.[1] This was the first time since the 1920s that direct foreign investment in the Soviet Union became possible.[2] The Decree on Joint Ventures was heralded as the beginning of a new era in Soviet foreign trade and investment, which indeed it was in many respects. Much has happened since then. In the summer of 1990, for example, the USSR Council of Ministers issued Regulations on

Due to the rapid and constant change in the legislative area, it is impossible to provide an analysis of the situation, except at a specific time. This paper takes account of materials and information available as of June 15, 1991.

As a result of the pace with which new laws and regulations are introduced, there are considerable delays in their publication in the official gazette. The new laws are usually published in *Izvestiia, Ekonomika i Zhizn,* and other newspapers and journals fairly quickly. That is why many citations are to such newspapers and journals, rather than the official gazette.

1. "On the Procedure for the Creation within the Territory of the USSR and the Activities of Joint Enterprises with the Participation of Soviet Organizations and Firms of Capitalist and Developing Countries, Sobraniye Postanovleny Pravitelstva SSSR," no. 9, item 40, 1987, 183.

2. During the New Economic Policy (NEP), Western companies invested in so-called mixed companies; there were 161 such companies in 1925. See Hobér (1989, 174–76) and the sources referred to there.

Joint Stock Companies and Limited Liability Companies,[3] and at
the end of that year the Fundamentals of Legislation on Investment Activity in the USSR were adopted.[4] At the same time, we
have witnessed a remarkable outpouring of new, interesting, and
generally favorable economic legislation at the republican level.
Particularly in the Russian Republic (RSFSR) many of the individual pieces of legislation were originally part of Stanislav Shatalin's
500-Day Plan. Despite the gloomy picture of the Soviet economy
today and the uncertain political situation,[5] it is important to keep
in mind the enormous progress that has taken place in the legislative field since the beginning of 1987. Significantly, in February 1991, the Draft Fundamentals on Privatization Legislation
were published, and there are reports that the RSFSR is in the
process of drafting a number of laws aimed at privatizing state
enterprises and property.[6] This legislative activity represents—at
least at the conceptual level—nothing less than a revolution.

We have thus seen a very ambitious legislative agenda in the
field of foreign trade and investment. Unfortunately, however, reality has not changed as quickly. One explanation for this is the
power struggle between Moscow (the "center") and the individual
republics, which has been going on for the last couple of years and
has manifested itself, *inter alia*, in the so-called war of legislation.
It would therefore seem necessary to analyze this constitutional crisis of the Soviet Union. Indeed, it is necessary today to evaluate all
new laws and regulations in light of this power struggle. Another
recent trend that permeates every aspect of change in Soviet economic and commercial life is the pronounced desire to transform
the Soviet economy into some form of market economy. Even
though there may be differences today in the Soviet leadership in
this respect, these differences would seem to concern the methods

3. The text was first published in *Ekonomika i Zhizn*, no. 27, July 1990, 14.
4. The text was first published in *Izvestiia*, December 17, 1990, 2.
5. Soviet Prime Minister Valentin Pavlov caused some concern among Western
business leaders and observers when he said, in an interview on February 12, 1991,
with the trade union newspaper *Trud*, that Austrian, Swiss, and Canadian banks
had acquired billions of rubles illegally and planned to flood the Soviet economy
with them. Mr. Pavlov later softened his tone in meetings with Western media.
6. See the discussion on the shift to a market economy in Section III.

to be used to transform the economy, rather than the goal.[7]
Although we have recently seen a large number of new laws
and regulations, in order to properly understand what is going on
and to put recent developments in perspective, we must disentangle
the constitutional crisis, its origins and affects. Hence, this paper's
focus on that topic. To complete the picture of what is presently going on in the foreign trade and investment area, I shall also discuss privatization as a condition for shifting to a market economy,
as well as some of the most recent laws in this area.

II. THE CONSTITUTIONAL CRISIS IN THE SOVIET UNION

Setting off a war of legislation that threatens to tear apart the Soviet
Union, and that indirectly led to the crackdown by Soviet troops in
the Baltics in early 1991, all of the fifteen republics had by the fall
of 1990 proclaimed that their laws, not those of the Soviet Union,
govern their territories.[8] In an attempt to restore the priority of
USSR laws, the USSR Supreme Soviet on October 24, 1990, enacted a
law declaring the primacy of USSR law over republican law.[9] On
the same day, however, the Supreme Soviet of the RSFSR responded
with a law claiming that USSR legislation would affect its territory
only if ratified by the RSFSR Supreme Soviet. A week later, on
October 31, 1990, that body passed a law declaring the economic
sovereignty of the republic. Elsewhere, Estonia passed on October
22, 1990, the Law on the Economic Border of the Estonian Republic,
with the purported object of protecting Estonia's internal market.
Other republics have taken similar measures to prevent the export
of goods beyond their borders. This hopeless mess of legislation
sends conflicting signals to interested business people. The uncertainty created by the present situation is already today one of the
major stumbling blocks for potential foreign investors.

7. As late as March 25, 1991, President Gorbachev, during an interview published
in the German magazine *Der Spiegel*, confirmed his commitment to the market
economy (*Der Spiegel*, no. 13, March 25, 1991, 177).
8. See Appendix 6-A for a list in chronological order of the various declarations of
independence and/or sovereignty (Sheehy 1990).
9. "USSR Law on Ensuring the Effectiveness of Laws and Other Legislative Acts of
the USSR." Text published in *Izvestiia*, October 28, 1990, 3.

Background

The Soviet state represents an unusual combination of confederate and federal principles. The Union of Soviet Socialist Republics officially came into being on the basis of an international treaty concluded on December 30, 1922, by the RSFSR, Ukrainian, Belorussian, and Transcaucasian Republics (Georgia, Armenia, and Azerbaidzhan), later joined by the other union republics. Each union republic was regarded as a sovereign socialist state with a constitutional right to secede freely, to have its own Constitution, to enter into relations with foreign states, and to conclude treaties and exchange diplomatic and consular representations. Two union republics, the Belorussian SSR and the Ukrainian SSR are members of the United Nations. The aforementioned elements of confederation, however, are outbalanced by elements of centralized federalism in the USSR Constitution, which delineates the jurisdiction of the USSR and leaves to the union republics those powers not reserved to all-union jurisdiction.

Today it is clear that the 1977 Constitution, even in its latest form, is a document of only transient importance. The revision of the Soviet constitutional system is far from complete, and its structure will undoubtedly be affected by future events. A complete overhaul of the federal system, including a new union treaty, would seem inevitable. Such an overhaul is prompted by, among other things, the necessity of resolving the war of legislation and the now accepted necessity of a shift to a free-market economy. It is also prompted by the commitment of President Gorbachev to the rule of law, to the creation of a *Rechtsstaat.*

In tracing the origins of the constitutional crisis in the Soviet Union, it is instructive to start out with the claims from the Baltic republics for sovereignty, because they have presented the first clear challenge to central authority.

Baltic Claims for Sovereignty

On November 16, 1988, the Estonian Supreme Soviet introduced an amendment to its Constitution declaring all-union law valid on Estonian territory only after approval by the Estonian Supreme

Soviet.[10] Based on Article 76 of the 1977 USSR Constitution, this amendment required that all changes to the Soviet Constitution be approved by the Estonian Republic.[11] On May 18, 1989, the Lithuanian Supreme Soviet issued a similar declaration of independence and introduced important changes to the Lithuanian Constitution, declaring that laws and other legal acts must be ratified and registered by the Supreme Soviet of Lithuania in order to be valid on Lithuanian territory, and that all land and other natural resources belong to the republic (Vardys 1988, 66). A few days later, a Latvian proposal for similar amendments was published.

Moscow vigorously denounced the Baltic initiative, basing its counterclaims on various articles of the 1977 Constitution, which by then had proved its inadequacy in regulating relations between Moscow and the republics. The Presidium of the Supreme Soviet of the USSR, in a special session on November 22, 1988, refused to recognize the Estonian declaration and claims to natural resources, and it proclaimed several of the amendments to the Estonian Constitution unconstitutional.[12] That body also denied any obligation to register all-union laws and reaffirmed Article 73 of the 1977 USSR Constitution, which upholds the primacy of union legislation over republic legislation. The Presidium also said that the question of state property is an all-union issue and that private property is not envisaged by the 1977 Constitution, referring to Articles 10 through 13 and Article 173. Finally, the Presidium pointed out that changes in the Constitution require a two-thirds majority (Article 174) and that the sovereignty of the union extends to the entire territory of the USSR (Articles 74 and 75).

Analysis of the 1977 USSR Constitution

Using the Baltic initiative as an example, let us try to analyze the relationship between the center and the union republics on the

---

10. Narodny Kongress, Sbornik materialov Kongressa narodnogo fronta Estonii, October 1 and 2, 1988, 194, 216.
11. The text of this and subsequent articles cited in this paper can be found in Appendix 6-B.
12. *Vedomosti Verkhovnogo Soveta SSSR*, no. 48, Art. 70, 1988.

basis of the provisions of the 1977 USSR Constitution. The starting point is that the union republics are entitled to legislate in areas that do not fall under union competence (Article 76, second paragraph). This principle is supplemented by the rule that if the union does not use its competence, it may be used by the union republics.

Article 73 outlines the competence of the union by enumerating in twelve subsections the areas of union competence. It not only enumerates vast areas of union competence, including establishing the frontiers of the Soviet Union and ensuring uniformity of legislation on Soviet territory, but adds in Section 12 that the union also decides all other questions considered to be of all-union significance. The Constitution does not draw any clear borderline between the competence of the union and that of the union republics but rather gives general priority to the union.

This is particularly true in the economic and commercial spheres: centralist elements provided for in the Constitution were even more permeating in practice, because economic questions were entrusted primarily to the USSR Council of Ministers and its Presidium. Article 6 of the 1978 Act on the Council of Ministers granted that body far-reaching control over the establishment and operation of economic agencies. Notably, no distinction was ever made between all-union ministerial agencies and those of the union republics (see Maslov 1989, 57–60).

Clearly, the union's power prevailed over the republics, thanks not only to the 1977 Constitution, but more importantly also to the far-reaching and arbitrary powers of the top leadership and the Communist Party. What possibilities, then, did the Constitution offer to change the division of power between the center and the union republics? Which agency has the ultimate power to effect such a change?

The supremacy of the USSR Constitution is laid down in Article 173, which goes on to say that "all laws and acts of state organs are issued on the basis of and in accordance with the Constitution of the USSR." While Article 173 does not explicitly mention the constitutions of the union republics, it could be argued that it includes their constitutional amendments as well, because these are adopted in the form of laws. Consequently, the legality of changes of union republic constitutions should be judged against the union Constitution. This conclusion seems to follow from Article 173 read together with Article 73 (which gives the union the right to ensure legislative uniformity), and Article 174 (which stipulates that changes in the USSR Constitution must be made by a two-thirds majority). The most recent amendments to the 1977 USSR Constitution mentioned above do not challenge this conclusion. Moscow's refusal to accept the Baltic claims thus has constitutional support; economic sovereignty of the union republics does, from a constitutional point of view, require the consent of the relevant all-union agencies. However, applying this analysis to the Baltic states presupposes acceptance of the occupation of the Baltic republics in 1940 and their inclusion in the Soviet Union. The Baltic initiatives proceed from the assumption that their occupation contradicted international and municipal law and the belief that they should be treated as equal sovereigns in their relations with Moscow (see, for example, Shtromas 1985/86, 459–67). Under international law, however, the legality of legislative measures making earlier legal acts retroactively illegal is a very complicated issue, particularly in light of the uncertainty prevailing with respect to recognition of states and governments.[13] While most Western states do not recognize *de jure* Soviet rule of the Baltic states, some Western countries recognize it *de facto* and act in accordance therewith.

---

13. See, generally, Brownlie (1979, 89, et seq.). With respect to retroactivity, Brownlie states: "When a state makes a late acceptance of the existence of a state, in the field of basic rights and duties of existence, this recognition *ex hypothesi* cannot be 'retroactive' because in a special sense it is superfluous" (id., 98). See also Kelsen (1966, 398).

On May 25, 1989, the first session of the Congress of People's Deputies opened in Moscow. The Congress decided to establish a commission headed by Alexander Yakovlev, a close ally of President Gorbachev, to evaluate the 1940 Molotov-Ribbentrop Pact. On July 23, 1989, Yakovlev officially acknowledged for the first time the existence of secret protocols that divided Poland between the Soviet Union and Germany and ceded the Baltic states to the Soviet Union. On September 29, 1989, the commission published a document according to which twenty-one of the twenty-eight members recommended that the secret protocols be declared invalid. Yakovlev, while condemning the secret protocols, has refused to recognize any connection between the present status of the Baltic states and the secret protocols, stating that "requests" were made by the Baltic three to be admitted to the Soviuet Union in 1940. See, for example, Kaiser (1991, 300).

Katastroika

By the end of 1989, the Baltic initiative for economic sovereignty
had gained such momentum and support that the USSR Supreme
Soviet, on November 27, promulgated a law on the economic self-
sufficiency of the Baltic republics.[14] To inspire economic initiative,
the law transferred control over enterprises and economic organizations from central to local agencies; however, it also contained provisions stipulating that the legislative acts of these agencies not conflict with union law. The Baltic republics, however, felt
the law was too little, too late (Kavass and Griffen 1990, 1). Months
before the law was enacted, the Baltic republics had promulgated
laws allowing for the establishment of joint-stock companies and
foreign private ownership, all of which were more far-reaching
than union law.

During 1990, the Baltic republics continued to promulgate their
own laws without taking into account Moscow's protests, as did
most other republics. The RSFSR has challenged union law with a
number of legislative drafts, notably, the resolution on Rent,
Purchase, and Gratuitous Transfer of Government Property.[15] This
law stipulates, *inter alia*, that all property can be sold or leased, with
the exceptions explicitly prohibited by RSFSR legislation.

This could mean that even property that union legislation pro-
hibits for sale could be sold unless there is an RSFSR provision corresponding to union law. A further step in this direction was
taken on October 31, 1990, when the Law on Ensuring the
Economic Foundation of RSFSR Sovereignty was published.[16] The
law stipulates in Article 1 that all land, minerals (including gold,
diamonds, platinum, and other precious stones, oil and gas), water
resources, forests, and other raw materials "constitute the national
wealth of the RSFSR peoples." It goes on to say that the procedure
and conditions governing the ownership of these objects are to be
laid down in legislation promulgated by the RSFSR.

All these legislative enactments by the RSFSR and other republics introduced in the wake of perestroika threaten to create

14. Text published in *Izvestiia*, December 2, 1989.
15. *Vedomosti Verkhovnogo Soveta SSSR*, no. 1249, item 385, 1988.
16. An English translation appears in *Soviet Business Law Report* 1, no. 8,
December 1990, 8–9.

katastroika. For example, in the middle of November 1990, the central government decided to liberalize prices on "luxury goods" (jewelry, fur, furniture, and radios). The RSFSR vetoed this resolution and prohibited the sale of these goods until the dispute had been settled. These and similar measures have catapulted the Soviet economy into a state of virtual chaos where there seems to be a shortage of everything except rubles. On December 7, 1990, directors of 3,000 state enterprises voiced their concerns. The directors, assembled in the Kremlin for a two-day meeting, read the riot act to Soviet politicians. One of them is reported to have said: "We have four conductors at the moment—Gorbachev, Yeltsin, our regional council, and our city authorities. They are all playing a different tune, but we want one tune: a presidential one."[17]

Similar expressions of frustration are often voiced by Western business leaders involved in the Soviet Union or contemplating investments there.

In December 1990, the RSFSR adopted a new tax system in the form of the Law of the RSFSR on the Procedure for the Application within the Territory of the RSFSR in 1991 of the Law of the USSR on Taxes on Enterprises, Associations, and Organizations.[18] The 1990 USSR Law on Taxes on Enterprises, Associations, and Organizations[19] granted only limited taxing powers to the republics. This did not satisfy those within the RSFSR who aimed for greater taxing powers and fiscal autonomy for the republics. This disagreement over the nature of fiscal relations between republics and the federal government has now been manifested in the above-mentioned law adopted by the RSFSR in December 1990. The Russian law, among other changes, offers preferential tax rates for foreign joint ventures registered in the Russian republics. It also offers a 38 percent general tax rate, rather than the 45 percent rate stipulated by the USSR tax law.

The most important conflict between the USSR and RSFSR laws on enterprise taxation concerns the allocation of revenues. Under Article 4 of the USSR law, 22 percent of taxable profits will be paid

17. *Financial Times,* December 7, 1990, 20.
18. The law that was enacted on December 1, 1990, was published in *Ekonomika i Zhizn,* no. 1, January 1991, 22–23.
19. "Law on Taxes on Enterprises, Associations, and Organizations," *Vedomosti Syezda narodonykh deputatov SSSR i Verkhovnogo Sovieta SSSR,* no. 27, item 522, 1990.

into the union budget, and each republic may impose an additional 23 percent tax to be paid into republic and local budgets.   The Russian law, however, provides for the inclusion of virtually all en-terprise tax revenues within the republic and local budgets and makes no provisions for revenues to be included in the union bud-get, thereby directly challenging USSR legislation.   It is still un-clear how the Soviet Union will react to the new Russian rules, but it is inevitable that Western investors will face substantial uncer-tainty.   The rationale underlying the new Russian law seems to be the idea that each republic is entitled to its portion of the national income.   As a result of this attitude, at the beginning of 1991, *katas-troika* was about to break out also with respect to central government spending—including defense, law and order, foreign aid, and the environment—as a result of the refusal of the RSFSR to back an economic agreement worked out between President Gorbachev and the republican leaders.   Boris Yeltsin was reportedly withholding 27 billion rubles, thereby extracting further concessions from the federal government.   While no details of the agreement that was eventually reached have been released, it would seem clear that the federal government will be at the mercy of the republics for its spending, because the base for direct federal taxation is diminish-ing.

The Solution

Only a new union treaty can end the war of legislation and sort out the relationship between Moscow and the union republics. Proposals range from one end of the constitutional spectrum to the other.   Some politicians advocate a new form of "soft" federalism, rather than a confederation, based on the argument that a federa-tion of equals is unrealistic due to the centralized power still in the hands of the Communist Party.   At the other end of the spectrum, the Shatalin Plan assumed that the country would become a volun-tary economic union of equal sovereign republics.

A viable approach, in my opinion, would be to introduce clearly defined but limited republic sovereignty, leaving defense, foreign policy, and security to union authority.   It cannot be emphasized enough that it is of vital importance to agree on clear demarcation lines between republic and federal authority. This is particularly true with respect to foreign investors: business leaders can cope with almost any set of rules, as long as they know what those rules are and provided they are reasonably clear. Furthermore, time is of the essence. The constitutional crisis in the Soviet Union requires urgent resolution before the situation deteriorates beyond remedy. At present it would seem to be a Herculean task and, it is submitted, virtually impossible from a political point of view to divide authority in such areas as defense, foreign policy, and security. Therefore, the only realistic solution would seem to be to leave these areas to union authority, at least for the time being.

The RSFSR seemed to accept this limitation in its October 24, 1990, law claiming that union legislation would be valid only if ratified by the RSFSR Supreme Soviet. The possibility of a differentiated federal structure also merits serious examination. For example, there is little doubt that the Baltic republics' long-term goal is full independence, and Moscow should acknowledge this fact in the process of amending the draft union treaty. But the constitutional solution reached with the Baltic states need not necessarily be applied to other republics.

Given the tensions between Moscow and the republics—the result of years of a highly centralized system—negotiating a new union treaty will be a difficult and lengthy task. Whatever approach is taken, it is of critical importance that the government recognize the degree of decentralization that has already occurred. However, President Gorbachev most likely will not accept the radical decentralization of power that most republics are demanding; Gorbachev's recent call for a moratorium on laws asserting the supremacy of republic law over union law is evidence of this, as is, of course, the military crackdown in the Baltics.

Gorbachev's latest rearrangement of the Soviet system of government, produced like a rabbit from a hat, contains seeds of authoritarianism unlikely to engage the republics.[20] In the new system, the Council of Federation, whose members will include the Soviet president and a number of republic presidents, is the top decisionmaking body. It is unclear, however, how many republic

20. The USSR Law on Amendments and Additions to the USSR Constitution in Connection with the Refinement of the System of State Administration was adopted on December 26, 1990, and published in *Izvestiia*, December 27, 1990, 8.

presidents will join the council, and poor participation would doubtless diminish its effectiveness. Furthermore, the Council should operate on the basis of some form of consensus, yet this also seems elusive. Most republics are concentrating on their own future rather than that of the union, and some republics have signed treaties of their own recognizing each other as virtually independent states. The new system of government also presupposes an existing and functioning union treaty, yet there is little to prevent Gorbachev from trying to impose rule by his own will.

As usual, a good deal of confusion is built into the system, making it difficult to comment on its affect. Nonetheless, to an outside observer, it is abundantly clear that the time has come to declare a cease-fire in the war of legislation and to conclude a peace treaty in the form of a union treaty. The only alternative seems to be to declare a state of emergency and to introduce presidential rule.

The latest draft union treaty appeared about a week before the referendum of March 17.[21] This draft consists of three sections, and like previous ones it bears the hallmarks of a federation: one currency, the primacy of federal law in areas within federal competence, single citizenship, and federal budget and taxes. The first section contains a list of "basic principles," which interestingly enough never mentions the word "socialist." The second section is crucially important: it enumerates the powers of the federal government—including defense, security, and foreign policy—and those executed by federal and republican governments jointly. However, it does not list the powers executed by the republics exclusively. The third section outlines the institutions of government and law, foreseeing the abolishment of the Congress of People's Deputies and its replacement with the Supreme Soviet, as well as the creation of a Constitutional Court, which would try questions concerning the constitutionality of legislative acts and hear dis-

---

21. Published in *Izvestiia*, March 9, 1991. Judging from pronouncements made during the interview with *Der Spiegel* (see note 7, supra), President Gorbachev interprets the outcome of the March 17 referendum as support for the draft union treaty. He does so despite the fact that six republics (the Baltics, Armenia, Georgia, and Moldavia) boycotted the referendum, that Kazakhstan altered the question, and that the RSFSR, the Ukraine, and Uzbekistan added their own questions. Thus, only five of the fifteen republics held the whole referendum without any alterations and/or additions. These five remaining republics were: Azerbaidzhan, Belorussia, Kirghizia, Tadzhikistan, and Turkmenia.

putes between the federal and republican, as well as among republican, governments on the constitutionality of their respective legislative acts. It is probably reasonable to assume that a Constitutional Court, or the equivalent, will in practice play a key role in the future. In all likelihood, there will be numerous disputes concerning delineation of power and authority between federal and republican governments and government bodies. It is therefore of utmost importance that a comprehensive and reliable mechanism be created to handle and resolve such disputes.

Unfortunately, much of the language is vague—deliberately so, it would seem—leaving almost every article subject to dispute. It is therefore difficult to escape the unfortunate conclusion that this draft will not put an end to the war of legislation, in particular because six republics—the Baltic three, Georgia, Armenia, and Moldova (formerly Moldavia)—have declared that they will refuse to sign under any conditions.

However, one recent event may turn out to be a watershed in the war of legislation. On April 23, President Gorbachev and nine of the fifteen republics signed an agreement—the so-called nine-plus-one agreement,[22]—which has resulted in a truce, at least temporarily, in the war of legislation. The agreement, which refers to the republics as "sovereign states," may result in a significant enhancement of the role of the republics in government and foresees an increased responsibility of the republics in developing economic ties at different levels.

The agreement itself, however, is not enough to bring about the much-needed peace in the power struggle between Moscow and the republics. Among other things, the agreement calls for the adoption of a new Constitution that should incorporate the provisions of a new union treaty. While the nine-plus-one agreement acknowledges the right of republics to secede, it leaves open the crucial questions of the future economic relationship among the republics. It is therefore clear that much work remains before the war of legislation is over. Minimally, the agreement shows that

---

22. The agreement was signed by President Gorbachev and the presidents of the RSFSR, the Ukraine, Belorussia, Azerbaidzhan, Kazakhstan, Kirghizia, Tadzhikistan, Turkmenia, and Uzbekistan. The three Baltic republics, Armenia, Georgia, and Moldavia refused to sign the agreement. An English translation of the agreement is reproduced in Appendix 6-C.

the nine republics that have signed it seem to be willing to remain part of the Soviet Union, albeit a different Soviet Union, one
with greater independence for the republics. Another open question is the role to be played in the future by the republics that did
not sign the agreement, that is, the Baltic three, Armenia, Georgia, and Moldova.

If a new union treaty is eventually signed along the lines envisaged in the nine-plus-one agreement, it will entail a considerable decentralization of commercial activities, which will have
broad implications for foreign investors. The center of gravity of
foreign investment legislation will shift from Moscow to the republic level, and republics will gain more control of commercial
and economic activities within their territories. As a consequence,
Western investors will need to familiarize themselves with the
commercial and investment legislation in each republic to a much
greater extent than is necessary today. It may also be necessary in
the future to develop an "internal" conflict-of-laws system that will
determine which republic law is to be applied in any given situation.[23]

III. THE SHIFT TO A MARKET ECONOMY

As I have suggested earlier, it is probably fair to say that most political leaders in the Soviet Union today—both at federal and republican levels—favor some kind of market economy. The crucial question is what do these political representatives understand by the
term "market economy"? Does this once-forbidden concept mean
the same thing to all of them? The short answer is that even at
the highest levels of Soviet government there is a very poor understanding of what a market economy is and what it takes in terms
of legal and organizational infrastructure to establish one.

23. Statutory provisions concerning the regulation of conflict of laws within the
Soviet Union already exist. See, for example, Article 18 of the "Fundamental
Principles of Civil Legislation of the USSR and of the Union Republics," *Vedomosti
Verkhovnogo Soveta SSSR,* no. 50, item 525. However, such provisions have been of mi-
nor practical importance due to the fact that legislation of all republics has been vir-
tually identical as a result of the binding character of the Fundamental Principles.

In 1987, with the adoption of the Law on the State Enterprise[24] it seemed as if the Soviet economy took a small, cautious step toward a market economy. The law proclaimed the independence of the state enterprise and tried to replace the Plan by contracts between state enterprises. Unfortunately, the law only did away with the Plan in theory; it survived in the form of so-called state orders (*gosudarstvennye zakazy*), which were still binding on the enterprises.

Even though the Law on State Enterprise in many respects meant a radical change for Soviet enterprises, it soon became clear that it would do little in the way of taking the Soviet economy a further step toward a market economy. This required changes in the ownership structure.

At the beginning of 1990, the USSR Supreme Soviet issued a number of legislative acts purporting to change the ownership regime in the Soviet Union, namely the new USSR Law on Ownership,[25] the Fundamentals of the USSR and Union Republics Legislation on Leasing,[26] and the Fundamentals of the USSR and Union Republics Legislation on Land.[27] This legislative package taken as a whole in principle contained all the elements to demonopolize the Soviet state economy. However, many of the individual provisions were fraught with uncertainty regarding their actual meaning and scope. During the rest of 1990, we witnessed an unprecedented outpouring from the Soviet government of legislative acts in general, and in the commercial field in particular.

Despite ambitious legislative attempts to introduce at least market economy concepts, real life did not change very much. One explanation is that the power and bureaucratic structure of the planned economy remains and still permeates Soviet economic life. However, there can be no market economy until all the markets, in particular capital and labor, are freed. There is no such thing as a capital market without capitalists.

---

24. *Vedomosti Verkhovnogo Soveta SSSR*, no. 26, item 385, 1987.

25. *Vedomosti Syezda narodnykh deputatov SSSR i Verkhovnogo Soveta SSSR*, no. 11, item 164, 1990.

26. First published in *Pravda*, December 1, 1989, 1, 3.

27. *Vedomosti Syezda narodnykh deputatov SSSR i Verkhovnogo Soveta SSSR*, no. 10, item 129, 1990.

The most pressing point on the legislative agenda should be
the introduction of comprehensive privatization legislation; this is
really essential for the introduction of a market economy in the
Soviet Union.

Indeed, there has been some movement in this field.   In
February 1991, *Ekonomika i Zhizn* published the Draft Fundamentals
for Legislation on Privatization of State Property and State Enterprises.[28]   At about the same time, a legislative package on privatization was worked out by the Committee on Economic Reform of
the Russian Republic for presentation to the Supreme Soviet of the
Russian Republic.[29]

The Draft Fundamentals are quite general in character and
leave many questions to be determined by federal and republican
legislation, which as of today does not exist.   One such important
question is the privatization of land.   Article 2:4 of the Draft
Fundamentals simply states that these questions are to be determined "by other legislative acts."   Another important question left
open is the role of foreign investors in the privatization process.
While Article 6 of the Draft Fundamentals includes foreign citizens and foreign firms among those that may acquire state enterprises and state property, no further provisions address this issue.
Both the questions of land and the role of foreign investors must be
covered in a comprehensive way to make privatization an effective
tool of transforming the Soviet economy.   It is reasonable to assume
that the role of foreign investment must play an important role in
any successful privatization process in the Soviet Union, in particular in light of the funding and financing difficulties that many
potential Soviet buyers will face.

The legislative package prepared for the RSFSR is much more
comprehensive and detailed.   In fact, compared to most Soviet legislation, it is well thought out, well written, and well organized.
The proposal consists of a framework law and four sets of rules covering, respectively, details of the State Committee for Adminis-

28. *Ekonomika i Zhizn,* no. 7, February 1991, 18–19.
29. Simultaneously, two other draft laws on privatization seem to have been prepared and submitted to the Supreme Soviet of the Russian Republic for its consideration. The draft discussed in the text is the one prepared by a working group head by
Grigorij Yavlinskij under the auspices of the Committee on Economic Reform of
the Russian Republic.

tering State Property, provisions covering tender offers for the acquisition of state property, provisions on auctions for the acquisition of state property, and provisions on the transformation of state enterprises into state-owned joint-stock companies.

The proposal creates an organization and several mechanisms for privatizing state-owned enterprises and organizations. Only organizations connected with defense, security, health, welfare, and government functions are exempted from the scope of the bill.

The proposal creates a Russian Federation State Committee for Administering State Property ("Committee") consisting of seven members who are not to include legislators or government or party officials. The Committee is charged with preparing an annual privatization plan and also with regulating specific privatization transactions. The proposal also authorizes the creation of similar committees at the regional and local level under the authority of the Committee.

The proposal establishes three means of privatizing state-owned enterprises: (1) reorganizing them as state-owned joint-stock companies whose shares then are sold; (2) selling them at closed-door "contests" based on more than simply the highest bid; and (3) selling them at open auctions based on highest bid. The Committee determines which mechanism to use in any instance, but reorganization is intended for viable enterprises that will keep operating as before, contests are intended for smaller enterprises or those that hold monopolies in any given geographical region, and auctions are intended for larger enterprises or those that are bankrupt or liquidated.

The proposal permits all individuals and nongovernmental (less than 50 percent state-owned) organizations to act as buyers. The role of foreign individuals and companies is not clear. The bill refers to the Russian foreign investment law, which has not yet been adopted. It also provides that foreigners may bid at auctions only if the opening price exceeds 100,000 rubles. In addition, the bill provides for so-called intermediary organizations to assist the Committee in conducting privatization transactions pursuant to commercial contracts.

Privatization transactions shall occur according to the Committee's annual plan. In addition, any individual or organization can initiate a privatization transaction by filing an application to the Committee. Also, the labor collective of the enterprise may initiate the transaction by a petition of at least 50 percent of the employees, as may the administration of the enterprise. The application may include a proposal for what privatization mechanism to use.

Pursuant to the proposal, the Committee must determine within one month whether a privatization transaction is to occur and, if so, what mechanism to use. It may reject the application only if the applicant is ineligible or for some other reason provided by law, and its rejection may be appealed. If the Committee proceeds, it establishes a commission to administer the transaction, though such a commission may not be necessary in the case of auctions. The commission may consist of between five and nine members, including a representative of the Committee, a representative of the local council (Soviet), and financial specialists. A representative of the labor collective must participate in the case of reorganizations and a representative of the antitrust agency (which is being created separately) in the case of contests.

The commission is charged with preparing a privatization plan including the mechanism to be used, the value to be set, and the means of payment to be sought. To determine the value, the commission is to review the assets and liabilities of the enterprise and attempt to determine market value or book value. The commission's plan must have the support of the labor collective and the local council and must be approved by the Committee, which has two weeks to review it after it is submitted. In the case of reorganizations, the commission must prepare draft documents for registration, which the Committee must then review within one week. In the case of contests and auctions, the proposal requires advertisement of the privatization transaction at least thirty days beforehand.

Detailed procedures are laid down for the three privatization mechanisms. For auctions, the Committee may hire an auctioneer who receives bids and concludes the sale, which may be at a price no more than 15 percent below the opening price. For contests, the commission reviews offers in private and chooses what it views as the best, though the final price cannot be more than 30 percent below the opening price. In both instances, after the bidding, the buyer signs a protocol after which payment must be made within the next thirty days; after full payment, the buyer concludes a sales-purchase agreement. In the case of reorganizations, a majority of the labor collective must approve proposed registration documents, after which the documents are submitted to the Ministry of Finance, which must register the new joint-stock company within thirty days. Upon registration, shares are issued to the Committee, which determines how to sell them based on the recommendation of a board of directors that it appoints. After shares are sold to buyers, the general shareholders' meeting becomes the decisionmaking body.

The proposal provides subsidies for current and in some cases former employees of the enterprise to participate in privatization transactions; however, the bill limits the amount of the subsidies and the extent of their use in any transaction. One source of subsidies is various funds that the enterprise may already have on hand. The bill also requires the new owner of a privatized enterprise to conclude a labor agreement with the employees within six months of assuming ownership.

There are several matters of potential concern in the proposal. It does not adequately delineate the respective responsibilities and relationships of the Committee and its regional and local counterparts. It also raises questions about the role and opportunities for foreign companies in privatization transactions; it restricts participation in auctions to those at which the opening price exceed 100,000 rubles, but otherwise defers to the anticipated law on foreign investment of Russia.

In the absence of foreign investment, the bill does not indicate or suggest potential sources of funding for buyers to effectuate privatization transactions, other than minimal employee subsidies; it does not establish a coupon system or provide for government credits for buyers. Similarly, the bill lacks any criteria for the Committee to follow in promulgating annual privatization programs, and the criteria for the Committee to use in choosing among available privatization mechanisms are overly general.

It should be emphasized that the Draft Fundamentals briefly discussed above purport to cover all-union as well as republican property. This means, that before a meaningful privatization process can be initiated, the center and the republics must agree on how to divide the existing state property between themselves; in

other words, it requires a resolution of the war of legislation discussed above. Indeed, I believe that the entire future direction of
economic reform in the Soviet Union turns on this issue. The
uncertainty over the legal relationship between the center and the
republics also casts its shadow on the large number of new laws
and regulations that have been promulgated both at federal and republican levels during 1990 and 1991. Until there is a clearly defined relationship between the center and the republics, we cannot
properly judge the significance of all the new laws and regulations.

IV. RECENT LEGISLATION IN THE AREA OF
FOREIGN TRADE AND INVESTMENT

As I have previously noted, we have during 1990 and 1991 witnessed a steady flow of new legislation, both federal and republican, in the economic and commercial field. All these new legislative acts are potentially of great importance for foreign trade
and investment. However, due to the constitutional crisis in the
Soviet Union today, many of them exist in a legal vacuum that
makes it difficult, indeed sometimes impossible, to predict what
impact they will have in real life. This notwithstanding, I shall
briefly discuss some of the more potentially important legislative
acts.

Let us start with the infamous decree on dealing with economic sabotage, or the so-called KGB decree. On January 26, 1991,
faced with increasing pressure to respond to food shortages and
widespread economic crime, President Gorbachev issued a decree
enabling the police and the KGB to inspect and search the premises of various forms of enterprises, including joint ventures and
representative offices of foreign firms.[30] The decree authorizes the
KGB, in the course of carrying out "operational investigation
measures in accordance with Article 29 of the Fundamentals of
Criminal Procedure" (Article 1), to enter business premises, seize
records, documents, samples of merchandise, money, and receipts.

30. The Decree on Joint Action of the Militia and Special Units of the USSR
Armed Forces in Maintaining Law and Order and Fighting Crime was published
in *Izvestiia*, January 30, 1991, 1.

The decree is, in my opinion, primarily intended for domestic consumption and seems to be aimed at Soviet speculators acting as middlemen and engaging in questionable ruble exchange transactions. To Western observers, the sweeping language of the decree is ominous. The decree itself offers virtually no rights for the subjects of the investigation and does not contain any procedure to halt investigations. On the other hand, the decree does not explicitly dispense with the established procedural protections available under Soviet law today. The reference to Article 29 of the USSR Fundamentals may well be read, minimally it could be argued, to incorporate the generally prescribed procedural protections in the Fundamentals.

On balance, this decree is unlikely to affect foreign trade and investment in any dramatic or fundamental way. Some would say the decree adds nothing new, because the KGB has always been an aspect of doing business in the Soviet Union. Foreign exporters and investors that are engaged in export, production, or services in the Soviet Union with substantial Soviet counterparties who do not try to circumvent currency exchange rules have, in my opinion, little to worry about, provided there is no dramatic deterioration in the political climate.

Unfortunately, it is difficult to escape the conclusion that this decree, together with others, such as the highly sensitive price reform and the withdrawal from circulation of 50- and 100-ruble notes, provides evidence that President Gorbachev seems to be retreating from his previous positive position on economic liberalization, and is now prepared to rely on more traditional mechanisms to control the economy and law and order.

On June 19, 1990, the USSR Council of Ministers issued "Regulations on Joint Stock Companies and Limited Liability Companies."[31] When Moscow first announced the drafting of a corporate law in April 1988, the focus seemed to be primarily on a comprehensive act that would apply to joint ventures. However, the regulations do not apply to joint ventures, which continue to be regulated by the Decree on Joint Ventures of January 13, 1987, as amended, relevant ministerial instructions and regulations, and the USSR Law on Taxes on Enterprises, Associations, and Organi-

---

31. See note 3, supra.

zations, adopted on June 14, 1990.[32]   The regulations allow a
number of interesting investment opportunities.   For example, a
provision allowing individuals to acquire unlimited shares in
joint-stock companies may encourage private capital investment in
industrial activities.   Likewise, cooperatives may be transformed
into joint-stock companies, an opportunity that would free them of
many of the restrictions currently affecting them.   The foreign investors' role in Soviet joint-stock companies, however, remains undefined.

Under the regulations, Soviet citizens and legal entities may
form joint-stock companies provided the nominal aggregate value
of subscribed shares is at least 500,000 rubles.   There must be at least
two founders whose holdings comprise at least 25 percent of the
shares for a minimum period of two years.   The joint-stock company shares are characterized as securities, which are negotiable
instruments and may be issued either in bearer or registered
form.   Individuals can hold only the latter.   A joint-stock company
may issue both common and preferred shares, though the latter
may not be issued for an amount exceeding 10 percent of the share
capital.   The regulations also enable joint-stock companies to issue
bonds (*obligatsii*) in either bearer or registered form to legal entities or individuals under certain conditions.

The highest decisionmaking body of the Soviet joint-stock company is the general shareholders' meeting, which must take place
at least once a year.   Shareholders elect a supervisory and executive
board at that meeting with voting based on the principle of one
share–one vote.   The supervisory board controls the work of the executive board of the company.   Members may include representatives from the work collective or other social organizations, but
there is no guarantee that employees are entitled to appoint and
the shareholders obliged to accept such representatives.   An audit-
ing committee reviews the financial and commercial activities of
the joint-stock company.   This committee, however, is not entirely
independent of the company, because its members are to be elected
from among the company's shareholders and work collective.   The
committee prepares an annual report following its review of the
financial statements that it submits to the general shareholders'

---

32.   See note 19, supra.

meeting in conjunction with the annual company report. In addition to the share capital, the company need only establish a reserve fund. Annual transfers are to be made to the reserve fund until it reaches at least 15 percent of the share capital.

By and large, the regulations are permissive rather than restrictive. At present, however, it remains unclear what role joint-stock companies will play in the transformation of the Soviet economy. For example, the role of foreign investors in Soviet joint-stock companies is still undefined. Furthermore, there is at present no bankruptcy or antitrust legislation, both of which are critical elements in defining the goalposts for joint-stock companies operating in the Soviet economy (see Hobér 1990a, 2, 8; 1990b, 6).

On October 26, 1990, President Gorbachev issued two decrees of great importance for foreign investment in the Soviet Union. The first decree is the so-called Foreign Investment Decree, Decree of the President of the USSR on Foreign Investments in the USSR.[33] The Foreign Investment Decree says foreign investors may create 100 percent foreign-owned enterprises under Soviet law, and that, regardless of the form of the investment, foreign-owned enterprises will enjoy the same level of protection and operate under the same conditions that apply to Soviet enterprises and citizens. Furthermore, the decree allows foreign investors to invest freely the rubles generated by the Soviet investments and authorizes the creation of special economic zones. It should be noted, however, that the Foreign Investment Decree does not contain any details with respect to "wholly owned investments" in the Soviet Union. While the decree has clarified the position of foreign investors in relation to Soviet joint-stock companies, it still creates some uncertainties as regards joint ventures. By definition and proceeding from the language of the Decree on Joint Ventures, a joint venture in the Soviet Union requires at least two partners, one Soviet partner and one foreign partner. Thus, any wholly owned foreign legal entity in the Soviet Union must be in the form of a joint-stock company or a company with limited liability. No changes have as of yet taken place in this field as far as joint ventures are concerned.

---

33. "Decree of the President of the USSR on Foreign Investments," *Izvestiia*, October 26, 1990, 1.

In a companion decree issued the same day, President
Gorbachev announced a three-fold devaluation of the ruble to the
rate of 1.8 rubles to one U.S. dollar for foreign commercial transactions and investment, including contributions to Soviet joint ventures.[34] According to the decree, the exchange rate will thereafter
be subject to adjustment by Gosbank in accordance with fluctuations
in world currency values, "and other factors." This decree also
enables all Soviet legal entities, including joint ventures, to buy
and sell hard currency for rubles, starting on January 1, 1991, at
the currency exchanges and auctions that are to be operated or by
other forms of currency transactions permitted under Soviet law.
According to Soviet officials, this would permit foreigners to exchange ruble profits for foreign currency purchased at the new exchanges, thereby hopefully facilitating repatriation of profits. It
must be emphasized, however, that the amount of hard currency
available for purchase this way will indeed be severely limited.

A few months later, on December 10, 1990, the USSR Council of
Ministers adopted the Fundamentals of Legislation on Investment
Activity in the USSR, which took effect on January 1, 1991.[35] These
Fundamentals are intended as a comprehensive law to govern both
domestic and foreign investments. This law constitutes an attempt
to define general principles of investment law to be applied equally
to Soviet and foreign investors.

The Fundamentals, like all fundamentals, do not, however,
provide specific detailed provisions. These are expected to be introduced by the individual republics in promulgating laws on investment activity. It is therefore necessary to read the Fundamentals
together with other economic and commercial laws and regulations, including, for example, the Decree on Joint Stock Companies, the Law on Ownership, the 1990 Law on Taxes on
Enterprises, Associations, and Organizations, and the 1987 Decree
on Joint Ventures. The Fundamentals are quite interesting because
for the first time in Soviet legislative history the right to invest has
been elevated to the status of an inalienable right protected by law.

One of the most important features of the Fundamentals is that
they uphold the freedom of contract; the contract is the basic legal

---

34. "Decree on the Introduction of a Commercial Exchange Rate for the Rouble
and the Creation of a Soviet Currency Market," *Izvestiia*, October 26, 1990.
35. See note 4, supra.

document regulating the relationship between partners. This is a significant deviation from previous law, which made important aspects of a commercial relationship subject to government regulation, one way or the other.

The protection of investment is probably the primary concern of foreign investors. Pursuant to the provisions of the Fundamentals, investors will be given a year's notice to regroup and avoid losses due to unfavorable changes in law. State agencies that violate investors' rights must by decision of a court or arbitration panel pay compensation. Different state bodies have the right to restrict or halt investment activities, if a state of emergency is declared, or if the investment violates the rights and interests of citizens, corporate bodies or the state and "other norms established by legislation." Such imprecise language is very worrisome, particularly in connection with investment protection, because it can be used in ways that make investment very uncertain and unstable. Reimbursement procedures for such investments and investments that have been nationalized remain to be worked out and promulgated.[36] It is not until we see these detailed laws and regulations necessary to supplement the Fundamentals as well as the individual pieces of legislation on investment to be promulgated by the republics that we can form a final judgment on the importance and relevance of the Fundamentals.

In December 1990, two other important pieces of legislation were enacted by the USSR Supreme Soviet. These are the USSR Law on the State Bank and the USSR Law on Banks and Banking Activities.[37] The first law applies to the (new) central banks and their powers to effect national monetary and credit policies and to supervise commercial banking activities; the second governs the formation and operation of commercial banks on Soviet territory.

The Law on the State Bank transforms Gosbank into the Central Bank of the USSR independent of the USSR Council of Ministers and directly accountable to the USSR Supreme Soviet.

---

36. As far as the protection of foreign investments is concerned, the ultimate protection is to be found in international law, either in the general rules of international law or in so-called bilateral investment treaties. Even though the Soviet government has signed a number of such treaties, none has as of yet been ratified by the Supreme Soviet.

37. The statutory texts were published in *Izvestiia*, December 18, 1990, 3, 4.

Gosbank's republic branches will be reconstituted as Union Republic Central Banks, with executive boards composed of members appointed jointly by Gosbank and the Union Republic Supreme Soviets.

As of today, it is not clear what affect, if any, the break-up of Gosbank will have on the specialized state-owned banks, that is, Vnesheconombank, Promstroibank, and Agroprombank. Except for Sberbank, which now is a specialized commercial bank under the supervision of Gosbank, the law does not address this question. The remaining specialized banks are likely to be treated in the same manner as other commercial banks and be granted full operational independence, despite state ownership. Vnesheconombank, for example, will in all likelihood remain a strong player in the international field, due to its size and expertise.

Gosbank and the Republic Central Banks will together form a single so-called reserve system for the Soviet Union. The reserve system is responsible for carrying out a uniform monetary and credit policy. It will control the money supply and regulate the interest rates it charges commercial banks on interbank loans and other transactions for which the reserve system acts as a central clearinghouse.

The Law on Banking Activities governs the establishment and operations of commercial banks. It should be pointed out, however, that several years ago Soviet commercial banks began operating in the Soviet Union without the benefit of any specific enabling law. The (new) Law on Banking Activities confirms the right of both Soviet and foreign individuals and legal entities to engage in the business of banking. Soviet banking, however, is now in a state of transition from an exclusive state monopoly to a market-oriented sector run largely by private companies. This transformation will require further regulations clarifying the banks' independence and the competitive environment in which they will operate.

In addition, the conflicts of authority between union republics and central government that continue to undermine stability in virtually every sector of the Soviet economy will also plague Soviet banking. The division of power between republic central banks and Gosbank, for example, is far from being resolved in the new banking legislation.

As far as the actual banking activities are concerned, the law allows Soviet banks to engage in any banking operation that does not contradict law. These operations include maintaining bank accounts and performing settlements of other banking operations on behalf of its clients and correspondent banks, financing capital investments, issuing payments and other negotiable documents, purchasing and selling government and other securities, foreign currencies, and precious metals and stones. The only areas that banks are expressly prohibited from entering into are insurance activities, manufacturing activities, and trade. It is noteworthy that Soviet banks, like most West European banks but unlike U.S. banks, may engage in investment banking activities.

A commercial bank may be founded by any legal entity or individual, provided that no shareholder owns more than 55 percent of the total share capital. Foreign shareholders forming a bank must include at least one banking institution. Foreigners may invest in Soviet banks pursuant to the Fundamentals on Investment Activities in the USSR.[38]

Finally, I would like to mention one law issued by the RSFSR, which dramatically highlights the war of legislation between the center and the individual republics, namely the RSFSR Law on Enterprises and Entrepreneurial Activity, which was enacted on December 25, 1990, and entered into force on January 1, 1991.[39] This law purports to be an attempt to support market economy activities in the form of different entrepreneurial activities. It is indeed interesting to note that throughout the text no mention is ever made of union authority.

The RSFSR claims exclusive rights of ownership, use, and disposal not only over the natural resources located on its territory but over all state enterprises located on Russian soil that are currently under union subordination.

The law grants equal rights to all types of property, including state, municipal, individual, collective, joint-stock, and various mixed forms. Foreign owners are to be treated the same as domestic owners. Enterprises are granted a wide variety of rights, including the right of court appeal to prevent state agencies from abusing their authority. Indeed, the law erodes the authority of

38. See text accompanying note 35, supra.
39. Published in *Ekonomika i Zhizn*, no. 1, January 1991, 16.

many agencies by giving no role whatsoever to any aspect of central planning. On the other hand, the law forbids enterprises from producing such commodities as weapons, narcotics, toxic or radioactive substances, liquor, and tobacco products. In addition, the Russian Council of Ministers reserves the right to require licensing for certain products. Pursuant to the law, enterprises have complete freedom to engage in foreign economic activity, and after paying republic and local taxes, they dispose of ruble and hard currencies as they see fit. Unless Russia imposes steep taxes, this law theoretically allows citizens of all countries to operate profitably in the RSFSR.

Even though the political strength of the RSFSR in relation to the center has yet to be determined, it is sufficiently powerful for this law to be taken seriously. On the other hand, the RSFSR would not yet seem powerful enough actually to carry it out on its own. There are reports that the central government views this law as highly provocative, and that it intends to fight its implementation. Thus, the only guaranteed consequence of this law will be to add yet another log on the bonfire of uncertainties presently burning in the Soviet Union.

CONCLUSION

In the area of foreign trade and investment, there are at present two trends permeating every aspect of the Soviet economy: the war of legislation and the shift to a market economy. During 1990 and 1991, we have seen a large number of new laws and regulations both on the federal and republic level. By and large, they all constitute, though in varying degrees, steps toward some kind of market economy. A key role will be played by any privatization legislation that may be promulgated. In fact, a comprehensive privatization legislation is essential for the introduction of a market economy in the Soviet Union. True, privatization is, and will in all likelihood continue to be, a highly sensitive issue from a political point of view, but it is absolutely necessary.

The war of legislation raging in the Soviet Union today casts its dark shadow over all aspects of Soviet commercial and economic life. It creates considerable uncertainty among Western business leaders and thereby hampers foreign investment. Many of the new laws and regulations issued during 1990 and 1991 are quite promising. However, unless and until the war of legislation has been put to an end, many of them will exist in a legal vacuum, and it is impossible to properly judge their significance. The nine-plus-one agreement may prove to be a first step—a cease-fire—to end the war. However, this agreement is not enough. It must be followed by a new union treaty and a new Constitution, which both must take account of the *de facto* decentralization that has taken place. This will not be an easy task, but it is necessary. There is no other way out!

REFERENCES

Brownlie, Ian. 1979. *Principles of Public International Law.* 3d ed. Oxford: Oxford University Press.

Feldbrugge, F. J. M. 1990. "The Constitution of the USSR." *Review of Socialist Law* 16, no. 2.

Hobér, Kaj. 1989. "Joint Enterprises in the Soviet Union." *1989 Yearbook on Socialist Legal Systems.*

———. 1990a. "Joint Stock Companies a la Russe." *Soviet and East European Law* 1, no. 6, August, 2, 8.

———. 1990b. "Soviet Company Law Reform: Quo Vadis?" *Soviet and East European Law* 1, no. 7, September, 6.

Kaiser, Robert G. 1991. *Why Gorbachev Happened.* New York: Simon & Schuster.

Kavass, Igor, and Andrew Griffen. 1990. "Baltic Autonomy Law: Too Little, Too Late?" *Soviet and East European Law,* no. 2, March.

Kelsen, Hans. 1966. *Principles of International Law.* 2d ed. New York: Stevens.

Maslov, Alexander. 1989. "O pravovykh osnovakh ekonomicheskogo suvereniteta." *Kommunist,* no. 7, May.

Sheehy, Ann. 1990. "Fact Sheet on Declarations of Sovereignty." *Radio Liberty Report on the USSR,* no. 45, 23–25, and no. 46, 23.

Shtromas, Alex. 1985/86. "Soviet Occupation of the Baltic States and Their Incorporation into the USSR: Political and Legal Aspects, Part II: Legal Aspects." *East European Quarterly*, no. 4.
Vardys, V. Stanley. 1988. "Lithuanian National Politics." *Problems of Communism*, July–August.

APPENDIX 6-A

Below follows a list in chronological order of the various declarations of independence and/or sovereignty (Sheehy 1990).

November 16, 1988	Declaration of Supreme Council of Estonian SSR "On Sovereignty of Estonian SSR"
May 18, 1989	Declaration of Supreme Council of Lithuanian SSR "On State Sovereignty of Lithuania"
July 28, 1989	Declaration of Supreme Council of Latvian SSR "On State Sovereignty of Latvia"
September 23, 1989	Constitutional Law of Azerbaidzhan SSR "On Sovereignty of Azerbaidzhan Soviet Socialist Republic"
November 18, 1989	Georgian Supreme Soviet adopted amendments to Georgian Constitution giving republic right to veto all-union laws and declaring natural resources republic property
March 9, 1990	Decree of Supreme Soviet of Georgian SSR "On Guarantees of Defense of State Sovereignty of Georgia"
March 11, 1990	Act of Supreme Council of Lithuanian Republic "On Restoration of Independent Lithuanian State"
March 30, 1990	Decree of Supreme Council of Estonian SSR "On State Status of Estonia"
May 4, 1990	Declaration of Supreme Council of Latvian SSR "On Restoration of Independence of Latvian Republic"
June 12, 1990	Declaration "On State Sovereignty of Russian Soviet Federated Socialist Republic"

June 20, 1990	"Declaration on Sovereignty" adopted by Supreme Soviet of Uzbek SSR
June 23, 1990	Declaration "On Sovereignty of Soviet Socialist Republic of Moldavia"
July 16, 1990	Declaration "On State Sovereignty of Ukraine"
July 27, 1990	Declaration of Supreme Soviet of Belorussian SSR "On State Sovereignty of Belorussian Soviet Socialist Republic"
August 22, 1990	Declaration "On State Sovereignty of Turkmen Soviet Socialist Republic"
August 23, 1990	Declaration "On Independence of Armenia"
August 25, 1990	Declaration "On State Sovereignty of Tadzhik Soviet Socialist Republic"
October 25, 1990	Declaration "On State Sovereignty of Kazakh Soviet Socialist Republic"
October 31, 1990	Kirghiz Supreme Soviet approved first reading of declaration on state sovereignty

APPENDIX 6-B

The text of articles of the 1977 Soviet Constitution cited within this paper follows.[40]

Article 10. The economic system of the USSR develops on the basis of ownership of Soviet citizens and of collective and state ownership.

---

40. All translations of articles of the 1977 Soviet Constitution in this paper are from Feldbrugge (1990, 163, et seq.).

The state creates the conditions necessary for the development of diverse forms of ownership and guarantees their equal protection.

The land, its mineral wealth, water resources, and the plant and animal world in their natural state are the inalienable property of the peoples on the territory concerned, are under the jurisdiction of the Soviets of People's Deputies, and are granted to citizens, enterprises, institutions, and organizations for their use.

Article 11. The property of a citizen of the USSR belongs to him personally and is used to satisfy material and spiritual needs and to carry out autonomous economic and other activities, not forbidden by law.

Any goods for consumption and production purposes acquired out of earned income and on other lawful grounds may be in the ownership of a citizen, with the exception of those kinds of goods, the acquisition of which in ownership by citizens is not permitted.

Citizens are entitled to hold plots of land in inheritance life tenure and also in use in order to engage in farming and personal subsidiary economic activities and also for other purposes provided by law.

The right of inheritance of a citizen's property is acknowledged and protected by law.

Article 12. Collective property is the property of lease-holding enterprises, collective enterprises, cooperatives, joint-stock companies, economic organizations, and other associations. Collective property is created through the transformation, by methods provided by law, of state property and through the voluntary amalgamation of the property of citizens and organizations.

Article 13. State property is all-union property, the property of union republics, and the property of autonomous republics, autonomous provinces, autonomous areas, territories, provinces and other administrative-territorial units (municipal property).

Article 73. The jurisdiction of the Union of Soviet Socialist Republics, through its highest organs of state power and administration, encompasses:

(1) admitting new republics into the USSR; confirming the formation of new autonomous republics and autonomous provinces within the union republics;

(2)   determining the state border of the USSR and confirm-
      ing changes of boundaries between union republics;

(3)   establishing general principles for the organization and
      functioning of republic and local organs of state power
      and administration;

(4)   ensuring the unity of legislative regulation within the
      entire territory of the USSR and establishing principles
      of legislation of the USSR and the union republics;

(5)   conducting a unified socioeconomic policy and directing
      the economic system of the country; determining the ba-
      sic directions of scientific-technical progress and the
      general measures for a rational utilization and protection
      of natural resources; formulating and confirming the
      state plans of economic and social development of the
      USSR and confirming reports on their fulfillment;

(6)   formulating and confirming the integrated state budget
      of the USSR and confirming the report on its fulfillment;
      directing the uniform monetary and credit system; estab-
      lishing the taxes and revenues that go to form the state
      budget of the USSR; determining a price and wage policy;

(7)   directing the branches on the national economy and the
      associations and enterprises of union subordination; the
      overall direction of the branches of union republic subor-
      dination;

(8)   questions of peace and war, the defense of the sovereignty
      and the protection of the state borders and territory of the
      USSR, organizing defense, and directing the Armed
      Forces of the USSR;

(9)   ensuring state security;

(10) representing the USSR in international relations; the
      contacts of the USSR with foreign states and international
      organizations; establishing a general procedure for and
      coordination of the relations of union republics with for-
      eign states and international organizations; foreign

trade and other forms of foreign economic activities on the basis of the monopoly of the state;

(11) supervising the observance of the Constitution of the USSR and ensuring the conformity of the constitutions of the union republics with the Constitution of the USSR; and

(12) resolving other questions of all-union importance.

Article 74. The laws of the USSR have equal force within the territory of all the union republics. In the event of a discrepancy between the law of a union republic and all-union law, the law of the USSR prevails.

Article 75. The territory of the Union of Soviet Socialist Republics is one and includes the territories of the union republics.

The sovereignty of the USSR extends to its entire territory.

Article 76. A union republic is a sovereign Soviet socialist state that has united itself with other Soviet republics in the Union of Soviet Socialist Republics.

Outside the limits indicated in Article 73 of the Constitution of the USSR, a union republic independently exercises state power within its territory.

A union republic has its own Constitution, which conforms to the Constitution of the USSR and takes account of the special character of the republic.

Article 173. The Constitution of the USSR has supreme legal force. All laws and other acts of state organs are issued on the basis of and in accordance with the Constitution of the USSR.

Article 174. The Constitution of the USSR is amended by a decision of the Congress of People's Deputies of the USSR adopted by a majority of not less than two-thirds of the total number of people's deputies of the USSR.

APPENDIX 6-C

Following is the translation of the "nine-plus-one" agreement entered into on April 23, 1991.[41]

The crisis in our society continues to deepen. Society is torn apart by social and inter-ethnic conflicts. Production decline is worsening. Living standards are falling, and the supply of the most essential goods to people is in jeopardy. There are serious breaches of law and order and discipline in the country. The most acute problems, which have been building up for decades, the painful difficulties of the transitional period, and the mistakes committed in the curse of perestroika have all come to a head.

The USSR president and the leaders of supreme state organs of the union republics of the RSFSR (Russian Soviet Federated Socialist Republic), the Ukraine, Belorussia, Uzbekistan, Kazakhstan, Azerbaidzhan, Tadzhikistan, Kirghizia, and Turkmenia, having discussed the situation in the country at their meeting April 23, 1991, deemed it necessary to immediately implement coordinated actions.

First. The meeting participants believe that the adoption of resolute measures to restore constitutional order everywhere and the unconditional observance of laws currently in force, until the new union treaty and a Constitution of the union are adopted, are an absolute condition for stabilizing the situation in the country. union and republic organs of power, local soviets and executive committees, officials in all organizations and enterprises, and citizens must proceed from this premise in their activity.

Second. The paramount task for overcoming the crisis is the conclusion of a new treaty of sovereign states taking into account the result of the all-union referendum that has been held. In this context, the meeting participants deem it necessary:

- to complete in the immediate future the work on the draft new union treaty so that the agreed document could be signed by delegations of the aforementioned republics;

---

41. The translation appeared in *Soviet Business Law Report* 2, no. 1, May 1991, 12–13.

- not later than six months after the treaty has been signed, to prepare and adopt at a Congress of USSR People's Deputies a new Constitution of the union whose basis must be provided by the provisions of the treaty on the Union of Sovereign States;

- after the new Constitution has been adopted, to prepare and hold elections for union organs of power as provided by the treaty and the Constitution;

- normal operations by union and republic organs of power and by soviets of people's deputies at all levels must be ensured throughout the transition period;

- the supreme leaders of union republics participating in the meeting, recognizing the right of Latvia, Lithuania, Estonia, Moldavia, Georgia, and Armenia to autonomously decide the question of joining the union treaty, at the same time deem it necessary to establish a most-favored-nation regime for the republics that have signed the union treaty within the framework of the single economic space created by them; and

- discrimination along nationality lines, the fanning of inter-ethnic conflicts, and violations of the rights of Soviet citizens wherever they may live are impermissible. All such occurrences must be resolutely terminated by law enforcement organs.

Third. To confirm the obligations of union bodies and republics enshrined in the economic agreement for 1991 and the need for their unconditional fulfillment, primarily as regards budgets and the formation of extra-budgetary funds.

There was unanimous support for the implementation of joint anti-crisis measures, taking the exacerbated socioeconomic situation into account.

It is necessary to ensure further intensification and development of economic ties between enterprises, regions, and republics, and the USSR Cabinet of Ministers and the union republic governments will bear greater responsibility for this.

With a view to stabilizing the situation in the country's national economy, the meeting participants advocated the introduction of a special work regime in industry's base sectors, at enterprises producing consumer goods, and in railroad transport.

Whenever necessary the republics' organs of power will adopt additional measures ensuring the national economy's normal work.

The meeting participants believe that the provision of foodstuffs for the population is the paramount task. Central and republican organs will implement coordinated actions to fulfill the planned deliveries of material resources to agriculture and the agroindustrial complex enterprises. During the second quarter, the USSR Cabinet of Ministers and the union republic governments must elaborate and adopt decisions on the maintenance of equivalent relations between agriculture and agroindustrial complex enterprises and the other sectors of the national economy.

Fourth. Recognizing that not all the factors having a negative effect on the population's living standards were taken into account when implementing the retail price reform, the meeting participants deem it necessary to adopt a series of additional measures in the interests of social protection for citizens, especially those on low incomes. Specifically,

- to abolish the 5 percent sales tax on goods in daily demand. The USSR Cabinet of Ministers and the republic governments must compile a list of these goods within one week;

- the USSR Cabinet of Ministers and the republic governments must within two weeks examine the real situation concerning prices and adopt coordinated decisions on the questions creating the greatest social tensions;

- measures must be taken to compensate higher prices in students' cafeterias and school canteens, and to review downwards the new rates in railroad and air transport; and

- a decision on the indexation of incomes must be adopted within one month.

Bearing in mind the aforementioned agreed decisions, the leaders of the union and the republics address miners and all working people with a call to halt the strikes for economic and political reasons and to apply efforts to make up for the losses in the immediate future.

Fifth. Taking into account the exceptionally acute crisis situation in the country, the leaders of the union and the republics perceive as intolerable the attempts to attain political goals by incitement to civic disobedience and strikes or by calls to overthrow the existing and legitimately elected organs of state power.

They advocated cooperation and collaboration between all social and political forces within the framework of the law, utilizing the opportunities offered by the development of democracy, the activity of representative organs of power, and glasnost.

Moreover, it was especially emphasized that, at the present crucial time, the interests of the people, the practical work to extricate the country from the crisis, the continuation of democratic transformations in society, and the further radicalization of economic reform with simultaneous implementation of measures for the population's social support must be the paramount goal.

The meeting participants are aware that all these measures to stabilize the situation and overcome the crisis would be unimaginable without a radical enhancement of the union republic's role.

Signed by Soviet President M. Gorbachev; Chairman of the RSFSR Supreme Soviet B. Yeltsin; Ukrainian SSR Premier V. Fokin; Chairman of the Belorussian SSR Council of Ministers V. Kebich; Uzbekistan President I. Karimov; Kazakhstan President N. Nazarbayev; Azerbaidzhan President A. Mutalibov; Kirghizia President A. Akayev; Tadzhikistan President K. Makhkamov; and Turkmenia President S. Niyazov.

7

Local Government: Structure and Economic Regulation

Emily Silliman

LOCAL GOVERNMENT AUTHORITY

When asked, the mayor of Surgut, a town in Siberia, says that Surgut is subordinate to the Khanti-Mansi Autonomous Okrug, and that he is not subordinate to the Tiumen Oblast, within whose borders the Khanti-Mansi Autonomous Okrug lies. The new First Secretary of the Tiumen Oblast Communist Party, when elected to office, declared in an interview how much he appreciated the support of his good constituents out in Surgut.[1] Tiumen Oblast government as well as party officials prefer to pretend that Khanti-Mansi is a mere administrative subdivision under their purview. The mayor of Surgut is probably correct, but that will not stop the Tiumen Oblast from making various efforts to assert its control.

The structure of local government bodies in the Soviet Union is complicated, and the relationship among the various bodies is by no means clear. This paper will discuss the structure of local governments in the Soviet Union and describe some of the areas of regulatory authority exercised by them. The goal is to understand the nature of these organizations and the extent of their respective authority.

1. "New Tiumen Oblast First Secretary Interviewed," *Rabochaya tribuna*, April 28, 1990, 1, 2, as excerpted in *FBIS*, May 10, 1990, 89.

THE STRUCTURE OF LOCAL GOVERNMENT

The following discussion relies heavily on Soviet legislation, both because the structure found there is the starting point from which future events will deviate and because the Soviet government wields considerable authority. One can assume that local governments have at least the powers that USSR legislation grants them. They can try to wield additional authority, the status of which is shaky indeed. As will be seen below, when there is a conflict between USSR and local regulatory authority, the USSR wins. Figure 7-1 summarizes the layers of government, which will be discussed below.

In the term "local soviet of people's deputies," found in the Constitution of the Soviet Union, the word "soviet" refers to the elected body within a given territorial unit. "Local" refers to any territorial unit that is not the Soviet Union itself, a union republic, or an autonomous republic.[2] Therefore, this local government discussion does not include an entity such as the Republic of Estonia, or any of the twenty autonomous republics, such as the Komi or the Yakut autonomous republics (fifteen of which are found within the borders of the Russian Republic). The term "local government" does encompass subdivisions of both Estonia and the Yakut Autonomous Republic.

Higher-Level Local Government

The term local government includes the major subdivisions, roughly akin to American states, which are called oblasts, krays, autonomous oblasts, or autonomous okrugs. The four types of major subdivisions are roughly equivalent in size; the smallest is the Southern Ossetian Autonomous Okrug, and the largest is the Khanti-Mansi Autonomous Okrug. The Khanti-Mansi Autonomous Okrug lies within the borders of the Tiumen Oblast, but it is not subordinate to Tiumen Oblast authority. The two soviets of

2. Adopted by the Supreme Soviet of the USSR on October 7, 1977, "Konstitutsiia (osnovnoi zakon) SSSR" (Constitution [basic law] of the USSR), *Svod zakonov SSSR* 1, art. 90, 14–42. All references to the Constitution of the USSR include the amendments of March 14, 1990, *Vedomosti SSSR*, no. 12, item 189, 1990.

Figure 7-1. The Layers of Soviet Government

The Layers of Soviet Government

USSR	USSR Supreme Soviet
Republic	Russian Republic Supreme Soviet
Local Govt (higher)	Oblast, Kray Soviet of People's Deputies
Local Govt (middle)	Rayon, City Soviet of People's Deputies
Local Govt (lower)	Microrayon, Village Soviets

people's deputies, those of the Tiumen Oblast and Khanti-Mansi, are roughly equivalent in power and authority, and they are equally subject to Russian Republic law. Moscow and Leningrad are two cities that wield local government authority equivalent to an oblast or a kray.

Five republics—Estonia, Latvia, Lithuania, Moldova (formerly Moldavia), and Armenia—do not have major subdivisions within them. Thus, there are no powerful local rivals to republic authority as in the Russian Republic, though internal divisions within Moldova indicate that major local subdivisions could develop.

Middle-Level Local Government

The middle level of local government authority is made up of "rayons" and small cities.[3] An oblast, kray, autonomous oblast, or autonomous okrug is subdivided into rayons.[4] If a city is relatively small, it will be treated as a rayon. A major city such as Moscow or Leningrad is subdivided into many rayons. It should be noted that the five above-mentioned republics are divided into rayons and cities. They lack an entire level of local government (no higher-level local bodies), which is probably a strategic advantage.

Each rayon or city has its government structure, including a so-viet of people's deputies and an executive committee. As will be seen below, the trend is to grant considerable authority to the local soviets at the middle level. One senses a fear that oblasts and krays are large enough to threaten the state as a whole if they are given too much authority. Whatever the reason, this middle level is now extremely important.

Low-Level Local Government

Within rayons there are village and settlement councils of people's deputies. Within cities, microrayon, or neighborhood, soviets also

---

3. Soviet legislation refers to this level as the "rayon, city (rayon within a city)" level.
4. The author resists using the English word "region" here, because the term "region" is confusingly used to mean an oblast in many English-language texts.

exist. This is the lowest level of local government. Organizations at this level elect soviets, though they are not legal persons, and receive budget allocations at the discretion of higher authorities.[5]

DIRECT LOCAL GOVERNMENT OWNERSHIP

Under the USSR Law on Ownership, local governments exercise the rights of communal ownership, which is a type of state owner- ship.[6] Property that is held as communal property by a given local government includes the local administrative bodies, the funds making up the local budget, housing, and utilities. It also includes agricultural enterprises, trade enterprises (that is, shops, ware- houses, and distribution systems), transportation, industrial, con- struction, and cultural, medical, and educational institutions.[7]

According to the USSR Law on Local Self-Determination and the Local Economy (the Local Government Law), a local govern- ment may request the transfer of other types of government prop- erty to its communal property. The request may be made if the property is "particularly important to meet the everyday living and the social-cultural needs of the population."[8] The transfer is made on a paid or nonpaid basis.

Thus, the scope of organizations under the direct control of lo- cal government authorities becomes clear. An organization such as Mosobshchepit, attached to the city of Moscow, actually operates a large proportion of the public restaurants and cafeterias in the city. The main administration to which Mosobshchepit is attached also regulates public health in the restaurant industry.[9] This example

---

5. Law of the USSR of April 9, 1990, "Ob obshchikh nachalakh mestnogo samou- pravleniia i mestnogo khoziaistva v SSSR" (On the basis for local self-determination and local economy in the USSR), *Vedomosti SSSR*, no. 16, item 267, art. 21, para. 2, 1990.
6. Law of the USSR of March 6, 1990, "O sobstvennosti v SSSR" (On ownership in the USSR), *Vedomosti SSSR*, no. 11, item 164, art. 23, 1990.
7. Ibid.
8. Local Government Law, supra, note 5, art. 10.
9. "Perechen komitetov, glavnykh upravlenii, upravlenii i obedinenii Mosgoris- polkoma i obedinenii komitetov i glavkov" (List of committees, main adminis- trations, administrations and departments of the Moscow city executive committee and enterprises attached to the committees and departments), *Vestnik ispolkoma Mossoveta*, no. 1, 1989, 12.

shows how much control the local government regulators exercise in certain areas of activity.

Two Western-looking stores on Tverskaia ulitsa in Moscow, Christian Dior and Estee Lauder, are actually owned and operated by Moscow City's department of trade (Krasnyansky 1990, 36–37). Although hard currency to stock the stores comes from central budget allocations, and the purchases are made through an all-union foreign trade association, the stores are actually run by local government authorities.

This tight control over retailing and restauranting may change under a recent proposal to privatize a large number of small businesses.[10]   Should that happen, many stores and restaurants would shift from wholly owned status to merely regulated status. Judging from the above-cited Local Government Law, however, there appears to be a trend in the opposite direction, toward shifting more enterprises to local government ownership. Rather than privatize industrial enterprises outright, in some cases Soviet authorities are exploring the virtues of local government control, in response to local demands for greater autonomy. Just which enterprises come under local "communal" ownership will depend on the outcome of ongoing power struggles.

LOCAL GOVERNMENT RELATIONS WITH ENTERPRISES NOT UNDER DIRECT COMMUNAL OWNERSHIP

The basic areas of regulatory authority at the local level are the power to allocate land or rescind a land allocation, the power to register organizations, and the power to tax. Beyond these basic powers, the level of local involvement depends on the sector of the economy in question. Although the specific sectors are not explored in this paper, it is worth noting that local governments have almost no role in running the post office and the local telephone and telegraph service, whereas in agriculture, local governments are increasingly in the lead. The following is a discussion of the basic areas of regulatory authority.

---

10. "Soviets Pin Hopes on Mom 'n' Pop Stores," *Wall Street Journal,* April 23, 1991, A13.

Allocation of Land and Other Property

The Soviet Constitution, as amended in 1990, states that land is provided by the soviets of people's deputies for use by citizens, enterprises, institutions, and organizations.[11] Every level of government
in the Soviet Union has a soviet of people's deputies, and clearly all
levels can become involved at some point in the governmental
process.

The Fundamental Principles on Land Legislation, in Article
13, state that the soviets of people's deputies of the "autonomous
oblasts, the autonomous okrugs, krays, oblasts, and other administrative-territorial units" are given jurisdiction over allocation of
land for use and over allocation of land by leasing, and they are
required to keep a registry of land users.[12] Land in the Soviet
Union may not be bought and sold, and in most cases private ownership is not allowed. Therefore, use allocations and leases are the
primary means of acquiring property.

The Russian Republic land code states that land allocation decisions are to be shared by the middle-level local governmental
bodies (rayons and cities) and higher-level bodies (oblasts and
krays). The language is vague, but it seems to indicate that smaller
plots are allocated by rayons and cities, whereas larger plots are
handled either by an oblast or a kray, or by the Russian Republic
Council of Ministers.[13]

In practice, the rayon-level governments are taking the lead in
all land negotiations with consultations in the background going
on with other local government officials. An amendment to the
Local Government Law late in 1990 made it clear that any decision
made by a local soviet of people's deputies would be considered

---

11. USSR Constitution, supra, note 2, art. 10.
12. Adopted by a Law of the USSR of February 28, 1990, "Osnovy zakonodatelstva
SSSR o zemle" (Fundamental principles of USSR legislation on land), *Vedomosti
SSSR*, no. 10, item 129, 1990.
13. Adopted by Law of the Russian Republic on July 1, 1970, "Zemelnyi kodeks
RSFSR" (Land code of the RSFSR), *Svod zakonov RSFSR* 4, art. 13, beginning at 37. At
least as of 1990, the 1970 code was still in use. See Ukaz of the Presidium of the
Supreme Soviet of the RSFSR of April 25, 1990, "O nekotorykh voprosakh pre-
dostavleniia i iziatiia zemel," (On several questions concerning the allocation and
rescinding of land), *Vedomosti SSSR*, no. 18, item 587, 1990.

binding on lower-level soviets.[14] In any case, if the oblast or kray thus expressed an official opinion, the rayon would be obligated to listen.

Often when land allocation decisions were made in the past, they were made informally, presumably at Communist Party meetings, and no one ever bothered to put down on paper that a land allocation had been made. More than one joint venture has been given space as a charter fund contribution of a Soviet partner, only to find out that the space had never been allocated to the Soviet partner in the first place. Such a situation strengthens the hand of the local government authorities, who then have an opening to come into the negotiations as the landlord.

Local governments are using their land allocation authority to their greatest benefit. The Moscow City Council took a 40 percent participation share in the Sheraton Hotel to be built on Gorky Street in exchange for providing the site. One rayon government in Siberia accepted US$1 million worth of frozen meat in exchange for allocating land for oil and gas development. Other rayon governments in Siberia have caught on, and they are asking for royalties in the 35 percent participatory share range. A 35 percent royalty is not unheard of in the United States, but for that 35 percent you actually get mineral rights. The topic is too large to receive full attention here, but mineral rights are still controlled by USSR organs, and the local government is currently in a position to provide the land only.

Limitations on the Power to Allocate Land and Property

The ability to allocate land and other property such as buildings gives a local government body a hammerlock on virtually all activity. Needless to say, there are limitations on this power, which again are poorly defined. In an area such as telecommunications, where the local-level enterprises are run by a USSR ministry, the

14. Law of the USSR of October 23, 1990, "O vnesenii izmenenii v Zakon SSSR ob obshchikh nachalakh mestnogo samoupravleniia i mestnogo khoziaistva v SSSR" (On amendments to the USSR law on the basis for local self-determination and local economy in the USSR), *Vedomosti SSSR*, no. 44, item 914, 1990.

local government organizations are required to provide buildings that meet certain specifications and housing for designated managers for each local telephone and telegraph office.[15] Other areas where local governments are subject to required allocations include transportation (such as the railroads), the forestry industry, and fishing.

In some cases, local governments allocate land but do so only with approval at the all-union or republic level.[16] The Law on Ownership indicates that certain property is all-union property if it falls within certain categories of use (seaports and the above-described areas such as telecommunications and railroads), or if it is used by an enterprise created by USSR funds or by an enterprise that operates under USSR jurisdiction. Likewise, a republic has jurisdiction over the property of those enterprises that belong to it.[17]

There are also limitations on the ability of local governments to rescind a land allocation. Land allocations may be rescinded if the current user agrees to the change, if the time limit of an allocation has expired, if the land is used for a purpose other than its designated purpose, if taxes are not paid, if the use harms the quality of the land, and if it is not used at all for two years (one year for agricultural land).[18] Legislation may provide other bases for rescinding land allocations, and, of course, within these rules local government officials tend to have their own interpretation of when a plot of land may be rescinded.

Registration of Companies

Interestingly enough, the registration of all enterprises in the Soviet Union is now carried out by the middle-level local governments, unless otherwise stipulated in USSR and republic legisla-

---

15. Established by Decree of the Council of Ministers of the USSR on May 27, 1971, "Ustav sviazi SSSR" (Communications charter of the USSR), *Svod zakonov SSSR* 8, art. 14, 365, at 368.

16. Fundamental Principles on Land, supra, note 12, art. 14.

17. Law of the USSR of March 6, 1990, "O sobstvennosti v SSSR" (On ownership in the USSR), *Vedomosti SSSR*, no. 11, item 164, arts. 19 and 21, 1990.

18. Fundamental Principles on Land, supra, note 13, art. 9.

tion.[19] So far, other USSR legislation and Council of Ministers decrees have reiterated that enterprises will be registered at the rayon or city level. The local registration rule includes the registration of enterprises with foreign ownership participation, unless the Soviet Union decides to adopt a law on foreign investment that holds otherwise.

The Russian Republic Law on Enterprises and Entrepreneurial Activity also provides for rayon and city (middle-level) registration.[20] A Russian Republic decree has stated that enterprises with foreign participation should be registered with the RSFSR Ministry of Finance, though since the RSFSR Law on Enterprises was issued, this decree is considered overruled (Patterson 1991, 10–11).

"Enterprise" as used here is a general term meaning any organization, either state-owned or not state-owned. State enterprises that choose to become lease-based (*arendnye*) enterprises also register with the local rayon. Thus, the rayon plays a key role in the privatization process, though a state enterprise must also have the permission of its superior organ to change its status. I have seen a registration document for a lease-based enterprise, and the primary concern expressed in it by the Sverdlovsk Rayon of Moscow was that the enterprise be added to the rayon state tax inspectorate.

Local governments are authorized to deny registration only if the registration documents are improperly submitted, or if the enterprise is in violation of USSR or republic law. A refusal to register on the basis of disagreement with the goals of the enterprise is not valid and can be challenged in court. A local government has only thirty days to act on a submission for registration.[21]

Obviously, there will be wide differences of opinion concerning what activities would be considered legal, and some local governments will make the paperwork requirements easier than others. Putting the registration power at the rayon level encourages local experimentation.

---

19. Law of the USSR of June 4, 1990, "O predpriiatiiakh v SSSR" (On enterprises in the USSR), *Vedomosti SSSR*, no. 25, item 460, art. 6, para. 1, 1990.

20. Law of the RSFSR of December 25, 1990, "O predpriiatiiakh i predprinimatelskoi deiatelnosti" (On enterprises and entrepreneurial activity), as published in *Ekonomika i Zhizn*, no. 4, 16, art. 34, January 1990.

21. Law on Enterprises, supra, note 19, art. 6.

Taxing Authority

Considerable controversy surrounds the question of how much and which types of tax revenues should be allocated to local government use. The Law on Local Governments lists the sources of local revenue, but unfortunately the list includes virtually every type of tax levied in the USSR, without going into how the revenues are to be divided among levels of government.[22] Presumably, as Soviet tax legislation develops, a designated portion of all tax revenues will be given to local government authorities.

According to joint venture sources in Moscow, local governments have shown a penchant for innovation in the taxation area. The chairman of the Executive Committee of the Moscow City Council wrote a letter encouraging the rayon governments to collect land and building rent as well as utility bills from joint ventures (enterprises with foreign capital participation) in hard currency. He promised that 50 percent of the money would stay in the rayon budgets, thus encouraging rayon officials to go knocking on doors. From the point of view of USSR legislation, such a move would be illegal. So far, taxes levied on joint ventures have been payable in rubles, with the exception of the 15 percent tax on hard-currency profits carried abroad. By no means has the issue of local taxing authority been settled, and there will be many rounds of debate to come.

OVERLAPPING JURISDICTIONS

There is a Moscow city organization in charge of all hotels in the city, which determines access to scarce hotel space.[23] Nevertheless, numerous hotels in Moscow were built and are controlled by other organizations, such as the State Committee on Foreign Tourism or the USSR Council of Ministers. If you want to reserve a block of rooms in Moscow, you would have two possible routes—one is to go to the Moscow hotel authorities, and the other is to go directly to another organization that runs a hotel. Travelers caught in the

22. Local Government Law, supra, note 5, art. 17.
23. Supra, note 7, 12.

cross fire between the dual masters have found themselves without expected rooms.

Local governments actually rent out most living space within their jurisdiction. At the same time, many industrial enterprises that seek to attract a good work force build and pay for their own apartment buildings. The buildings are turned over to the local government authorities, though the units are designated for use by the enterprise that built them. For a short period of time in 1990, when the city of Moscow was experimenting with privatizing the housing market, industrial enterprises were allowed to purchase from the city those buildings that they were using to house their employees.[24] The enterprises able to make these purchases were those that had nonstate funds at their disposal. Moscow held the opportunity open for only a few days before changing its mind, though one plant manager I know bought two apartment buildings during that time.

Thus, there are pressures mitigating in favor of removing overlapping jurisdiction. One owner means one set of decisionmakers and an increased ability to respond to changing economic opportunities. Nevertheless, to relinquish control over hotels and housing would mean a major reduction in local government power, and many local governments would be reluctant to take that step.

DIRECT CONFLICT BETWEEN LOCAL GOVERNMENTS AND USSR AUTHORITIES

Showdowns between USSR authorities and local government authorities are inevitable, if one considers the vast number of incidents of conflicting or overlapping authority that exist. Moscow authorities have been the focus of much conflict, since a relatively liberal soviet of people's deputies was elected about a year ago.

News reports in February 1991, for example, stated that the Moscow City Soviet had appointed a new police chief. The appointee was considered politically unacceptable by the USSR Ministry of the Interior, which has veto power over the appointment of the police chief, and was replaced by a more reliable, con-

24. Mossovet decree, August 1990.

servative figure (Rutherford 1991, A10). The police chief of Moscow works for the city but is also a deputy interior minister within the Ministry of Interior of the USSR.

In another incident, the Moscow City Council sponsored the creation of a mercantile exchange, called the Moscow Goods Exchange.[25] The founding statute declared the intention to organize trade in shipments of goods for hard currency, and to attract foreign firms and joint ventures for this purpose. Nonetheless, the USSR Council of Ministers issued a decree forbidding the Moscow Goods Exchange from engaging in foreign currency trades.[26] New hard-currency regulations have firmly reinstated the regulatory control of the central USSR banks over all hard-currency transactions.[27]

Conflicts between local governments and their republican masters have also become a factor in the past year. The Ossetian Autonomous Oblast within the Georgian Republic declared its independence from Georgia and claimed the status of an autonomous republic. As an autonomous republic, it would be subordinate only to USSR authority. Georgia responded by legislating the dissolution of the Ossetian Autonomous Oblast. Gorbachev tried to step in and declare the dissolution unconstitutional, but with very little effect.[28]

THE TRADITIONAL ROLE OF LOCAL GOVERNMENTS

When trying to understand the role of local governments vis-à-vis the center, one naturally looks to the USSR Constitution. There

---

25. Established by the General Meeting of the Founders on June 1, 1990, "Polozhenie o Moskovskoi tovarnoi birzhe" (Statute of the Moscow goods exchange).

26. Decree of the USSR Council of Ministers of July 20, 1990, "O sovershenstvovanii roznichnoi torgovli . . . na inostrannuiu valiutu" (On retail trade in foreign currency). (Official copy).

27. Law of the USSR of March 1, 1991, "O valiutnom regulirovanii na teritorii SSSR" (On currency regulation on the territory of the USSR), *Izvestiia*, March 16, 1991, 2.

28. Ukaz of the President of the USSR of January 7, 1991, "O nekotorykh zakonodatelnykh aktakh, priniatykh v dekabre 1990 goda v Gruzinskoi SSR" (On several legislative acts passed in December of 1990 in the Georgian Republic), *Izvestiia*, January 8, 1991, 1.

one finds the undying refrain of an unreformed Soviet Union. Article 93 states:

> The soviets of people's deputies directly and through their established organs direct all branches of state, economic and so-cial-cultural development, make decisions, facilitate their implementation, and exercise regulatory control over their implementation.[29]

This system contemplated a unified governmental system, where the lower levels were the implementors of upper-level decisions. In order for such a system to function at all, an organization such as the Communist Party was needed to ensure that implementation at the lower levels would be unquestioning.

As party authority has disappeared completely in some areas, and waned seriously in others, obvious problems have arisen. One level of local government may be given a certain set of responsibilities, but the potential for meddling from above is ever-present. All government agencies are ultimately responsible for everything that happens in the country. One might call this a "total responsibility" system of government.

The most serious problem, of course, is that with the coming of free, or relatively free elections at all levels of government, people are being elected who represent different constituencies. The total responsibility system of government is not equipped to handle conflict of this type. The conflict manifests itself in relations among different government bodies, but also within local governments themselves.

The Executive Committee of the Moscow City Soviet, when the liberals were elected in 1990, was a bastion of the old system of party authority. It became clear that the city soviet would not have effective influence over Moscow's administrative departments. In a bold move, some key departments were shifted from Executive Committee jurisdiction to direct City Soviet jurisdiction.[30] The list

---

29. USSR Constitution, supra, note 2, art. 93.
30. Joint Decision of the Moscow Soviet of People's Deputies and the Executive Committee of the Moscow City Soviet of May 15, 1990, "O perepodchinenii otdelnykh strukturnykh podrazdelenii i organizatsii neposredstvenno Mossovetu" (On the reassignment of certain structural subdivisions and organizations directly to the Moscow City Soviet).

included the main architectural administration, which approves all new construction, the religion department, the building inspectors, and several others.

Obviously, a legislative body such as the soviet encounters difficulties when it tries to run city offices directly. The move points out, however, that internal power struggles are going on and will continue to go on at every level of local government.

TOTAL REGULATORY AUTHORITY

The total responsibility system of government, of course, is disturbing not only because of the organizational confusion it causes, but for the implications it has for the role of government in general. Government purports to regulate every aspect of life in the society.

Tremendous strides have been made toward making local government soviets freely elected bodies. This is a popular move, because a freely elected local government body is more responsive to the public than an unelected dinosaur (that is, a national ministry).

Local governments want, and may be able to win, however, an amazing amount of control—through the allocation of housing, land, production space, retail trade, restaurants, production of many types of goods, and so on. When the ability to regulate local industry becomes almost total, the image one conjures up is that of a nineteenth-century American company town. Company towns were at least prosperous, and the grip on power eventually loosened, but one assumes that this is not an attractive model for most Soviet citizens. The ultimate question remains whether any government agency should retain direct, comprehensive control over commercial activity and, through the allocation of housing and other services, over people's lives.

REFERENCES

Krasnyansky, Eduard. 1990. "Dior Under Police Protection." *Business in the USSR*, no. 4, September.

Patterson, Carol. 1991. "Putting Laws into Practice." *P.S.S.E.E.L.*, March.

Rutherford, Andrea. 1991. "City of Moscow Fears a Loss of Power to Kremlin After Police Chief's Ouster." *Wall Street Journal.* February 20.

8

Ownership Rights

Peter B. Maggs

In Chapter 6, Kaj Hobér has provided a comprehensive survey of what the USSR and some of the republics have done that is of interest to prospective foreign business partners. The present paper will start from a different perspective, by defining criteria for ownership rights essential to the encouragement of foreign investment. Unfortunately, neither the USSR nor the states that the USSR currently occupies with its troops have created systems of ownership rights sufficient to attract large amounts of foreign capital. To encourage foreign investment rights, states must not only define and protect ownership rights, they must ensure that information on ownership rights is available to prospective investors.

Prospective investors find definitions of ownership rights in Soviet legislation to be unattractive. Investors doubt the efficacy of republic legislation that conflicts with USSR legislation, despite republic declarations of sovereignty, due to the presence of USSR troops and the very recent history of their use to enforce USSR ideas of ownership rights. Furthermore, investors often do not know the content of ownership legislation of republics other than the Russian Republic, due to language and communications barriers.

OWNERSHIP RIGHTS AND MONEY

Ownership rights are meaningless unless they can be traded for money in the context of a market. This means that, before foreign trade and foreign investment can flourish, there must not only be laws guaranteeing ownership rights, but there must be a currency that has value because it can be converted into things that themselves have value. Unfortunately, even those republics that have declared sovereignty or independence from the Soviet system still use rubles as their currency.

The primary reason that rubles are worthless is that they cannot be effectively converted into ownership rights. There are two key reasons for this nonconvertibility. The first is the Soviet-imposed system of fixing maximum legal prices below those the market would set, with the result that owners prefer to engage in black-market transactions or barter rather than trade their goods for money. The second is Soviet-imposed legal barriers to the purchase of land, factories, and capital equipment. Even if a few small republics do allow the sale of all types of land and goods at free prices, the ruble will still be worthless, dragged down by the lack of a market economy in most of the Soviet Union. Thus, local reforms of laws on ownership will be ineffective as long as the ruble is without value.

There is another reason why the ruble cannot serve as the medium of exchange in those few republics that are really moving toward allowing full ownership rights: the USSR government is using the printing press as a major weapon in its "war of laws"— to counteract the republics' refusal to transfer taxes to the center. The resultant runaway inflation serves as a further barrier to the creation of meaningful, marketable ownership rights.[1]

---

1. This is not the first war the Soviet government has fought with paper money. Here is how a Soviet author praised the role of paper money during "War Communism":

> The paper money of the Soviet Republic has supported the Soviet government in its most difficult moments, when there was no possibility of paying for civil war out of direct tax receipts. Glory to the printing press! To be sure, its days are numbered now, but it has accomplished three-quarters of its task. In the archives of the great proletarian revolution, alongside the modern guns, rifles, and machine guns which mowed down the enemies of the proletariat, an honorary place will be occupied by that machine-gun of the People's Commissariat of Finance which attacked the bourgeois regime in its rear—its monetary system—by converting the bourgeois economic law of money circulation into a means of destruction of that same regime, and into a source of financing the revolution. (Preobrazhenskii 1920, 111)

Thus, it is very hard to conceive of a good climate for investment in any area where the ruble is the currency until such time as the Soviet Union as a whole moves to a true market economy with private ownership of the means of production and without price controls.

In principle, there is nothing wrong with using the currency of another country. Bermuda, for instance, uses the dollar as its currency. Because the dollar has a relatively stable value, the system works well. Bermuda is very prosperous, providing the United States with tourist, banking, insurance, and military base services in return for consumer goods and food.

OWNERSHIP RIGHTS AND NEGOTIATING COSTS

A party to a contract has rights only against its contract partner. An owner has rights against all the world. This distinction is the essence of the fundamental advantage of ownership rights, in that a simple transaction of transfer of ownership can affect relations with everyone. A fundamental flaw in the system that has prevailed to date under USSR law has been the fact that rights of foreign investors are more contractual than ownership by nature. As a result, making investments that can be subject to USSR law can be far more expensive in terms of negotiating time and lawyer time than investing in the United States or many other countries. Obtaining rights in immovable property, for instance, requires negotiating not merely with the owner, but with many layers of government. Becoming owner of an enterprise is not a matter of mere registration—it involves obtaining approval by a variety of government agencies.

OWNERSHIP RIGHTS AND RISK

Prospective foreign investors carefully weigh the risks they will be running. There are business risks and credit risks in all countries. There are also risks from fire, flood, and natural disaster in all countries. However, decades of Communist rule in the Soviet Union have created an additional variety of serious legal risks. It is difficult to determine rights in immovable property, to obtain security for loans, to contest arbitrary action by administrative authorities, and to be confident of protection against expropriation.

Land Title

In every country where land is bought and sold in the market, there is an effective system for determining land ownership rights. While systems differ from country to country, they generally have the common function of encouraging land transactions by providing assurance to buyers that they are getting what they think they are paying for. The most common system involves government maintenance of a public land register listing all ownership interests in land, fortified by a legal provision making unregistered ownership interests invalid. Often there are also private services, which provide analyses and summaries of land ownership information to potential buyers. The removal of land from the market by Soviet authorities has prevented adequate development of such systems. An essential step in creating a market for immovable property is the re-creation of a system that can give confidence in ownership interests.

Needless to say, under conditions of the war of laws, the registration of ownership interests is not merely a technical matter. A prerequisite to the creation of an effective registration system will be the settlement of conflicting claims to ownership of resources among the USSR, the sovereign republics, the local authorities, and the military-industrial establishment.

Creditors' Rights: Security Interests and Bankruptcy

Security interests and bankruptcy is another area of ownership law that has atrophied during the period of Communist rule. Foreign investment projects generally require both low-risk bank financing and high-risk venture-capital financing. In return for the relatively low interest rates on their loans, banks want security. In other words, they want to be sure that there is specific property that they can seize and sell if the loan is not repaid. Assume that the other aspects of a market economy have been achieved—the right of private ownership of land and means of production, a system of recording ownership interests in immovable property, free sale of ownership rights without price controls, and a decent monetary system. These rights are not enough. There has to be a system that will allow creditors to have confidence that their interest in particular property of the debtor will be protected even if the debtor goes bankrupt. (It is when the debtor becomes bankrupt that they really need the protection.)

Restrictions on financing and the *de facto* absence of bankruptcy under Soviet planning led to the atrophy of two necessary institutions. First, there must be some system of mortgage and security interests registration, or one runs the risk that a borrower may pledge the same property to several lenders. Second, there must be some system of guaranteeing the rights of creditors who have mortgage or security interests against other creditors in case of bankruptcy.

Administrative Interference

Under Soviet planning every enterprise was subordinate to some superior agency. Under such conditions, enterprise property rights were meaningless. While Soviet lawmakers from time to time passed legislation purporting to protect property rights of individual enterprises, in fact superior agencies were able to interfere with property rights at will. This tradition of interference has not formed a propitious basis for providing protection of enterprise ownership rights against government agency interference.

During recent years, several legal devices have developed in Soviet law for providing protection to independent enterprises. However, these mechanisms have proved inadequate. Therefore, to encourage foreign investment republics must find political and legal ways to curb interference by USSR authorities and at the same time provide adequate safeguards against interference by their own authorities.

A wide variety of Soviet government and party organizations have long overregulated the uses owners make of their property. The Soviet government from time to time attempted to curb excesses of this regulation. For instance, a 1987 decree required State Arbitration approval of regulations issued by ministries relating to contracts made by organizations subordinate to other ministries.[2] As economic entities without superior government agencies began to play an increasing role in the Soviet economy, the emphasis in legislation shifted more and more from protection against superior agency meddling to protection against unwarranted interference in general. Legislation in the 1980s enhanced the power of the Procuracy by allowing it to suspend illegal acts of administrative agencies.[3] The laws on cooperatives, ownership, enterprises, and the rights of citizens adopted in 1987–1990 expanded protection against government regulatory agencies.[4] The 1990 Law on Enterprises was based on the important premise that certain minimum rights should be granted to all types of enterprises, whereas prior law had treated individual, cooperative, and state enterprises quite differently.

Soviet legislation on protection of rights of economic entities developed rapidly in the period 1988–1990, though it remains to be seen if entities will be able to exercise these rights in practice. The 1986 Law on Individual Labor Activity contained no explicit provisions on rights against government interference. General legislation adopted in 1987 and substantially strengthened in 1989, however, granted citizens the right to appeal illegal administrative actions. The legislation in the 1988 Law on Cooperatives exhorted state agencies to act legally, but it provided relatively little

2. Decree of the CPSU Central Committee and the USSR Council of Ministers, February 12, 1987, "On Further Improvement of the Activities of Organizations of State Arbitration and Raising Their Role in the Strengthening of Legality and Contractual Discipline in the National Economy," *SP SSSR*, no. 15, item 5, 1987.

3. USSR Law on the USSR Procuracy, *Ved. SSSR*, no. 49, item 843, 1979; as amended, *Ved. SSSR*, no. 49, item 935, 1982; *Ved. SSSR*, no. 25, item 349, 1987; *Ved. SSSR*, no. 2, item 2, 1988. The Procuracy is the government agency responsible for supervising the legality of the actions of other government agencies.

4. USSR Law on the Procedure for Appeal to Court the Illegal Actions of Bodies of State Administration and of Officials Infringing on the Rights of Citizens, *Ved. SSSR*, no. 22, item 416, 1989, replacing USSR Law on the Procedure for Appeal to Court of Illegal Actions of Officials Infringing on the Rights of Citizens, *Ved. SSSR*, no. 26, item 388, 1987; as amended, October 20, 1987, *Ved. SSSR*, no. 42, item 692, 1987. Also see Edict of the Presidium of the USSR Supreme Soviet, January 7, 1988, "On Amending Certain Legislative Acts of the USSR in Connection with the USSR Law, On the Procedure for Appeal to Court of Illegal Actions of Officials Infringing on the Rights of Citizens," *Ved. SSSR*, no. 2, item 2, 1988.

in the way of enforcement mechanisms, with the notable exception of the right of founders to go to court if a cooperative was refused registration. The 1990 Law on Enterprises provided economic entities general rights to complain of illegal pressures by administrative agencies.

The following section of the 1988 Law on Cooperatives was not only weak and unsatisfactory in wording, but by failing to provide effective remedies to cooperatives, it left them largely at the mercy of local officials.

Article 53. *On The Guaranty of Observance of the Rights of Cooperatives*

Central and local state bodies bear responsibility for the observance of the provisions of the present Law, shall be guided by them in the adoption of normative documents connected with the practical activity of cooperatives, shall build their relations with them in strict accordance with this Law.

The 1990 Law on Enterprises contained a similar provision, also without an explicit enforcement mechanism:

Article 24. *On the Guaranty of Observance of the Rights of Enterprises (or Associations)*

Bodies of state authority and administration bear responsibility for the observance of the provisions of the USSR Law on the State Enterprise (or Association) in the adoption of normative documents affecting the practical realization of the present Law, and shall build their relations with the enterprises and associations in strict accordance with the aforementioned Law.

The 1990 Law on Enterprises had a number of provisions that did offer means for enforcement:

Article 6. *State Registration of An Enterprise*

3. A refusal of state registration of an enterprise may occur on ground of violation of the procedure for founding an enterprise established by legislative acts of the USSR, the union republics, and the autonomous republics, and also for the noncorrespondence of the founding acts (or documents) to the requirements of legislation. Refusal of state registration

of an enterprise on motives of the inexpediency of its founding is not allowed. If state registration is not made within
the established period or if it is refused upon grounds which
the founder of the enterprise considers baseless, he may go
to court.

Note the important limitation that registration can be refused
only on the basis of legislative acts. In other words, administrative regulations cannot be a ground for refusing registration. The
market, rather than officials' discretion, is to determine which
enterprises are registered.

Article 30. *Guarantees of Rights and Interests of Enterprises*

1. The state guarantees the observance of the rights and legal
    interests of enterprises. An enterprise, in the conduct of eco-
    nomic and other activity, has the right, on its own initiative,
    to take any decisions not contradicting legislation in force.

    Interference in the economic and other activity of an enter-
    prise on the part of state, societal, and cooperative bodies is
    not allowed if it does not involve the right of state agencies
    for the exercise of supervision of the activity of enterprises
    provided by the legislation of the USSR, the union republics,
    or the autonomous republics.

This is a milestone in Soviet legislation. It appears to forbid Communist Party interference in enterprise operations. It also forbids
individual ministries and state agencies to issue regulations not
based on "legislation."

2. Union, republic, and local and local state and societal bod-
    ies and their officials, in the adoption of decisions involv-
    ing enterprises and in their relations with them, bear re-
    sponsibility for the observance of the provisions of the pre-
    sent law.

This provision talks about "responsibility," but it does not make
clear the procedural mechanisms for enforcing the responsibility.

State bodies and officials may give instructions to an enterprise
only in accordance with their competence established by law.
In case of issuance by a state or another body of an act not corresponding to its competence or to the requirements of law, the

enterprise has the right to turn to court or State Arbitration with
a suit to have such an act recognized as invalid.

Does this imply that the enterprise does not have the right to just
disobey the instruction and to contest its validity when the state or
another body tries to enforce it?

> Damages caused to an enterprise as the result of fulfillment of
> instructions by state or other bodies or their officials violating
> the rights of the enterprise, and also as the result of improper
> exercise by such bodies or their officials of the obligations pro-
> vided by law with respect to the enterprise, are subject to com-
> pensation by these bodies. Disputes on compensation for harm
> shall be decided by a court or State Arbitration in accordance
> with their competence.

Damages are hard to prove. State arbitration or court proceedings
may be slow. Thus, the right to sue for damages is a poor substitute
for the right to disobey illegal orders.

The Law on Ownership promises effective protection of enterprises' property rights:

Article 31. *Guarantees of the Right of Ownership*

1. The State guarantees the stability of the relations of ownership established in accordance with the present Law.

2. In case of adoption by the USSR, a union or an autonomous
   republic of legislative acts terminating the right of ownership,
   the damages due to an owner as the result of the adoption of
   these acts, by decision of a court, shall be compensated to the
   owner in full measure by the USSR, or the respective union
   or autonomous republic.

3. The state shall provide by legislation equal conditions for the
   protection of the right of ownership to citizens, organizations, and other owners.

Article 34. *Invalidity of Acts Violating the Rights of Owners*

If as the result of the issuance by a body of state administration
or a local body of state authority of an act not corresponding to
law the rights of the owner and other persons for the possession,
use, or disposition of property are violated, the act shall be rec-

ognized as invalid on suit of the owner or the person whose
rights are violated.

Damages suffered by citizens, organizations, and other persons
as the result of the issuance of these acts shall be subject to compensation in full amount at the expense of funds at the disposition of the respective agency of authority or administration.

Despite the improvement in the wording of USSR legislation,
the recent decision of the USSR Supreme Court in the case of
General Kalugin suggests that there is still no effective judicial
remedy against USSR administrative interference with ownership
rights. In that case, the Supreme Court held that it could not question a decree issued in the name of the Council of Ministers de-
priving General Kalugin of his pension rights, even though he
proved that the Council of Ministers had never actually adopted the
decree. The circumstances strongly suggested political influence
on the court. While that case concerned a particular property
right, General Kalugin's right to a pension, and its implications
as to the lack of judicial protection of property rights, is much
broader. Until a system of constitutional courts or of judicial review by ordinary courts is firmly in place and "telephone law" is a
thing of the past, property rights will be insecure. The task of protecting property rights in a future market economy while dismantling the property rights of the old system is a complex one.
Literal enforcement of the more recent USSR legislation could create real threats to privatization. Suppose a republic decides to distribute the land, buildings, equipment, and livestock of a collective
farm to individuals willing to take up private farming. Read liter-
ally, the law would require the republic to compensate the collective
farm. Republics will have a very difficult time privatizing property
of the USSR military-industrial complex.

BALANCING OWNERSHIP AND PUBLIC INTERESTS
THROUGH TAXATION

In an early and famous Supreme Court decision dealing with the
allocation of power between the United States and the individual
states, the court stated, "the power to tax involves the power to de-

stroy."[5] Legislation at the USSR level and in many republics has placed such a high tax on income generated by owners of business property as to effectively destroy the rights of ownership. The result may reflect Communist ideology, or it may be a mere by-product of the current financial crisis.

While taxes on income are far too high, taxes on property ownership are far lower than in other countries. Property taxes, in particular taxes on immovable property, can form an important source of government revenue. Governments with revenues from property tax have a strong interest in encouraging private ownership and development of property and a market economy. Without private ownership and markets, property has little or no value, and thus there is nothing to tax.

Market-oriented economists generally agree that an optimum tax system must raise sufficient government revenue while being economically neutral, fair, and simple (McLure 1986).

Plan- and market-oriented economists differ on the issue of economic neutrality. Under an economically neutral tax system, tax would not affect economic decisionmaking.[6] Advocates of a planned economy, faced with failure of an administrative-command planning system, typically retreat to suggesting that planning be done indirectly through tax incentives and disincentives, that is, through a tax system that is not economically neutral. For instance, the top economist in the Soviet government, Academician Leonid Abalkin, called in 1989 for "severe tax regulation" of excess profits (Abalkin 1989, 3 at 5). Market-oriented economists argue that any deviation from economic neutrality will lower economic efficiency. They would argue, for instance, that Abalkin's proposal would discourage investment in innovations. If a company tries a high-risk new technology and fails, it will bear the loss. If it succeeds, the tax-collector will take the profits, calling them "excess profits." Even market-oriented economists may concede that non-neutral taxes are appropriate in some cases, for instance where there are specific, measurable externalities. Tobacco companies cost society huge amounts in medical care costs (though they do reduce old-age pension payments). Arguably, they should pay higher

5. McCullogh v. Maryland, 17 U.S. (4 wheat.) 316, 431, 1819.
6. Except, of course, for the effect of the reduction in the wealth of the decision-makers.

taxes. Property taxes are neutral, in that they tend not to divert property from its best and highest use. Income taxes, in contrast, strongly discourage entrepreneurial activity.

Tax fairness is not exactly the same as tax neutrality. A tax may be unfair, but neutral, if it does not affect behavior. A high tax on corporations and a low tax on partnerships would not only be unfair, it would be non-neutral in effect, because it would lead many corporations to reorganize as partnerships. However, a poll tax levied at the rate of 100 rubles a year for men and 50 rubles a year for women would be unfair but neutral, because it would be unlikely to lead to many sex-change operations.

Economists divide tax fairness into horizontal tax fairness and vertical tax fairness. Horizontal tax fairness requires that individuals in similar situations receive similar treatment. Vertical fairness requires that the tax burden in some sense be equitably distributed among those with differing incomes. Vertical fairness is very much a political question. A government must prevent a public perception of unfairness if it is to maintain legitimacy. However, public perception that high incomes should be taxed at a confiscatory rate may lead to taxes so high as to destroy chances for a successful market economy.

Property taxes based on the market value of land and buildings could meet the tests of both horizontal and vertical fairness. Horizontal fairness requires a system of appraisal that will ensure that tax records accurately reflect the value of each parcel of land. By taxing property at a flat percentage rate, one can be sure that the rich, who own more property, will pay higher taxes.

Simplicity often leads to greater neutrality and fairness; unfortunately, sometimes simplicity conflicts with these other goals. For instance, a tax of 50 percent of enterprise income is simple. However, it is not neutral in that unprofitable enterprises use public resources but contribute nothing in return. Former Prime Minister Margaret Thatcher's poll tax was very simple. However, widespread public evaluation of the tax as unfair is one of the reasons that she is the *former* prime minister. Property taxes also would have the value of simplicity, because they could be applied as a fixed percentage of the value of all immovable property. This assumes that property can be valued—but such valuation will be possible, of course, only once there is a market in the land.

TAX PROCEDURE

In evaluating the Soviet tax system as a threat to incentives for ownership of business property, it is important to consider procedural tax law as well as substantive tax law. Soviet tax law has gone much further in the direction of substantive fairness than in the direction of procedural fairness. Procedural fairness would require that only the people's elected representatives could adopt important tax legislation; that administrative regulations on tax be published in draft form for public comment before their adoption; that these regulations be published in final form before they take effect; and that taxpayers have a judicial forum in which to contest the legality of tax regulations and the correctness of the application of these regulations by tax enforcement agencies. The new personal income tax law now extends the right of judicial review of administrative action to allow citizens to contest income-tax assessments in court. However, the Enterprise Tax Law follows the old system by denying access to court to aggrieved organizations, thus creating yet one more disincentive for investment.

INFORMATION ABOUT THE LAW

Companies planning investment need information about the law. However, the system for distributing this information is extraordinarily poor. At the USSR level, for instance, the total volume of tax laws currently in effect that were adopted by Soviet legislative bodies amounts to only a few dozen pages. Tax administrative regulations adopted by the Ministry of Finance must come to hundreds, perhaps thousands, of pages. The vast majority of these regulations are secret from the general public. Years of Soviet rule by secret decree have created a clandestine legal culture. As the victims of Soviet rule fight their way free of Soviet laws, they must also strive to overcome the aftereffects of Soviet legal culture. Constitutions should provide that no law and no administrative regulation is effective until it is published. Constitutions should guarantee citizens free access to public records. To encourage foreign investment and trade among the republics, laws should be published not only in the language of the individual republic but in good translations in more widely known languages. The republics should use modern computer techniques for dissemination. The author of this paper already regularly receives information in English on new Lithuanian legislation through an unofficial computer network. This practice needs to be emulated and expanded, so that as the republics create legislation for a market economy foreign investors will perceive the changes that are taking place.

CONCLUSION

While the creation of a legal system of ownership rights suitable for a market economy is a complex task, it is relatively simple compared to the tasks of preparing public opinion for the transition to a market economy and managing the transition process. As suggested in this paper, the lessons of long and successful experience of market economies suggest both right ways and wrong ways to organize property relationships for such an economy. In contrast, the transition in the Soviet Union will involve undoing centuries of popular attitudes and decades of ideological conditioning. It will mean challenging the many who benefit from the system of public ownership.

Unfortunately, foreign investment cannot thrive as an island of healthy business activity in a sick economy. In order to obtain really significant foreign investment, the Soviet Union will have to revamp its entire system of property rights to create the basis for a working market economy. Once such an economy exists, many of the most difficult questions of foreign investment policy will disappear. If factories, land, buildings, goods, and services are freely available for rubles, the ruble will easily become a convertible currency. If all enterprises' property rights are guaranteed by law, foreign enterprises will not need special privileges. Thus, while the tasks are truly challenging, the potential reward, that of a healthy Soviet economy participating fully in the world economy, is truly great.

REFERENCES

McLure, Charles E., Jr. 1986. "Where Tax Reform Went Astray." *Villanova Law Review* 31: 1619.

Abalkin, Leonid I. 1989. "Radikal'naia ekonomicheskaia reforma: pervoochrednye i dolgovremennye mery." *Ekonomicheskaia gazeta*, no. 47.

Preobrazhenski, E. 1920. *Bumazhnye dengi v epokhu proletarskoi revolutsii.* Moscow, 4. Quoted in *Soviet Policy in Public Finance 1917–1928.* Gregory V. Sokolnikov, et al., eds. Stanford, 1931.

Part III

Gateways to Socialist Economies

9

The Role of Austria, Finland, and Hong Kong in East-West Economic Relations

Josef C. Brada and Ali M. Kutan

INTRODUCTION

It is generally recognized that international economic relations, whether trade or resource flows, are more costly and more difficult to transact than are comparable domestic transactions. In part the costs are higher because the transaction involves parties in two different countries, necessitating the use of two different currencies and financial systems, satisfying the legal systems of two countries, and requiring that products meet standards and codes in both markets. Distance also plays a role in increasing the costs and time required for communications, thus compounding barriers thrown up by differences in language. Distance also throws up psychological barriers.[1] First, differences in business culture and practice may make reaching agreement on transactions more difficult and the resulting contracts more ambiguous in their interpretation by the two parties. Greater distance also means that the potential parties to a transaction know less about each other's intentions and capacities. Finally, greater distance means that exporters in one country know much less about the true needs of consumers in the importing country than they do about the needs of domestic consumers; they are also less knowledgeable about the importing

---

1. For a general discussion of these barriers, see Fayerweather (1989, ch. 6). For an overview of their significance in East-West economic relations, see Brada and Jackson (1978).

173

country's distribution networks and means of influencing consumer behavior.

The fact that international trade has grown more rapidly than world output in the post–World War II period, the emergence of the multinational corporation (MNC), and the growing globalization of capital flows suggests that these barriers have, to some extent, yielded to the potential gains that exist in international trade. Nevertheless, continuing efforts to reduce such barriers, including the movement toward creating a unified market within the European Community and the effort to create free trade among Canada, the United States, and Mexico, suggest that barriers to trade continue to hamper the international flow of goods and services.

Perhaps the segment of international economic relations most severely hampered by both objective and psychological barriers has been that between the developed market economies and the socialist planned economies of Eastern Europe, the Soviet Union, and the People's Republic of China. Among objective factors, systemic differences have played a major role. The system of economic planning in these countries has generally tended to be trade averse, because trade flows generally involved greater uncertainty for planners than did recourse to indigenous production (Brown 1968). Moreover, trade among these countries tended to replace trade with market economies (Biessen 1991). The state trading monopoly also comprised a system of protection, which both lowered the volume of East-West trade and altered its structure in a way that protected certain domestic consumers and industries at the expense of others (Brada 1991). Finally, there was a virtual ban for many years on foreign direct investment in these economies, which was only partially ameliorated by the introduction of joint venture legislation. Similarly severe restrictions existed on the Western side. Constraints were imposed on exports of technology and capital to the socialist countries, and a variety of tariff and nontariff barriers were raised against socialist exports.

The financial system of the socialist economies is a formidable barrier to effective international relations because currencies of these countries have been inconvertible. There are several consequences of this, the most important of which is that there has been a general shortage of foreign exchange, leading to its rationing and to the need to seek alternative ways of financing East-West trade. Moreover, the inconvertibility of the socialist countries' currencies has led to the creation of a variety of clearing accounts in their trade among themselves and with developing countries.

In addition to these systemic differences, there were also additional costs associated with distance and difficulties in communications. For Western business representatives, travel to the Soviet Union and to China was time-consuming and difficult due to limited transportation facilities, and expensive both due to the distances traveled and the limited and expensive hotel and business facilities in socialist countries. The poor communications infrastructure made follow-up communications difficult as well. From the socialist side, travel to the West was even more difficult, both because of the shortage of foreign exchange and because of politically motivated restrictions on travel to the West. This lack of interaction between businesspeople and trade officials exacerbated communications gaps created by differences in language.

These barriers to extensive interactions between the two sides contributed to the persistence of a variety of psychological barriers. On the part of Western traders, there was some concern that such trade would hurt their image in their home country, often on the basis of charges that they were "trading with the enemy." There was also some distrust of the motives and reliability of a bureaucratic state agency acting on behalf of a government hostile to capitalism. Popular, and probably professional, attitudes in the socialist countries were little better. The world market was viewed as a generator of chaotic instability and cyclical fluctuations and Western traders as motivated by short-term profits that were bolstered by numerous unsavory practices such as profiteering, monopolistic pricing, deceit, and corruption. Thus, contact with this market and its representatives had to be strictly regulated.

If outside observers were distrustful of those engaging in East-West trade, the participants themselves were equally subject to misperceptions and misunderstanding. On the socialist side, bureaucrats had little understanding of the objectives of their Western trading partners or of the constraints under which they operated. Their principal objective in executing trade transactions was to have them carried out in a way that maximized the convenience and benefits of the foreign trade apparatus. Both foreign trade officials and managers of firms producing for export were woefully ignorant of the needs of Western consumers and of Western distribution and marketing techniques. The inability to travel to the West and the lack of objective information about Western economic developments made it impossible to develop competitive exports. Western negotiators, too, found it difficult to free themselves from misconceptions about the locus of decisionmaking power in these countries as well as from the notion that their concept of the "bottom line" must also be the concept employed by their socialist counterparts.

Nevertheless, the potential gains to both sides from East-West trade, the importance of Western technology and know-how for the continued development of the socialist economies, the magnitude of the market provided by the populations of China, Eastern Europe, and the Soviet Union, and the productive potential of these countries have all served to provide powerful incentives for traders to overcome these barriers. Given the obstacles involved, it is not surprising that middlemen arose who specialized in overcoming these gaps and barriers, simultaneously facilitating this trade and reaping some of the profits that such trade generates. Although the specialized knowledge resides within firms, trading houses, banks, and specialized information-gathering and service organizations, it is quite remarkable that such specialization has taken place along national lines as well, with three countries in particular, Austria, Finland and Hong Kong, playing a special role in facilitating business between the East and the West.

AUSTRIA

Geopolitical Background

Austria is a relatively small country. Given its lack of many of the important natural resources required by modern industry and the limited size of its domestic market, it is highly dependent on international trade. As the summary data in Table 9-1 indicate, a significant portion of this trade is with the socialist countries of Eastern Europe and with the Soviet Union.

Austria's strong position in East-West economic relations is based in part on its location, which gives it borders with Czechoslovakia and Hungary, and, by means of the Danube, easy communications with Bulgaria, Romania, and the Soviet Union. Austria has long historical ties with the Eastern European countries, many of whom were part of the Austro-Hungarian empire, and thus it shares with the peoples of these countries some elements of a common business culture and past commercial practices.

Equally important to its role as a bridge between the East and the West is Austria's neutrality. After World War II, Austria was occupied by the Allies, and the Austrian State Treaty stipulated that the country remain neutral. Thus, though Austria has a market economy, albeit with a strong corporatist bent, it belongs neither to NATO nor to the now-disbanded Warsaw Pact. Austria's neutrality did not prevent it from joining the European Free Trade Area (EFTA), but it has prevented the country from joining the more supernational European Community (EC). This inability to join the EC has been overcome to some extent by special Austrian-EC arrangements on trade, but with the strengthening of EC integration as a result of the 1992 program, further problems for Austria will arise. Indeed, in the long-term the problem may be exacerbated if Hungary and Czechoslovakia are able to successfully transform their economic and political systems and gain admission to the EC.

The Importance of Soviet Trade for Austria

As Table 9-1 indicates, trade with Eastern Europe and the Soviet Union accounts for nearly 8 percent of Austrian exports. In this trade, the Soviet Union is Austria's largest partner, though as might be expected, Austria's neighbor Hungary is a close second. The importance of the Soviet Union has increased over time, as Table 9-2 shows. Nonetheless, the long-term growth of the Soviet share in Austrian trade has been modest, with the exception of the early 1980s, when the increase in oil prices sharply increased the Soviet share of Austrian imports.[2]

---

2. From the Soviet perspective, dependence on Austria is, of course, much less, with bilateral trade rarely reaching 1 percent of total Soviet foreign trade.

When viewed in terms of individual commodities, there is somewhat greater concentration, because each country is likely to export those commodities in which it has a competitive advantage vis-à-vis the other. Table 9-3 indicates that the Soviet Union does not account for a particularly large share of any individual category of Austrian exports. On the import side, the dependence of the Austrian economy is somewhat greater, because Austria obtains approximately 25 percent of its imports of fuels and energy from the Soviet Union. Given the general dependence of Austria on petroleum and natural gas imports, this reliance on the Soviet Union does represent an important form of dependence, although the recent problems with Soviet energy production have led Austria to diversify its sources of energy imports.

With the exception of Austrian energy imports, Soviet-Austrian trade is not at a level where severe dependencies on the Soviet market exist. However, this trade is sufficiently concentrated in its commodity structure and in terms of participating agents that these agents may indeed face a much greater dependence on economic relations with the Soviet Union than the aggregate data would suggest. As Table 9-4 indicates, Soviet-Austrian trade consists to a large extent of exchanges of fuels for manufactures. Indeed, the share of manufactures in Austria's exports to the Soviet Union significantly exceeds their share in Austria's trade with developed market economies (Richter 1989, 23–24).[3]

A further type of concentration is by individual firms. Even though Austria is a gateway to the Soviet Union, its firms face many of the same costs and information gaps that face firms from other Western countries that wish to do business in the Soviet Union. Thus, large firms, which are better able to bear the cost of the added expense of doing such business, and which can expect to amortize these costs over larger transactions, predominate in Austria's trade with the Soviet Union. This tendency is reinforced by the preference of the Soviet foreign trade apparatus to deal with large Western firms in the belief that they are more reliable, technologically advanced, and able to undertake transactions on a scale commensurate with the size of the Soviet economy. Thus,

---

3. At the same time, though the Austrian trade structure is biased toward manufactured exports to the Soviet Union, the role of so-called technology-intensive goods is not higher in this trade than in Austria's trade with other countries.

Table 9-1. Economic Profile of Austria, 1990

Population	7,644,275
Area	83,850 km²
GDP Per Capita[a]	$13,600
GDP[a]	$103.2 Billion
Exports[a]	$31.2 Billion
As % of GDP	30.2%
Exports to Eastern Europe and Soviet Union[a]	$2.4 Billion
As % of Exports	7.9%

a. 1989.
Sources: CIA (1990); United Nations (1991).

Table 9-2. Share of the Soviet Union in Austrian Exports and Imports

Year	Exports	Imports
1971	2.2	2.6
1976	2.6	3.6
1981	3.1	6.2
1986	3.1	3.1
1989	4.6	1.9

Sources: Richter (1989); the author's calculations.

Table 9-3. Soviet Share of Austrian Exports by Commodity, 1986

Commodity	Soviet Share of Austrian Exports
Foodstuffs and Agricultural Products	5.1
Raw Materials and Fuels	0.1
Chemicals	2.7
Semi-Finished Manufactures	4.8
Machinery and Transportation Equipment	2.8
Other Manufactures	2.2

Source: Richter (1989).

only some 500 Austrian firms engage in trade with the Soviet Union. Of these, the twenty largest account for 80 percent of all Soviet-Austrian trade, and the largest five firms account for 66 percent (Richter 1989, 9). Four of these five firms, including the largest, VOEST-Alpine, are state-owned enterprises. The importance of the Soviet market for major actors in the Austrian economy is much more significant than an examination of the aggregate trade would suggest.

The Role of the Austrian Government

The Austrian government both supports and regulates transactions arising from the country's role as a middleman between the Soviet Union and the West. The Federal Ministry for Economic Affairs, jointly with the ministries of Finance and Agriculture, sets policy for this trade. The Federal Chamber of Commerce represents the interests of the business sector in the policymaking process and exercises overview over the agreements reached with Soviet trading partners. The framework for trade between the two countries is worked out through the Austrian-Soviet Joint Economic Commission. The Austrian State Bank once maintained a clearing account for Soviet-Austrian trade, but after Soviet-Austrian trade was converted to hard-currency payments in 1971 this practice was discontinued.

In general, the government has sought to position Austria as an international bridge between East and West, attracting international bodies such as the United Nations and regional bodies such as the Danube Commission. In addition, private organizations such as the United States East-West Trade Center, an office of the Japan External Trade Organization (JETRO) devoted to promoting Soviet and Eastern European trade, and the German Chamber of Commerce in Austria serve to promote East-West trade by providing contacts and specialized knowledge. The Austrian National Bank supports the Wiener Institut für Internationale Wirtschaftsvergleiche, which collects data on, and provides analyses of, the economies of Eastern Europe and the Soviet Union. Other government agencies that facilitate East-West trade include the Austrian Bureau for East-West Trade and the Austrian Evidence

Bureau for Foreign Trade Business, which facilitates countertrade transactions (Barisitz 1990a, 114).

Mechanisms for East-West Commerce

Financial Aspects. From the 1950s to 1971, Soviet-Austrian trade was settled in clearing dollars through an account maintained by the Austrian State Bank. Under this arrangement, Soviet exports would be priced and invoiced in dollars and credited to the Soviet Union's clearing account. Austrian exports would also be priced and invoiced in dollars and debited to the Soviet Union's clearing account. Austrian exporters could convert their export proceeds into schillings at the Austrian State Bank and deposit schillings to pay for imports from Soviet Union. Over time, the two countries would adjust their trade volumes to balance out the clearing account. Such a clearing system was attractive for the Soviet Union because it avoided the need for the Soviet State Bank to utilize foreign exchange to meet the transaction demand in Soviet-Austrian trade. It was also attractive to the Austrian government because it facilitated trade with the Soviet Union and gave Austrian firms a competitive advantage in the Soviet market. At the same time, this arrangement had some drawbacks for Austria, largely concerning the balancing of the clearing account.

One difficulty was that the clearing-account balance tended to favor Austria. This forced the Austrian authorities to impose a variety of restrictions on trade carried out within the framework of the clearing arrangement. Austrian firms had little difficulty in selling their goods to the Soviet Union, but Soviet goods did not find a ready market in Austria. Thus, to balance the clearing account, Austrian firms had to re-export Soviet goods, mainly to other Western European countries in order to earn hard currency. Moreover, the Austrian government imposed stringent local content restrictions on Austrian exports. In order to qualify for hard currency under the clearing balance, manufactured exports required 75 percent domestic value added and other exports 65 percent. In the case of goods that did not meet these criteria, the exporter had to purchase Soviet goods to a value equal to the difference between actual and required value added and re-export them to hard-currency markets (Richter 1989, 14–15). This mechanism, coupled with an ongoing trade deficit vis-à-vis the Soviet Union, suggests that Austria served as a middleman more for Soviet goods going to other market economies than for Western goods destined for the Soviet Union.

This cumbersome clearing arrangement was abrogated in 1971 and replaced by settlement of individual transactions in convertible currencies. This was largely due to the Austrian government's perception that the administrative costs of maintaining the special clearing arrangement and the economic distortions such a special arrangement created could not be compensated by whatever competitive advantage it gave Austrian exporters on the Soviet market. Nevertheless, many of the skills in middleman trade and financing developed in this period have continued to be utilized to promote East-West trade.

Transit Trade.[4] About seventy firms belong to the Austrian Transit Traders Association and engage in transit trade, often with the Soviet Union or the Eastern European countries. In transit trade, Austrian traders acquire title to goods in one country and ship them to another. Thus, the goods do not enter into Austria, though the Austrian trade balance reflects both the purchase and the sale of these goods. In 1988, transit transactions accounted for 14 percent of Austrian foreign trade. As Gabrisch and Stanlovsky (1989) point out, transit trade is a genuine middleman activity, not to be confused with transit and transportation services. The services provided by the middleman are, among others:

1. permitting countries that have clearing arrangements with the Soviet Union to export or import outside these arrangements;
2. facilitating countertrade agreements; and
3. allowing a Western exporter to benefit from the middleman's expertise in the Soviet market.

Austria was particularly active in this type of trade in the mid-1980s, with particularly intensive involvement by VOEST-Intertrading, the trading arm of the state-owned company, VOEST-

4. This is based to a large extent on Barisitz (1990b).

Alpine. After this firm suffered large losses in some of its more speculative transactions, the volume of transit trade subsided but continues to remain significant.[5]

Countertrade. The insatiable hunger of the Soviet Union and the Eastern European countries for Western goods and technology, coupled with the low quality of their exports and their lack of skill in penetrating Western markets, has led many of these countries to resort to countertrade in order to overcome their perennial lack of convertible currencies. Countertrade transactions, of which there are many types, tie the sale of Western goods, turnkey plants, or technology to an agreement by the seller to accept goods from the importing country as partial or complete payment for the Western firm's goods. In some cases, such as the sale of machinery, equipment, or turnkey plants, the output of these is offered to the Western exporter as compensation, while in other cases an assortment of potential exports, often unrelated to the Western export, will be offered.[6]

In many such cases the Western exporter will have great difficulty in selling the products offered as countertrade, in part due to their low quality and in part because they may be unrelated to the seller's normal business activities. In such situations, many sellers turn the goods over to a trading house, sometimes on the basis of agreements reached prior to the signing of the countertrade agreement with the socialist country.

Many of the trading companies that specialize in these types of transactions are located in Austria. Some of them developed their expertise during the period of Austria-Soviet dollar clearing, when compensation arrangements were necessary for goods that did not have sufficient Austrian value-added; others were attracted to Austria by its reputation as the center of this type of trade.[7] Indeed, because Austria is a bridge between East and West, its acknowledged reputation as a center for this type of activity concen-

5. Much of VOEST's middleman trade came to resemble commodity speculation, particularly through dealings in oil with less reliable producers such as Iran and Iraq.
6. For a detailed survey of the various forms of countertrade, see Verzariu (1980).
7. Gabrisch and Stanlovsky (1989) give the example of the Swedish firm Alfa-Laval, which set up a trading house in Vienna to handle the firm's countertrade transactions.

trates vital information flows and expertise, creating important benefits for all participants.

Banking and Finance. Austrian banks, as well as the Austrian branches of foreign banks, including those from the East, provide the capital and the expertise needed to finance economic relations between the East and the West. The Austrian Control Bank provides government guarantees for East-West trade transactions. Commercial banks, particularly the larger ones such as the Creditanstalt and the Genossenschaftliche Zentralbank, maintain representative offices in Moscow as well as in other Eastern European capitals (Barisitz 1990a). These banks are leaders in counterpurchase financing, having innovated, for example, the leasing of Western equipment to enterprises in the socialist countries, with the lease payments repaid in the form of output from the leased equipment. They also provide trade and investment financing, swing credits, and Euro-credits. There are active markets in Vienna for Eastern European currencies and for clearing currencies of Eastern countries and Third World countries. These enable Austria's banks and trading houses to put together creative ways of overcoming problems of inconvertibility and foreign exchange shortages in ways that benefit both the countries and traders involved in what are often complex, multiparty exchanges of goods and means of payment.

Advantages and Disadvantages of Austria as a Gateway

Barisitz (1990a, 116–17) cites a survey of the advantages and shortcomings of Austria as a gateway to the East that was conducted in the mid-1980s by the German Chamber of Commerce in Austria. The findings are summarized in Table 9-5.

Clearly, Austria's geopolitical advantages are somewhat unique. Austria's intimate contacts with the East stem from its history as governor of much of Eastern Europe as well as from the postwar Soviet occupation of the country. Neutrality, a somewhat liberal economic stance reflected in the country's extensive social welfare system, significant state ownership of large firms, and a pervasive corporatism, also tended to make Austria something of a halfway house between the East and the West. Whether other countries

Table 9-4. Concentration of Commodity Structure in Soviet-Austrian Trade

Year	Share of Fuels in Imports from the USSR	Share of Manufactures in Imports from the USSR	Share of Manufactures in Exports to the USSR
1971–1975	65.7	14.8	99.3
1981–1985	85.0	8.2	92.1
1986	75.1	15.7	93.2

Source: Richter (1989).

Table 9-5. German Businesses' Assessment of Austria as Gateway to the East—A Survey of Advantages and Disadvantages (In Order of Importance)

Advantages	Disadvantages
Geographic Proximity	Foreign Exchange and Capital Controls
Tradition of longstanding Trade and Business Relations with the East	Trade Regulations
Good Transportation Facilities to the East (and to the West)	Inadequate and Expensive Communications Infrastructure
Generally Accepted as an International Meeting Place for East-West Business	Tax Laws
Political Neutrality	
Familiarity with Eastern and Western Ways of Doing Business	
Absence of Travel Restrictions and Formalities	
Know-How of Banks and Trading Houses	

Source: Barisitz (1990b, 116–17).

can easily duplicate this set of geopolitical assets is questionable. Equally questionable is whether they can develop the business know-how and expertise in both directions, that is, both toward the East and toward the West. Without deep business and trade connections with Western countries, Austria's East-based advantages alone would not suffice to make it a gateway to that part of the world.

FINLAND

Geopolitical Background

Like Austria, Finland is a relatively small, industrialized country that is highly dependent on international trade, both for imports of vital raw materials and to provide the necessary economies of scale and division of labor required to maintain a productive industrial sector. As Table 9-6 indicates, Finland trades somewhat more intensively with the socialist countries than does Austria; and, moreover, the Soviet Union plays a predominant role in this trade.

This is due in part to the country's common border with the Soviet Union, and particularly its proximity to the more developed regions such as Leningrad and the Baltic republics. Another contributing factor is the historical and political ties between Finland and the Soviet Union.

Until 1917, Finland was part of Russia. More important, after World War II Finland was required to pay war reparations to the Soviet Union, which resulted in the creation of both major industries and a specialized trading system that enabled Finland to carry on extensive trade with the Soviet Union without seriously distorting its own market-based economy.

The Importance of Soviet Trade for Finland

Finland's trade with the Soviet Union is driven by several factors. One is that some parts of the Finnish economy, including forestry, papermaking, and shipbuilding, are dependent on the Soviet market. Finnish ability to export to the Soviet Union and to import goods in return depends on its ability to manage the balance of trade between the two countries, especially in the face of recent large changes in world energy prices. As Table 9-7 indicates, the Soviet Union's share in Finnish trade has fluctuated considerably with oil prices.

Exports of machinery and equipment to the Soviet Union account for one-third of Finnish exports in this category. Such a proportion suggests a strong dependency on the Soviet Union by firms in this sector. The dependency is even more marked due to the concentration of exports in this category into a few lines, ships being perhaps the most important one. Other manufactures, including consumer goods, are also dependent on the Soviet Union for a large share of their total exports. Because Finland is not a major agricultural producer, the relatively high share of agricultural exports shown in Table 9-8 is not of great importance to the Finnish economy. Many of these exports are resales of food to Western diplomats and business representatives stationed in the Soviet Union.

In terms of the commodity structure of Soviet-Finnish trade, Table 9-9 shows that it is much like that of Soviet-Austrian trade. Fuels dominate Soviet exports, and, in the case of Finland, they account for 75 percent of the country's imports of fuels. Finland, in fact, is a major re-exporter of Soviet petroleum and petroleum products. Manufactured goods take up a larger share of imports from the Soviet Union than is the case with Austria, largely because of the geographic proximity of Finland to the Soviet Union. On the export side, manufactured goods dominate Finnish exports to the Soviet Union.

In both its exports and imports, Finland is heavily dependent on economic relations with the Soviet Union. Maintaining these relations at a satisfactory level while continuing to diversify and expand relations with the West has been a prime concern of the Finnish government. Like Austria, Finland's neutrality has prevented it from joining the EC, which causes concern about the future of Finland's economic relations with Western Europe. Maintaining good relations with the Soviet Union has also impinged on domestic politics and on the evolution of the country's industrial structure.

The Role of the Finnish Government

In view of the importance of the Soviet Union for Finland's economy, the Finnish government is deeply involved in managing
this trade. The Trade Division of the Ministry of Trade and
Industry negotiates bilateral agreements with the Soviet Union
under the aegis of the Soviet-Finnish Interstate Committee. The
Ministry of Foreign Affairs and inter-Ministry working groups
participate in this process as well. Once this agreement is signed,
trade transactions between Finland and the Soviet Union are carried out under the approval of the Export-Import Licensing Office.
The central bank of Finland maintained, until 1990, a ruble clearing account through which Soviet-Finnish trade was cleared.

The involvement of the Finnish government in trade with the
Soviet Union is considerably more detailed and involves more *di-
rigisme* than is the case in Austria's trade with the Soviet Union.
Moreover, given the great dependence of Finland's domestic economy on exports to the Soviet Union, the main concern of the
Finnish government has been to manage this trade in such a way
that export obligations to the Soviet Union can be met. The
Finnish government also seeks a sufficient volume of imports from
the Soviet Union to allow that country to maintain its purchases
from those Finnish industries most dependent on the Soviet market. This has meant a concern largely for creating an ability to re-
export Soviet goods, including fuels, to Western markets rather
than to develop a broad-gauge middleman role in Soviet-Western
trade. While this has led to the development of a good deal of specialized trade expertise in Finland, as well as to some creative
transactions—for example, Finnish shipbreakers' purchases of
Soviet warships from PepsiCo—Finland does not appear to be bent
on developing the international reputation of a gateway that
Austria has.[8]

---

8. In 1990, PepsiCo's ruble revenues from sales in the Soviet Union exceeded its
ability to repatriate them by selling Soviet goods, mainly vodka, in hard-currency
markets. To generate greater hard-currency revenues, PepsiCo, in collaboration
with Finnish shipbreakers, acquired several Soviet cruisers and destroyers, which
were scrapped at Finnish yards, generating hard-currency revenues that PepsiCo
could use to repatriate its profits from the Soviet Union.

Table 9-6. Economic Profile of Finland, 1990

Population	4,977,325
Area	337,030 km²
GDP Per Capita[a]	$15,000
GDP[a]	$74.4 Billion
Exports[b]	$22.2 Billion
As % of GDP	29.8%
Exports to Eastern Europe and Soviet Union[b]	$3.7 Billion
As % of Exports	18.6%

a. 1989.
b. 1988.
Sources: CIA (1990); United Nations (1991).

Table 9-7. Share of the Soviet Union in Finnish Exports and Imports

Year	Exports	Imports
1971	10.8	13.7
1976	20.2	18.3
1981	24.8	23.4
1986	20.2	15.2
1989	14.8	12.0

Sources: Richter (1989); the author's calculations.

Table 9-8. Soviet Share of Finnish Exports by Commodity, 1986

Commodity	Soviet Share of Finnish Exports
Foodstuffs and Agricultural Products	31.7
Raw Materials and Fuels	4.2
Chemicals	20.0
Semi-Finished Manufactures	13.5
Machinery and Transportation Equipment	33.3
Other Manufactures	31.0

Source: Richter (1989).

Mechanisms for East-West Commerce

Financial Aspects. Like Austria, Finland maintained a clearing account to settle payments arising out of Soviet-Finnish trade. However, the Soviet-Finnish account is maintained in clearing rubles. Because these rubles were not convertible into other currencies, it was necessary to manage bilateral trade in such a way as to maintain bilateral balance over time.

In principle, trade between Finnish firms and the Soviet Union was priced in rubles to reflect world market prices. Thus, world market prices were converted into ruble prices at the official dollar exchange rate.[9] Because the ruble was seriously overvalued relative to the dollar, such a pricing system overvalued ruble receipts of Finnish exporters, who converted these receipts into the ruble clearing account into Finnmarks at the exchange rate implied by the dollar-Finnmark and dollar-ruble exchange rates. Similarly, Soviet exports to Finland would not be competitive. Thus, in reality Finnish and Soviet trading partners had to negotiate prices that made competitive sense within the existing clearing arrangements.

Despite these adjustments, it is evident that exports to the Soviet Union were very profitable and thus very attractive to Finnish exporters. As a result, there has been a chronic "oversupply" of Finnish exports to the Soviet Union. To maintain balanced trade, the Finnish government issued export licenses to interested exporters. These were issued in part to reflect the bi-national trade agreement with the Soviet Union and the Finnish government's requirement that export goods have at least 80 percent domestic value added. Only firms that received export licenses were permitted to exchange clearing ruble receipts for domestic currency. Unlicensed exports to the Soviet Union thus must be invoiced in convertible currency, making them much less competitive.

Although the Finnish government viewed the clearing arrangement as a viable way of financing trade with the Soviet Union, the clearing arrangement was terminated in 1990 and replaced by payments in convertible currencies. In large part, the

9. Since 1983, the exchange rate has been set on the basis of a market basket of western currencies in which the dollar predominates.

Table 9-9. Concentration of Commodity Structure in Soviet-Finnish Trade

Year	Share of Fuels in Imports from the USSR	Share of Manufactures in Imports from the USSR	Share of Manufactures in Exports to the USSR
1971–1975	69.9	14.8	85.4
1981–1985	86.0	8.2	89.4
1986	76.6	15.7	93.0

Source: Richter (1989).

Soviet preference for ending the clearing arrangement was due to the reform of the Soviet foreign trade system, which made the clearing arrangement more difficult to operate due to the decentralization of Soviet trade decisionmaking.

Commercial Relations. Finland has developed some unique means of doing business with the Soviet Union that reflect its locational advantages. Thus, for example, Finnish construction companies have been active in the Soviet Union, often in the construction of hotels either for the Soviet government or for joint ventures between Western hotel chains and the Soviet Union. Overall, Finnish firms have been particularly active joint venture participants in the Soviet Union, though the motivation for these ventures may be more to promote exports to the Soviet Union than the profits of the joint ventures themselves.

Advantages and Disadvantages of Finland as a Gateway

Finland has unique geographical and political advantages that are quite similar to Austria's. In terms of location, it is closer to the Soviet Union but more distant from Eastern Europe. On the other hand, it is in many ways both physically and psychologically more distant from Western Europe, and this may be one factor that limits its usefulness as a gateway. The Finnish banking and trading infrastructure also appears to be less well developed than Austria's. Therefore, it appears Finland comes up short as a middleman in terms of its westward connections.

Another constraint for Finland is its own very large dependence on trade with the Soviet Union. Finnish concerns about this trade, and the need to manage it, and the country's relations with the Soviet Union appear to be sufficiently pervasive that there is less time and energy that is devoted to fostering the kinds of institutions and infrastructure needed to perform an effective middleman function.

HONG KONG

Geopolitical Background

Like the other two gateway countries, as Table 9-10 shows, Hong Kong is a small, highly trade-dependent economy. By Asian standards, it is quite highly developed. Hong Kong has a variety of advantages as a gateway to the People's Republic of China. Its excellent port was one of the reasons the British sought to lease the territory from China. Moreover, Hong Kong has an outstanding trading and banking infrastructure, a result both of its role as the outpost of British business in the Orient and its system of sound commercial laws.

A significant development in international trade will take place on July 1, 1997, when the British colony of Hong Kong reverts to Chinese sovereignty. There is increasing concern over the effect that the Chinese takeover of Hong Kong will have on world trade in the near future. One important concern is over the prospective role of Hong Kong in China's trade after the takeover and the difficulties in managing the transition. Hong Kong has been the main business link between China and other nations of the world. Over 30 percent of China's foreign exchange comes through Hong Kong (Mun and Chan 1986, 67–73). Therefore, a discussion of the role of Hong Kong as a business bridge between China and the rest of the world provides perspectives on issues not explored in the foregoing sections.

The Pattern of Hong Kong's Entropot Trade

Hong Kong was opened as a trading outpost of the British Empire in 1842 and grew rapidly as an entropot for trade between Europe and Asia. Trade with China dominated Hong Kong's entropot trade. Other major trading patterns were the United States, the United Kingdom, French Indo-China, Japan, and Thailand.

Table 9-11 shows the re-exports of Hong Kong only from 1960 to 1985, because prior to 1959 re-exports were not distinguished from exports in the official series. Hong Kong's entropot trade increased until 1967 both in absolute terms and as a percentage of its world exports. The latter declined in 1968 due to riots in Hong Kong as well as to disturbances in Mainland China during the early stages of the Cultural Revolution. Re-exports from Hong Kong in 1973 increased significantly for two reasons. China joined the United Nations and widened its external trade horizon beyond its capacity by using Hong Kong as its major trading center. At the same time, Western countries made sizable purchases of raw materials from China through Hong Kong in response to the oil crisis. However, the recession of 1974–1975 brought about a 6 percent decline in the re-exports from Hong Kong in 1975.

The rapid increase in the growth of re-exports started in the years of 1978–1981 and continued until 1985. It is interesting to note that this acceleration in growth of re-exports from Hong Kong coincided with the economic reforms in China. From 1962 until 1978, most of the increase in Hong Kong's re-exports was due to the growth of trade among market economies.

Table 9-12 shows the share of re-exports of Hong Kong accounted for by the Chinese trade. Between 1968 and 1978, Hong Kong's re-exports of Chinese goods were about 25 percent of total re-exports; re-exports to China were insignificant; and re-exports predominantly from market economies to market economies account for over 70 percent of the total.[10]

China started to decentralize its foreign trade system in 1979. Between 1979 and 1985, the share of re-exports that China supplied increased from other countries to China to slightly more than 30 percent. The share of re-exports increased from 6.6 percent to al-

---

10. See Zou (1990) for details.

Table 9-10. Economic Profile of Hong Kong, 1990

Population	5,759,990
Area	1,040 km^z
GDP Per Capita[a]	$10,000
GDP[a]	$57 Billion
Exports[b]	$40.3 Billion[c]
	$63.2 Billion[d]
As % of GDP	70.7%[c]
	110.9%[d]
Exports to People's Republic of China	$8.8 Billion
As % of Exports	14.0%

a. 1989.
b. 1988.
c. Without re-exports
d. Including re-exports.
Sources: CIA (1990); United Nations (1991).

Table 9-11. Hong Kong's Re-Exports

Year	U.S. $ (Millions)	Percentage of World Exports
1950	187	0.15
1962	187	0.13
1964	237	0.14
1967	362	0.17
1970	477	0.15
1973	1267	0.22
1975	1412	0.16
1977	2108	0.19
1979	4002	0.24
1981	7463	0.38
1983	7740	0.43
1984	10681	0.56
1985	13497	0.70

Source: Sung (1988).

Table 9-12. Hong Kong: Distribution of Re-Exports
(Million U.S. Dollars)

Year	From China to:		From Other Countries to:		% of World Trade	Total
	China	Other Countries	China	Other Countries		
1968	–	91	96	257	0.11	353
		(25.8)	(1.4)	(72.8)		(100)
1970	–	114	5	358	0.12	477
		(23.9)	(1.0)	(75.1)		(100)
1973	–	309	43	915	0.16	1267
		(24.4)	(3.4)	(72.2)		(100)
1975	–	353	28	1031	0.12	1412
		(25.0)	(2.0)	(73.0)		(100)
1977	–	535	37	1536	0.14	2108
		(25.4)	(1.8)	(72.9)		(100)
1978	–	781	46	1990	0.15	2817
		(27.7)	(1.6)	(70.6)		(100)
1979	–	1132	263	2607	0.16	4002
		(28.3)	(6.6)	(65.1)		(100)
1980	–	1687	932	3424	0.17	6043
		(27.9)	(15.4)	(56.7)		(100)
1981	52	2243	1438	3782	0.19	7463
	(0.7)	(30.1)	(19.3)	(50.7)		(100)
1982	91	2329	1226	3659	0.20	7305
	(1.2)	(31.9)	(16.8)	(50.1)		(100)
1983	13.6	2570	1539	3495	0.19	7740
	(1.8)	(33.2)	(19.9)	(45.2)		(100)
1984	270	3325	3320	3766	0.20	10681
	(2.5)	(31.1)	(31.1)	(35.3)		(100)
1985	395	4050	5907	3160	0.16	13512
	(2.9)	(30.0)	(43.7)	(23.4)		(100)

Note: Figures in parentheses show percentage share of Hong Kong's total re-exports.
Source: Sung (1988).

most 44 percent, and the share of re-exports not involving trade with China declined from 65 percent to 23 percent.

To analyze changes in the direction of entropot trade over time, Tables 9-13 and 9-14 present the rankings and shares of major markets and principal suppliers of Hong Kong's re-exports, respectively. As Table 9-13 indicates, China in 1965 ranked eighth among the major markets for Hong Kong's entropot trade. However, China became the number-one market for this trade in 1981. The jump in the ranking was due to the policy shift that called for expanding trade with the West. Other important major markets for Hong Kong's re-exports were the United States, Indonesia, Singapore, and Japan.

Looking at the supply side, Table 9-14 shows that Hong Kong's entropot trade shifted in favor of the Asian countries over time. The largest supplier of Hong Kong's re-exports was China between 1963 and 1981. In 1981, Japan became the second largest supplier. The United States ranked second among the major suppliers of Hong Kong's re-exports in 1969, but its share declined over time, and it ranked third in 1981.

The Role of Hong Kong in China's Trade

Hong Kong is now China's largest market, and China is Hong Kong's second largest market after the United States. Hong Kong is also China's largest source of foreign investment. Re-exports from Hong Kong now almost match domestic exports, and 80 percent of that business involves goods coming from or going to China. The growing economic interdependence between China and Hong Kong may enable China's economy to become the largest in the world in the near future. Tables 9-15 and 9-16 show China's indirect trade through Hong Kong, in absolute terms and as a percentage share of total trade, respectively.

Trade in absolute terms increased significantly after 1979, indicating the importance of trade reforms in China's trade since 1979. Japan has been a long-time trade partner of China, and most of Japan's trade is handled directly. Therefore, in Table 9-16 the percentage share (the ratio of indirect to direct trade) of China's trade handled through Hong Kong is higher for noncommunist

Table 9-13. Rankings and Shares of Major Markets for Hong Kong's
Re-Exports, 1965 and 1981

Country/Area	Ranking		Market Share (Percent)	
	1965	1981	1965	1981
Japan	1	5	17.0	6.7
Singapore	2	4	13.7	7.8
Indonesia	3	3	9.7	10.2
USA	4	2	5.7	11.5
Malaysia	5	16	5.5	1.2
Taiwan	6	6	4.6	5.8
Macau	7	7	4.3	3.4
China	8	1	3.6	19.3
UK	9	11	3.1	2.2

Source: Hsia (1984).

Table 9-14. Rankings and Shares of Major Suppliers of
Hong Kong's Re-Exports, 1969 and 1981

Country/Area	Ranking		Share in Total Supply (Percent)	
	1969	1981	1969	1981
China	1	1	27.0	30.7
Japan	3	2	10.9	20.1
USA	2	3	13.6	9.7
Taiwan	9	4	1.7	8.1
S. Korea	a	5	b	4.7
Switzerland	7	6	2.8	2.3
W. Germany	8	7	2.6	1.7
Singapore	a	8	b	1.6
UK	5	9	3.7	1.4
Belgium/ Luxembourg	6	10	2.9	1.2

a. Ranked below 16th.
b. Insignificant.
Source: Hsia (1984).

countries excluding Japan than for those including Japan, and this share rose from 11 percent in 1970 to 34 percent in 1985 for exports, and from zero percent to 27 percent for imports. Overall, the increase in import shares was more dramatic than in export shares.

Table 9-16 suggests that China's dependence on the entropot activity of Hong Kong is significant and increasing. For instance, the percentage shares in 1970 with all countries, with all noncommunist countries, and with all noncommunist countries except Japan were 6.7, 10, and 10.8 percent for exports and 0.3, 0.3, and 0.0 percent for imports, respectively. The corresponding ratios in 1985 were 22.3, 25.3, and 33.5 percent for exports and 18.2, 20.1, and 26.9 percent for imports.

There are several reasons for China's increasing dependence on the entropot activity of Hong Kong. Most important is that the Chinese economy is rigidly controlled and regulated by the government, whereas there is little government intervention in the Hong Kong economy. The latter provides opportunities for flexibility, fast responses to a changing world environment, and easy identification of profits as demanded by entropot trade.

In 1979, as part of the general reform of the economy, China liberalized and decentralized its foreign trade. The previous system, consisting of several hundred state trading monopolies, was to a large extent dismantled. In its place, provincial and municipal authorities were given greater rights to export goods produced by enterprises under their authority and to import needed goods from abroad. Not only were firms and provinces allowed to engage in foreign trade, but the number of foreign trading companies increased as well. While this "open-door" policy facilitated the rapid expansion of China's trade, it also posed unique burdens for both Chinese and foreign traders. Foreigners could no longer seek to deal with the entire Chinese market through the intermediation of a single monopolistic Chinese trading company located in Beijing. Rather, they had to deal with a multitude of regional markets, each with its own array of trading companies, producing or consuming enterprises, and regional authorities. On the Chinese side, regional authorities and enterprise managers who previously had little or no experience with foreign trade were abruptly thrust into positions where they had to make arrangements to replace previously centrally determined trade flows. The

Table 9-15. China's Indirect Trade through Hong Kong
(Million U.S. Dollars)

Year	With All Countries		With Noncommunist Countries[a] Except Japan	
	Exports	Imports	Exports	Imports
1970	114	6	99	–
1975	353	28	326	–
1977	535	38	483	33
1979	1132	363	991	191
1981	2295	1438	2093	1176
1983	2706	1675	2554	1212
1984	3595	3590	3332	2377
1985	4445	5907	4075	4040

a. Excluding Hong Kong. China's indirect exports (imports) are taken to be Hong Kong's re-exports of Chinese origin (Hong Kong re-exports to China).
Source: Sung (1988).

Table 9-16. China's Indirect Trade through Hong Kong
(Percentage Shares)

Year	All Countries[a]		All Noncommunist Countries[a]		All Noncommunist Countries[a] Except Japan	
	Ex.[b]	Im.[c]	Ex.	Im.	Ex.	Im.
1970	6.7	0.3	10.0	0.3	10.8	0.0
1975	6.2	0.4	8.0	0.4	10.8	0.0
1977	8.3	0.6	11.1	0.6	13.9	0.9
1979	10.7	1.9	12.6	2.2	16.0	2.3
1981	14.1	8.9	15.3	9.8	20.1	12.6
1983	15.2	10.6	16.1	11.9	20.7	12.9
1984	19.2	16.0	21.1	17.8	28.3	20.4
1985	22.3	18.2	25.3	20.1	33.5	26.9

a. Excluding Hong Kong.
b. Exports.
c. Imports.
Source: Sung (1988).

contacts and knowledge of Hong Kong's entropot traders enabled them to bridge this gap between Chinese and foreign buyers and sellers and to facilitate trade dealings in these new circumstances. As part of the continuing reorientation of its economic policy, China has assigned a high priority to expanding trade with the West. Unfortunately, China lacks skills to accommodate its intended trade expansion. Hong Kong is very rich in trading services, including insurance, finance, communications, shipping, marketing, and legal services. In addition, the geographical setting and cultural diversity that Hong Kong enjoys makes it a natural candidate for meeting China's trade requirements. Moreover, a legal system based on English law in Hong Kong makes the job of international businesspeople easier. There is no income tax in Hong Kong, and the corporate profits tax was reduced from 39 to 17 percent in recent years; but, there is a salary tax of about 16 percent.

The Transition Period and Prospects

Hong Kong will become a Special Administrative Region under the 1984 Sino-British Joint Declaration. According to this declaration, signed by the British and Chinese governments in Beijing in December 1984, about 6 million free and capitalist people will be under communist rule starting in 1997. Now, halfway through the transition, there are some signs that China does not want to wait until 1997 to start taking over. For instance, China issued a statement to the Hong Kong government in January 1991 that it has to be consulted on all matters that concern 1997. Hong Kong's Governor, Sir David Wilson, rejected the Chinese demands and cited the 1984 Sino-British Joint Declaration on the future of Hong Kong that gives Britain and the present Hong Kong government responsibility to administer the colony up to 1997. The Chinese vice-premier responded that in transition to 1997 only Beijing was entitled to speak on behalf of the people of Hong Kong. After 1997, he added, Beijing would respect Hong Kong's autonomy.[11]

Another event took place in November 1990 that raises serious questions regarding Hong Kong's freedom of action in the future

11. *Economist,* February 16, 1991.

in international organizations. A Hong Kong delegation had to withdraw from a conference sponsored by the World Meteorological Organization, of which Hong Kong is a member. The reason for the withdrawal was China's insistence that Hong Kong's participation in the conference was not consistent with its non-sovereign status. Even though the joint declaration permits Hong Kong to join international organizations, the recent events raise concerns about China's intentions. The uncertainty associated with Hong Kong's freedom of action may very much hurt China's trade with other nations by decreasing the importance of Hong Kong as a gateway between China and the rest of the world. At worst, Hong Kong can become another Chinese city with low economic growth.

These fears are already causing serious problems, one of which is the brain drain. According to Hong Kong government statistics, 46,000 people emigrated in 1988, 42,000 in 1989, and 62,000 in 1990.[12] Over 60,000 people are expected to leave in 1991. Also, nearly half of the multinational firms based in Hong Kong are considering pulling out before 1997. In addition, financial institutions are not doing well. For example, Hong Kong & Shanghai Bank, the biggest bank in Hong Kong, reported a 35 percent drop in 1990 earnings, its first decline since 1967.[13]

As concern increases over the effect that the Chinese takeover of Hong Kong will have on the world, Chinese officials are pledging to do their best to ensure that Hong Kong remains prosperous after the transition. For instance, in a March 10, 1991, speech to the Hong Kong General Chamber of Commerce, Lu Ping, director of China's Hong Kong affairs office, said that the colony will remain an "oasis" of free trade after it returns to China's control in 1997.[14] He added that Hong Kong's participation in international trade agreements to which China was not a party would continue after 1997, and it would be allowed to negotiate its own trade agreements without interference. He also said that the post–1997 government would have a relatively free hand to continue develop-

---

12. *Statistical Bulletin*, 1990.
13. *Wall Street Journal*, March 13, 1991.
14. *Journal of Commerce*, March 12, 1991.

ing Hong Kong into an international financial and commercial center. Given the evolving economic interdependence between China and Hong Kong and the increasing dependence of China on Hong Kong's entropot trade, it seems that it is not so much that China is taking over Hong Kong as the colony is taking over the Mainland. Given the vital contribution that Hong Kong has made to China's trade and economy in recent years, China will need Hong Kong as it is. The future of China is the best guarantee of the future of Hong Kong.

CONCLUSION

It is undeniable that the three countries examined in this paper have benefited from their role as gateways. The creation of high-skill and high-wage jobs in banking, commerce, and trade has clearly been of importance for all, perhaps with Hong Kong the greatest beneficiary, followed by Austria. The inflow of capital from abroad, both to help construct infrastructure such as hotels and to establish office and production facilities for foreign banks and firms has also had a positive impact on these economies.

At the same time, all three countries have experienced some costs from their gateway status. In economic terms there has been some distortion of the economic system in order to accommodate the trading systems of the East. This appears to have been most costly for Finland and least costly, so far, for Hong Kong. There have also been structural costs, again most heavily borne by Finland, whose industrial structure had to be tailored, and then retailored, to meet Soviet needs. Moreover, not all gateway activities have proven to be profitable and beneficial for the gateway countries. Finnish shipyards suffered severely in 1987 when the Soviet Union was unable to pay for ship deliveries, thus imposing severe interest costs on the Finns. Austrian trading firms suffered large financial losses from speculative trading in oil in the 1980s. Many of these loss-making transactions involved purchases of petroleum from Iraq and Iran with a view toward reselling it to Eastern European countries at higher prices. In some cases, such sales did not materialize; in other cases, the trading houses received lower prices than they had anticipated. Revelation of losses in these transactions by VOEST-Alpine's trading subsidiary led to a government crisis. Moreover, Austrian firms hold about 12 percent of outstanding Soviet and Eastern European debt, even though Austria accounts for only 6.8 percent of East-West trade. Because a good part of this debt may not be repaid, it too must be added to the list of unprofitable gateway activities. All three countries have had to face severe readjustments as their East-West trade was buffeted by economic and political instabilities in the East and the ups and downs of East-West relations. Finland is now coping with the effects of the collapse of the Soviet economy, while Austria must deal not only with that but also with the trade problems of Eastern Europe.

All three countries have also paid a political price for their gateway role. Finland and Austria have been forced into a political neutrality that has interfered with their ability to take full advantage of trends in European economic and political integration. Domestic politics have also been influenced by these countries' special relationships with the Soviet Union. In the case of Hong Kong, the people have been a British colony, with limited self-government, and now are moving toward an unknown future with considerable interference from the PRC in their internal affairs. The middleman role clearly requires a certain degree of political self-abnegation.

Finally, it is worth noting that playing a middleman role requires a certain degree of cultural and ethnic heterogeneity and intercultural tolerance. Both Hong Kong and Vienna are truly international cities where people of many countries and cultures live, work, and mix. In that regard, some of their greater successes at being a gateway, relative to Finland, may be due to their more cosmopolitan populations and to their openness to foreign influences.

REFERENCES

Barisitz, Stefan. 1990a. "Austria: A Business Bridge between East and West." *Osterreichische Osthefte*, Jahrgang 32, Heft 1.
——. 1990b. "L'importance de l'Autriche dans les relations d'affaires Est-Ouest." *Forschungsbericht*, no. 164, Wiener Institut für Internationale Wirtschaftsvergleiche, June.
Biessen, Guido. 1991. "Is the Impact of Central Planning on the Level of Foreign Trade Really Negative?" *Journal of Comparative Economics* 15, no. 1, March.
Brada, Josef C. 1991. "The Political Economy of Socialist Foreign Trade Organization and Policies." *Journal of Comparative Economics* 15, no. 2, June.
Brada, Josef C., and Marvin R. Jackson. 1978. "The Organization of Foreign Trade Under Capitalism and Socialism." *Journal of Comparative Economics* 2, no. 4, December.
Brown, Alan A. 1968. "Toward a Theory of Centrally Planned Foreign Trade." In *International Trade and Central Planning*. Alan A. Brown and Egon Neuberger, eds. Berkeley: University of California Press, 1968.
CIA. 1990. *The World Factbook*. Washington: CIA.
Fayerweather, John. 1969. *International Business Management*. New York: McGraw-Hill.
Gabrisch, Hubert, and Jan Stanlovsky. 1989. "Special Forms of East-West Trade, Parts I–II." *Soviet and Eastern European Foreign Trade* 25, no. 1: 79, Spring.
Hsia, Ronald. 1984. "The Entropot Trade of Hong Kong with Special Reference to Taiwan and the Chinese Mainland." *Mainland China Economic Series*, no. 2. Chung-Hua Institution for Economic Research. Taipei, Taiwan, Republic of China: University of Washington Press.
Mun, X. C., and T. S. Chan. 1986. "The Role of Hong Kong in United States–China." *Columbia Journal of Business* 21, Spring.
Richter, Sandor. 1989. "The Economic Relations of Austria, Finland, Yugoslavia and Hungary with the Soviet Union." *Forschungsbericht*, no. 161, Wiener Institut für Internationale Wirtschaftsvergleiche, October.
Sung, Yun-wing. 1988. "A Theoretical and Empirical Analysis of Entropot Trade: Hong Kong, Singapore and Their Roles in

China's Trade." In *Pacific Trade in Services.* Leslie V. Castle and Christopher Findlay, eds. New York: Allen and Unwin Press.

United Nations. 1990. *Economic Bulletin for Europe* 42, 90. New York: United Nations.

Verzariu, Pompiliu. 1980. *Countertrade Practices in East Europe, the Soviet Union and China.* Washington: U.S. Department of Commerce.

Zou, Gang. 1990. "China's Coastal Development Strategy and Pacific Rim Economic Cooperation." *Forum of Young Chinese Economists* 5, no. 1, June.

10

The Baltics:
The Premier European Gateway
to the Soviet Union

Jenik Radon

FASHION SHOW OF WORDS

To the outside observer, the economic reform process steadily taking root in the nations of Eastern Europe, the Baltics, and the
Soviet Union, together the infamous East of the postwar period, in
part resembles a fashion show of words. It is an article of faith
throughout the East that economic change can only succeed with
the infusion of significant foreign capital, management skills and
technology. This infusion is expected to effect the longed-for cure
for aged and deteriorating, if not collapsing, economies and industries. Attracting foreign participation has thus become a goal unto
itself. But reaching this goal demands imagination to mask the
economic shock that is the East. Catchy, but accurate, words that
symbolize change, prosperity, and a shining future have served this
purpose well. Within the last few years, joint ventures, privatization, and gateway are some of the "in" terms that not only reflect
the ongoing reforms but also serve to beckon potential investors to
the East.

These words conjure up visions of opportunity instead of pictures
of decay. They dress up an otherwise dreary economic landscape
and drape a world littered by environmental disasters. It does not
seem to disturb anyone, whether government official or foreign
expert, that these trendy words are in perpetual search of univer-
sally accepted definitions. Even the ordinary citizen cites them

and uses them with aplomb, though they would be hard-pressed to explain them.

Joint ventures and privatization have become such common terms that conferences discuss them; doctoral dissertations dissect them; and the media publicize them. And lawyers fine-tune the details. Gateway is an ancient concept, but yet the newest term. It has become a fixture in the East's promotional jargon, and, in contrast to joint ventures and privatization, it does not constitute a lawyers employment act.

Joint ventures, a term that historically meant partnership in whatever form, in the East came to mean any undertaking where the participants included those from the West, as well as from the East, particularly companies from Western Europe, the United States, and Japan. But tax authorities, customs officials and academics in Eastern Europe worried about such an all-encompassing simplistic definition. They questioned whether an undertaking with only 1 percent foreign participation should constitute a joint venture, entitling the venture to tax exemptions and other privileges. Still, this popularized term, which symbolizes the availability of previously forbidden investment opportunity, successfully lured a stream of foreign investors to the East. Thousands of joint ventures were formed. Even the economic basket-case of the East, the Soviet Union, became home to over 3,000 joint ventures. Still, joint ventures could not alone provide a cure for the immense economic problems of the East.

Hope was placed in privatization, which would serve to simultaneously invigorate the local entrepreneurs and other businesspeople with capitalistic thinking and attract foreign investors. Privatization initially meant the transfer of the ownership of enterprises from the government or state to private persons and companies. Such a transfer is simple in theory only. Implementation is cumbersome, time-consuming, and difficult beyond imagination. Even the Germans cannot get it right, despite drowning the former East Germany in an ocean of Deutsch Marks.

Many politicians and experts in the East are now prepared to accept a watered-down or broadened definition of privatization that would include the commercialization of the management of existing enterprises. The focus is to be on self-financing, known in the West simply as profit.

Questions abound, particularly whether all enterprises, including utilities, have to be privatized. Arguments arise on whether the government should or can remain as a partner in a privatized enterprise. Nevertheless, the popularization of the concept caught the eye of the capitalistic West, and privatization has become a magnet drawing foreign capital to the East, as well as an army of Western professionals seeking to advise on its implementation.

The term "gateway" at first glance eludes even basic definition. According to the dictionary, it means entrance or access. It is positive, catchy, and promising, as well as elastic. It can mean almost anything anyone wants it to mean. It is a Madison Avenue dream word. It also raises a series of immediate questions: Gateway to what? Gateway for what purpose? And gateway for whom? Although modern academia, having eliminated the study of geography, can dismiss it as a geographer's attempt to be scientific, deciding on an entry point, a gateway location, forms the basis of pivotal business deliberations. Where one locates is obviously critical.

The fact that "gateway" is an illusive term has not stopped Poland and other countries of Eastern Europe, including reunited Germany, from proclaiming themselves the gateway to the East and its untapped market of budding consumers. The Baltic countries of Estonia, Latvia, and Lithuania have pinned their economic hopes on becoming the gateway to the Soviet Union. All of these nations are impressed with the economic success of Finland and Austria and are conscious of their historic gateway role to the East. They are enamored by the prosperity of Hong Kong as the entrance to China. This success is worth emulating, though no one seems to know what steps are necessary to duplicate it.

In essence, a gateway is a competitive or strategic location for a business. Finland, Austria, and Hong Kong offer locational advantages and specialized services, particularly useful in developing or exploiting the market area for which they serve as a gateway. A gateway location normally effects a particular purpose, whether as a financial, communications, or administrative center. There may well be more than one possible gateway, because there is usually more than one suitable location for a business. A gateway may be created by design or it may evolve over time. In short, a gateway is simply a better (or the best) location for engaging in a certain type of business. In the Soviet context, the issue of determining a gateway location can be rephrased: How does a Western businessperson get into the Soviet market? Or simply put, where should one locate? The Baltics offer a particularly attractive and competitive location for a variety of Western businesses seeking to do business with the Soviet Union. What makes a Baltic location competitive can only be understood by considering potentially alternative locations. In that regard, the situation of Poland, Germany (or specifically Berlin), and other areas is instructive. Moreover, it is obvious that competitive advantages can change over time, and that a successful gateway appealing to a broad spectrum of industries and services will have to be actively and continuously supported. Thus, the economic history of Finland, Austria, and Hong Kong, among others, can serve as a guide for Baltic economic development policy.

TRADITIONAL GATEWAYS TO THE EAST: FINLAND AND AUSTRIA

Finland and Austria during the postwar period have had little choice but to capitalize on their lot as political no-man's lands between East and West. They became a natural meeting place of the East and the West. Finland, spurred on by its desire to safeguard its political independence after its defeat by the Soviet Union during World War II, consciously established a tradition of trading with the Soviet Union by importing its raw materials and exporting Finnish finished goods. These transactions were financed by a sophisticated and unique monetarized barter system, which formed the basis of the development of modern Finnish industry.

Austria, eager to find advantage in the neutrality imposed on it by the four occupying Allied powers, developed extensive experience in working with the diverse nations of Eastern Europe as well as the Soviet Union. An army of bankers and business consultants in Vienna became adept in carrying out complex transit trade, countertrade, and barter transactions, as well as countless other types of deals that took into account the vagaries of a centralized and planned economy, the nonconvertibility of the East's currencies, and the maze of the bureaucratic practices of its ministries. Specialists created unique financing techniques applicable only to transactions with the East.

The niche expertise of the Finns and Austrians helped them gain a virtual monopoly in traditional post-WWII East-West business transactions. They easily sold their services, particularly to businesspeople from Western Europe and the United States. However, over the years, very few foreign companies found it necessary to establish a permanent office or representation in Helsinki or Vienna to avail themselves of such services. Business could effectively and easily be conducted long distance. Still, Austria in particular did draw the United Nations and other international organizations and private institutes that emphasized East-West relations.

Today Finland and Austria are looking to market their experience and know-how as "old-hand" experts. But since investment in the East was not a legal option until a few years ago, sophisticated knowledge of the business activities or products of Eastern enterprises or how-to-do equity deals with the East is not widespread, whether in Finland, Austria, or elsewhere. Moreover, the accumulated knowledge of how to deal with the ministries of centralized Eastern European nations or with the pre-perestroika Soviet Union is today of doubtful, or at least limited, usefulness. The ministries themselves have become revolving doors, as officials and employees, especially those with foreign trade experience or English-language skills, have left to join the emerging private sector. The revolving door common in the corridors of Washington has become almost an everyday occurrence in the East.

Nevertheless, the perception shaped by accumulated history of the Hapsburg Empire and the neutrality of the last forty years have drawn a horde of Japanese and other multinational corporations to settle in Vienna, traditionally only a trolley-ride distant from the Slovak capital of Bratislava. This is "because businessmen see the country [Austria] as a gateway to Eastern Europe,"[1] particularly Hungary and the Czech and Slovak Federative Republic. This perception is enhanced by the conscious efforts of Austria, Italy, Yugoslavia, Hungary, and Czechoslovakia, all of which were, at least in part, united in the Hapsburg Empire, to revive traditional patterns of trade and investment. In 1989 they joined together in a region-

1. *Economist,* June 22, 1991, 113.

al forum for mutual economic development, with particular emphasis on the development of its Eastern European members. Vienna, as the geographical center of this regional forum, will surely succeed in becoming its administrative and informational hub.

The success of Finland and Austria as gateways underscores the importance of in-depth knowledge of the pertinent market area and the development of a sophisticated service sector, especially professionals capable of applying such knowledge in business deals.

THE GATEWAY TO CHINA: HONG KONG

Hong Kong, with its Chinese and English-language skills, its dual Chinese and English cultural heritage, and its excellent commercial infrastructure, including a sophisticated administrative support staff, has attained a very prominent position in the economic development of China. It became the headquarters city for countless foreign companies doing business with China and also home to a significant number of Chinese enterprises and banks engaged in international business. Hong Kong, at least until 1997 when it loses its secure status as a UK dependency and comes under the permanent sway of China, has the advantage of being geographically "within" China but politically not a "part" of it. Hong Kong has thus been a tailor-made gateway to China.

The English administration endowed Hong Kong with a respected and reliable legal system, which has created an environment of certainty and stability. Although the decisions of the Supreme Court of Hong Kong constitute binding authorities in Hong Kong, the decisions of the courts of England, as well as that of the courts of other commonwealth nations, are a persuasive guiding authority. Hong Kong thus developed a very sophisticated legal system. Furthermore, judicial independence, a hallmark of the English legal tradition, has been followed in Hong Kong.

While Hong Kong has a highly educated native labor force, its resource base is otherwise severely limited. It has no natural resources other than a harbor that today ranks as the busiest container port in the world and as a major re-export center. In fact, more than half of Hong Kong's exports are re-exports from China. Hong Kong's port thus serves as a natural bridge or gateway to and from China. Moreover, Hong Kong, with a relaxed bank licensing policy and very low taxes, was able to entice a legion of foreign banks to set up offices in Hong Kong and make it the financial gateway to China, among other places. Such attendant services as accounting firms, investment banks, head hunters, and countless other businesses found it easy, convenient, and profitable to locate there and thus provided Hong Kong with a sophisticated service sector, second only to that of Japan in the Far East. The service sector, supported by a highly developed communications system, could be readily utilized in China-related transactions. Hong Kong also beckons foreign businesspeople with Western-style living conditions, serving as a buffer to the economic shock that is China. Simply put, Hong Kong is China without the disadvantages.

At the same time, Hong Kong, as *the* Chinese gateway, began to have competitors and saw its initial monopoly position steadily erode. Beijing, the capital of China and the home of its influential government officials, and Shanghai, with its port and historical international prominence, as well as Shenzhen, the Chinese region immediately adjacent to Hong Kong, also began to flourish as centers for international business and became the home of foreign investors. Beijing in particular attracted many foreign representative offices and saw a sizable foreign "colony" of businesspeople establish themselves there. The Shenzhen region saw the establishment of countless Hong Kong–managed and –financed manufacturing facilities, which gave employment to thousands.

Hong Kong's remarkable success serves as a model for aspiring gateways. It underscores the importance of cultural know-how, language fluency, a reliable legal system, and a professional service sector. Moreover, supporting infrastructure of modern communications and good transportation facilities is a necessary part of a gateway's economic base.

AN ASPIRING EASTERN EUROPEAN GATEWAY
TO THE SOVIET UNION: POLAND

Notwithstanding historical animosities and Soviet military occupation, most of the nations of Eastern Europe aspire to be the gateway to the Soviet Union. Poland expounds on its central position between Western Europe and the Soviet Union. Czechoslovakia echoes that refrain but in addition seeks to market itself as the crossroads between northern and southern Europe. Hungary expands that theme by also declaring itself to be the model for Eastern European and Soviet economic transformation. In other words, it beckons foreign businesspeople to establish themselves in Hungary to learn how to do business in Europe's newly emerging (or perhaps reemerging) economies of the East. Only troubled Romania and Bulgaria have not advertised themselves as gateways.

Poland is typical of what these aspirants offer (or do not offer). It has its own large market of almost 40 million people. Despite its early success in restructuring its economy, Poland is still burdened by rising unemployment, significant inflation, aged industries, a nonconvertible currency, and a legion of other problems, many not yet discovered. Its economy depends heavily on oil, gas, and other raw materials of the Soviet Union. The modernization needs list (or, more soberly, wish list) of Poland is almost without end: a new infrastructure; capital infusion; modern technology; a functioning telephone system; and environmental equipment.

Poland does, however, offer geographical proximity to the Soviet Union and a population steeped in the Russian language. Still, the only apparent objective of Poland's desire to be the gateway to the Soviet Union is to encourage Western investors considering the Soviet market to first locate in Poland and then to use Poland as a base or springboard for the investor's expansion into the Soviet Union. But with a legacy of centralized planning, a dearth of knowledge of Western management skills, and an antiquated communications system, Poland cannot at present expect to be no more than a transit route to the Soviet Union. In short, Poland does not have any obvious, natural, or competitive advantage that would cause a Western firm to locate in Poland simply because it wished to enter the Soviet market.

BERLIN: THE CAPITAL OF GERMANY AND THE EAST

In less than eighteen months after the Wall came down, Berlin has become a magnet for those companies interested in pursuing emerging opportunities in the East, including the Soviet Union.

There is little doubt in the minds of many experts that Berlin, besides again attaining prominence as "the" German city—given its
central European location, its one-hour distance from the Polish
border by car, and its ready access to Germany's financial institutions and modern communications—will establish itself as the
major center for East-West commerce and investment. In fact, the
Central European Development Corporation—the investment vehi-
cle of American businessman and former ambassador to Austria,
Ronald Lauder, the billionaire Reichmann brothers, and other
major Canadian real estate developers, and headed by Mark
Palmer, the former U.S. ambassador to Hungary—has quietly settled in western Berlin, notwithstanding the flashy public announcements that it would be headquartered in Eastern Europe,
specifically Prague, a city alive with the splendor of ages long past
and an infrastructure just as old.

Likewise, Japanese corporations seeking, as is their custom, to
espy the future, began to flock to Berlin already in the first months
of 1990. The initial impetus was their firm belief that Berlin
would again become the capital of a united Germany. The Germans themselves did not have such faith in the future of Berlin,
and they squabbled and dickered for months until the Reichstag at
long last confirmed on June 20, 1991, that Berlin would be restored
to its rightful place as the sole German capital. The Japanese further saw a significant role for Berlin in the East. Japanese banking executives were even so bold as to publicly declare Berlin to be
the future "capital" of the East. Consequently, the Japanese have
already, despite a lack of suitable commercial space, managed to
open hundreds of representative offices in Berlin.

Originally, when the Japanese started their commercial activities in Europe, they chose the fashionable, but internationally
unassuming, city of Düsseldorf as their unofficial headquarters for
their European operations. Düsseldorf offered a prime location in
the industrial heartland of Germany, a particularly suitable choice
for the citizens of a country that emphasizes manufacturing.
Düsseldorf soon witnessed the birth of all the amenities and services necessary to support a thriving overseas Japanese business
community, including Japanese language schools, Japanese restaurants and golf courses, and accounting and other professional services catering to their specialized needs. But now even Düsseldorf

is suffering from the competition with Berlin and has begun to witness an exodus of its Japanese residents to Berlin.

THE NEED FOR A LOCAL PRESENCE IN THE EAST

Despite the ease with which an office can be established in Berlin, Vienna, or Helsinki, firms currently interested in investing in the East contemplate their own full-fledged local office or subsidiary. Things are changing so rapidly that occasional commuting is no longer sufficient. Detailed local knowledge is imperative, as new investment and tax laws are enacted almost daily; new local companies are established; old entities are privatized; and new management emerges in ministries and enterprises. Convenient "one-stop shopping" for sweetheart deals at a ministry of foreign trade is no longer feasible.

Western businesspeople have no choice but to become sophisticated "traveling salesmen" and personally get to know the emerging markets of the East. Purchasers, clients, and partners must now be actively and individually sought out and evaluated. This search is no different than that conducted in the West, except in one major aspect: in the East, there is not sufficient knowledge or publicly available information about potential business opportunities or possible business partners. There is no Standard and Poor's or other ready reference work or data bank. The use of traditional highly specialized East-West intermediaries, required in transit trade and countertrade, are no longer adequate, or even necessary. As a result, a local presence is needed and the only question is where.

The foreign business community in Warsaw has already grown to several thousand. Some apartments in Budapest are as expensive as in the West. In the Soviet Union, Moscow has witnessed an explosion in the number of foreign representative offices located there, notwithstanding the daunting task of finding commercial and residential office space. Moscow has also become the home of more joint ventures than any other city in the Soviet Union. The Japanese and Koreans eagerly eye the opening of the Soviet Pacific rim city of Vladivostok, the Asian gateway to mineral-rich Siberia and the last stop of a future European-Asian highway starting in Madrid, if not Gibraltar. The organization of a local office has become a cost of doing business with the East.

THE HISTORICAL SOVIET GATEWAY: MOSCOW

The city of Moscow has a historically nurtured competitive advantage in attracting investors to locate there. As the capital of the Soviet Union, Moscow naturally became home to the only resident foreign community of note in the country. This community consisted of foreign diplomats and journalists as well as foreign businesspeople pursuing trade with a centralized economy. In fact, permission to locate an office in the Soviet Union was usually restricted by the authorities to Moscow.

In this new era, however, where uncertain and new opportunities drive the dreams of Western businesspeople, the city of Moscow remains the mecca for those foreign companies that feel economic decisionmaking in the Soviet Union is still (and will remain) so government influenced, oriented, or controlled that ready access to Soviet (or Russian Republic) ministries is a must. (In fact, as long as government access is perceived to be essential for doing business in the Soviet Union, a presence in Moscow will not be an option for most international corporations.) By being the Soviet city of choice of foreign tourists, Moscow has had to accustom itself to the presence of a continuous stream of foreigners and has developed a system (even if basic or inadequate) to service the needs of its transient and resident foreign population.

Despite its prominence as the international Soviet city and the home of the largest international community in the Soviet Union, Moscow does not possess the necessary infrastructure or offer any of the inherent benefits associated in the West with being a major urban center. There is no consistently working communications system. There is no local army of qualified professionals, whether commercial bankers, investment bankers, business consultants, accountants, or lawyers. Moscow does, however, house an uncountable number of Third World–type intermediaries, namely "fixers," who arrange meetings with government officials and move a joint venture application through the bureaucratic labyrinth for approval. But even such fixers have failed to move the Moscow bureaucracy to approve construction projects in less than two to three years. Still, a mini–foreign army of professionals with beginners' enthusiasm has already set up shop in Moscow.

The monopolistic position of the city of Moscow as "the" gateway will inevitably erode, even if its position remains pivotal within the Russian Republic or the USSR. The sheer size of the Soviet Union and the inevitable political and economic (both macro and micro) decentralization process will spur the development of various places as alternate gateways to the Soviet Union. Prospective foreign investors will come to realize that they must meet enterprise management on location and that most government approvals (especially for small and medium-sized undertakings) can be secured locally. Moscow officials from centralized Soviet ministries no longer have a monopoly on information. Glasnost has sparked an explosion of information so that it is impossible for the ministries to know of most potential business opportunities in the Soviet Union. The authority of centralized ministries has been further diluted, as they are no longer exclusively empowered to negotiate on behalf of many Soviet trading or investment partners. Consequently, a foreign investor will now be able to more objectively determine which location can best serve as its base of operations and administrative headquarters.

Competition among regions and cities will invariably be a natural consequence of the decentralization process and the transformation (no matter how slow or difficult) of the centralized Soviet economy into a market economy, notwithstanding the possible political division of the Soviet Union into a number of independent nations. From an investment or commercial point of view, it is almost inevitable that all of the republics that today constitute the Soviet Union will for the foreseeable future remain economically (though not necessarily politically) interdependent, even if some will enjoy special or most-favored-nation status within a reconstituted, but smaller, Soviet Union.

The pattern of regional change in Poland is instructive and may well foreshadow changes in the Soviet Union and the altered role of Moscow. Krakow, a landmark European city, is now beginning to compete head-to-head with Warsaw for international corporations, especially Austrian firms. Poznan, a former Prussian city with a legacy of Teutonic efficiency, is advertising itself as the

"capital" of western Poland. Gdansk, with its port and Hansa traditions, sees itself as Poland's future Rotterdam and as a major service center. Regionalization and decentralization are processes
that have already begun, albeit slowly, to undermine the foundation that made Warsaw Poland's sole commercial hub, especially
for foreigners.

THE BALTICS TODAY

The Baltics, seafaring nations located on the Baltic Sea, constitute
the European coastline of the Soviet Union. Together they are almost the size of New York, New Jersey, Connecticut, and Massa-
chusetts combined. Their population of approximately 7.8 million,
which constitutes 2.7 percent of the population of the Soviet Union,
is only about 1.25 times that of Hong Kong and is comparable to
that of Sweden or the state of New Jersey. Although the Baltic
people speak three different languages and have distinct cultures,
all three are fluent in the language of their eastern neighbor,
Russia, and have shared a common history, or similar fate, for
more than 200 years. They have been conquered by nations from
the West and the East, each of which has left its legacy. During
Czarist times, the Baltic cities of Riga and Tallinn and the Russian
city of St. Petersburg (present-day Leningrad) were Russia's win-
dows to the West. Today they serve the same function for the Soviet
Union. Moreover, the Baltics realize and understand that their future economic prosperity depends directly on the stability and
growth of the Soviet market.

    As the Soviet Union is largely surrounded by a coastline of ice,
the warm-water port of Riga and other Latvian harbors have made
Latvia the major export-import center of the Soviet Union, with
more than 50 percent of the Soviet Union's exports to Western
Europe shipped through Latvia. Riga is also a major air hub, with
flights departing to more than sixty Soviet cities as well as to the
Scandinavian cities of Stockholm and Copenhagen and in the near
future the United States. Tallinn serves Helsinki and Frankfurt
and more than forty Soviet cities by air and, thanks to Soviet
planners, has become the Soviet Union's largest grain port. Even
with independence, these geographical advantages cannot be

denied, let alone taken away. It should be kept in mind that a major "German" port is in fact a Dutch city, Rotterdam. Therefore, as Western trade with the Soviet Union increases, ancillary service businesses will flourish in the Baltic ports, including freight forwarders, storage and distribution facilities, and insurance brokers. A natural economic and employment multiplier effect will occur.

The Baltic nations of Estonia, Latvia, and Lithuania, unlike Poland and the others nations of Eastern Europe, became an integral part or cog of the centralized Soviet economy and planning system with the result that their economies are almost totally dependent on imports of oil, gas, timber, and other raw materials, parts, and supplies from the Soviet Union. For example, 90 percent of Latvia's heating fuel, 100 percent of its oil, and 50 percent of its electricity are imports from the Soviet Union. Even the Baltic's agricultural production depends on seeds from the Soviet Union. Their economies would collapse if these goods were not available. As the Soviet economic boycott of Lithuania so surprisingly and vividly demonstrated, however, the city of Moscow and other parts of the Soviet Union also rely on specialized goods, food, and essential supplies from the Baltic nations. As a result of the boycott, Lithuanians had a surplus of meat because they were prevented from exporting their farm produce to the Soviet Union. The centralized Soviet economy is a chain economy; no link can be removed without harming and shortcircuiting each and every other part of the chain.

The interlocking Soviet economic system made distinctive parts of the Soviet Union "niche" or specialized producers. Latvia, for example, became a major Soviet industrial area and a center for Soviet high-tech consumer products. Its stereo sound system is world class and has been exported to western Germany. Further, Latvia produces all of the Soviet Union's train and diesel cars and 43 percent of its automated milking equipment. However, the necessary inputs for such production came from various areas of the Soviet Union. At least for the foreseeable future, this mutual economic embrace is a modern-day Gordian knot. For better or worse, the Baltics and the Soviet Union are (and will remain) economic partners. Russia's first popularly elected president, Boris Yeltsin, who openly and unequivocally supports Baltic independence,[2] confirmed on American television to millions of American viewers in an interview with Ted Koppel that even with Baltic political independence, there will be no change in the underlying economic relationship.[3] Thus, a historically forced partnership today offers the Baltics unique opportunity.

The Baltics, with their Western ambience that makes living relatively comfortable and relaxing, possess certain competitive advantages (both natural and Soviet created) that will enable them to flourish as the premier gateway to the Soviet market: (1) proximate location next to the West, especially Scandinavia; (2) a relatively well-educated and language-skilled people; (3) a culture that understands both the East and the West; (4) major transportation centers for the Soviet Union, including ice-free harbors; (5) access to the Soviet Union; and (6) a positive business climate.

What constitutes such a climate is one of those frustrating concepts that is difficult to describe but instinctively recognized when encountered. It is the willingness of a people to learn, adapt to changes, and accept new ways. It is a confidence in the future. It means an open government that permits entrepreneurs to test new

2. ABC News Nightline, Show #2627, June 18, 1991:

Koppel: If you were president of the Soviet Union, and the president of Lithuania came to you or the president of Estonia, or Latvia, and said, "Mr. President, we want to go our own separate way, we want complete and total independence." What would you say to them?

Pres. Yeltsin [through interpreter]: I spoke about this with Gorbachev two and a half years ago. I said: "Give independence to the republics of the Baltic. If you don't give this degree of economic independence now, tomorrow they're going to ask even more, and then they're going to simply ask to get out of the union." Once we had that in the Constitution, it can't be prevented. You can't create chains for the union. It has to be a voluntary union. By armies, tanks, and batteries, you can't create a union, or by exerting pressure or using violence. So, undoubtedly I am in favor of giving them the sort of independence they want.

Koppel: Even if that means total independence, complete independence, they move out of the union altogether?

Pres. Yeltsin [through interpreter]: Even that. They will be connected with us economically, of course, because Russia has signed a treaty with Latvia, Estonia, and is now preparing a contract, a treaty, with Lithuania. But they'll be bilateral economic relations. Whether they belong to the union or not, our economic relations would remain as they are, our economic market would remain. And I would not be in favor of preventing any sovereign republic, which is entitled to self-determination, and we can't prevent them enjoying that right, whether it be a citizen, a person, or a republic. They're sovereign.

3. Id.

ideas and make mistakes. It is an absence of excessive bureaucratic obstacles. In short, it is that combination of tangible and intangible factors that makes a businessperson exclaim, "I can do business here."

THE BALTIC STRUGGLE

Under the present fluid and chaotic circumstances throughout the Soviet Union, it is admittedly difficult to envision the three Baltic nations as a commercial gateway or entrance to the Soviet Union. These nations are locked in a bitter and protracted struggle with the Soviet Union for the restoration of their independence. Although the United States and other nations of the West have never recognized the 1940 incorporation of the Baltic nations by the Soviet Union, which was a consequence of the infamous Molotov-Ribbentrop Pact, or, more appropriately, the Hitler-Stalin Pact, the West has *de facto*, by its actions, for most of the post-WWII period, acknowledged the annexation. Only recently has the West begun to provide tentative political support for the Baltic struggle.

Sweden and Denmark have encouraged and permitted the opening of Baltic information offices, which function as unofficial embassies and commercial offices. The U.S. House of Representatives has passed an amendment to the State Department Appropriations Bill calling for the establishment of U.S. information offices in the Baltics. Even Germany, until recently preoccupied with obtaining Soviet consent to the reunification of West and East Germany, is no longer a reticent observer. Germany at last signaled its public support when the Reichstag voted to permit the opening of an Estonian information office. A number of countries of the West, led by the Scandinavians, are supporting observer status for the three Baltic nations at the Conference on Security and Cooperation in Europe. Iceland is the first nation ready to exchange ambassadors with Lithuania. Such open Western support took on momentum on the heels of the shocking Baltic slayings in January 1991.

The Baltic people are justifiably smarting over the New Year slaughter of unarmed civilians in Riga and Vilnius by special Soviet forces (not to mention the agonizing litany of pre-pere-

stroika horrors and injustices) and the continuing, at times vio-
lent, takeover of press, border posts, and other buildings by troops
stationed in the Baltics. The Baltic nations by choice have refused
to join with USSR and republic leaders in formulating a new
union treaty or any other agreement seeking to politically recon-
stitute the present-day Soviet Union. As mentioned, President
Yeltsin supports this decision.

Moreover, on the economic front, deliveries of goods and raw
materials to the Baltics, including critical energy supplies, are subject to at least the same significant disruptions prevalent throughout the Soviet Union. Admittedly, there is the fear that these disruptions vis-à-vis the Baltics will intensify and worsen as the Soviet
Union presses on with demands that independence-seeking republics pay for such supplies in hard currencies, which they obviously do not have.

The current uncertain situation clearly does not encourage doing business in the Baltics or the Soviet Union, let alone even using a Baltic location as the administrative headquarters or base for
a Soviet-focused investment. As is commonly known, business, pre-
ferring a stable and predicable environment, is politically risk-
averse or neutral. But stability sufficient to attract an avalanche of
foreign investment in the Baltics is not a thing for the immediate
present but for a day in the not too distant future when de jure and
de facto independence of the Baltics converge and some semblance
of order emerges in the Soviet Union. Only then will the rules of
the game for the foreign businessperson become clear and the confusion and pressures caused by the "war of laws" between the centralized Soviet government in Moscow and the Baltics be settled.

TALLINN: THE "WORLD" TRADE CENTER
OF THE SOVIET UNION

The Baltic nations can (and do) not sit idly by and wait for
Western-style stability to spontaneously emerge. They are actively
seeking to create the necessary institutional framework for a modern market-oriented society and also have focused their efforts on
entering into bilateral, or so-called horizontal, economic agreements with each other and with Russia and other parts of the

Soviet Union. Undoubtedly, they will have to enter into a detailed economic agreement with the Soviet Union at the time that Baltic political independence is restored.

The three Baltic nations have signed agreements to create a Baltic common market by 1993. The aim is to create an integrated economy and to coordinate economic activity in a manner similar to that of the European Community. In January 1991, they entered into political treaties with the Russian Republic pursuant to which they recognized each others' rights to sovereignty. They previously had entered into bilateral economic treaties with Russia as well as other Soviet republics.

Tallinn, Estonia, will be the home for a bureau to coordinate economic development, independent of centralized Soviet control, for the three Baltics nations and Armenia, Belorussia, Russia, the Ukraine, the city of Moscow and any other republic or administrative unit that may wish to join. Kazakhstan and Kirghizia have already expressed interest. The bureau will not just coordinate committee meetings of its members but will also collect and distribute information. With the expansion of such horizontal ties with Soviet republics, Tallinn will become an invaluable economic "know-how" center for many parts of the changing Soviet landscape. With some imagination, it is not difficult to foresee Tallinn's developing an economic database drawing business consultants, international organizations, and financial institutions, many of which may well chose to establish a local presence there. Furthermore, if such a bureau is to function effectively, the various Soviet republics and areas will have to establish cultural, business promotion, and other representative offices in Tallinn. Several republics, including the two largest Soviet republics, Russia and the Ukraine, have already done so. Tallinn's emergence as a "world" trade center for the Soviet Union appears assured.

It is not surprising that Tallinn has become a meeting place for representatives of the various Soviet republics. Because of its proximity to the West, namely Finland, Tallinn was developed as a major Soviet showcase for the West. More Western tourists visit the Estonian capital than any other Soviet city, except Moscow and Leningrad. Fashion shows have become common, especially as Raisa Gorbachev reportedly proclaimed Tallinn the fashion capital

of the Soviet Union. It regularly hosts major international conferences, and in 1988, for example, this old Hansa city held the first
conference in the Soviet Union on the establishment of joint ventures in the Soviet Union. The list of Soviet, Baltic and international congresses and exhibitions that have been held there is
pages long and even includes an international cybernetics congress. Tallinn has become a place where East meets West and also
East.

THE BALTICS' (RE)INTEGRATION INTO THE WEST

The Baltics have not been hesitant in embracing Western business
practices and customs. In fact, the only private (nonstate) chamber
of commerce in the Soviet Union is located in Estonia. Considerably more joint ventures on a per-capita basis are located in
the Baltics, especially Estonia and Latvia, than any part of the Soviet
Union. These joint ventures encompass a full range of economic
activity, including housing construction, consultancies, hotels, and
business service centers.

Estonia has already become a mini-colony of neighboring
Finland, which has a virtual monopoly on the joint ventures established in Estonia. This is easy to explain, given the fact that the
two nations are separated by a mere sixty miles of sea and are ethnic cousins, speaking related languages. Moreover, the wage dif-
ferential between Finland and Estonia is even more extreme than
that between the United States and Mexico, which makes Estonia
an especially attractive low-cost producer for high-cost Finland.

Companies from Sweden and Denmark are also increasingly
seeking Baltic partners. Approximately 10 percent of the registered joint ventures in Latvia, for example, are with Swedish
firms. Close geographic proximity permits effective integration of
Baltic production facilities with Scandinavian home-office activities. Joint ventures will be a mini-boom for Scandinavian export
businesses because the management of a joint venture will look
first to the home country of the non-Baltic partner for needed
Western inputs. These joint ventures will thereby further cement
expanding Baltic-Scandinavian economic ties.

As regular air links have been established between Scandinavia and the Baltic nations, the number of businesspeople from Stockholm and Copenhagen looking for potential Baltic partners will invariably increase. Management exchange programs are sprouting everywhere. Information or commercial centers, in some sense unofficial embassies, have been set up by a number of Scandinavian countries in Riga and Tallinn, which will further deepen commercial, cultural, and other contacts. Further, most important in today's rapidly changing business world, Scandinavian companies are working on integrating the Baltics into the Scandinavian (and therefore international) telephone and communications network. Swedish banks are laying the groundwork for expansion into the Baltics by acting as advisors to newly created Baltic financial institutions. These developments are indicative of the steady reintegration of the Baltics into the Nordic or Scandinavian trading area. As in the case of the former lands of the Hapsburg Empire—namely Austria, Hungary, Czechoslovakia, Poland, Italy and Yugoslavia—dormant (but not forgotten) economic relationships are reviving after more than fifty years.

The major investors in Eastern Europe and the Soviet Union, the Germans, have also rediscovered the Baltic Sea region and the Hansa traditions of Riga and Tallinn, which thousands of Germans called home for 700 years. The Germans are now establishing joint ventures throughout the Baltics, including in Lithuania with its productive agricultural lands. Some joint ventures are with Baltic enterprises that are the successors of previously owned German companies. Surprisingly, some of these enterprises continue to effectively utilize basic know-how developed by German industrialists more than fifty years ago.

For the Scandinavians and the Germans, there is also the lure of the untapped Soviet market, readily reachable by plane from the Baltic capitals. By working with the Balts, a traditionally Western people, who are fluent in Russian and have learned (from almost fifty years of common living) to understand the culture of the people living in the Soviet Union, the Scandinavians and Germans have come to realize that they can employ Balts as a bridge in expanding Soviet operations.

THE BALTICS: PRACTITIONERS OF THE MODERN KOREAN ECONOMIC PROVERB "SAME, SAME"

The Baltics will profit from the influx of Scandinavian and German investors because they will learn by example from some of the most advanced economies of the West. The Scandinavian and German businesses serve as a model of exacting Western industrial and service standards and a continuous challenge to the Balts to learn the most modern techniques. Estonia and Latvia had a living standard comparable to Finland in the 1930s and are motivated by the goal of reattaining that standard (and ultimately surpassing it). The Baltic view of Scandinavia is similar to Korea's analysis of Japanese economic achievement and Korea's answer on how it can be duplicated: "Same, Same." This simply means first copy, then improve. This competitive spirit will invariably have a positive snowball effect. The Baltics will become even more attractive as an investment location as soon as they master these world-class commercial standards and offer Western living standards.

Baltic knowledge of the language of international commerce, namely English, is already widespread, while continuous interaction with Scandinavia will significantly improve these already good language skills. English specialized schools abound. A service staff fluent in English will itself attract American and potentially even Japanese investors to locate in the Baltics. More than twenty countries, including, surprisingly, such East Asian powerhouses as Taiwan and Malaysia, have organized or are in the process of establishing representative offices in Tallinn. This follows the opening of the Estonia-American Chamber of Commerce in June, 1990 the first foreign chamber in the Soviet Union not part of any Moscow ministry or centralized all-union organization. But the Japanese will, for a change, have to follow in the footsteps of their East Asian neighbors, because the Japanese have not yet opened a Baltic office. Still, in a private report, a major Japanese research group, impressed by the fact that its researchers did not as a matter of course need translators as so many people spoke English, has recommended a Baltic location to its clients.

The Balts will come to be the interpreters of newly learned Western methods, particularly to the more isolated cities in the interior of Russia and the Soviet Union. Representatives of Kazakhstan, for example, have requested the Estonian Management Institute to assist in the establishment of a similar management training program in that Central Asian republic. Tallinn already has business consultancies that are advising the distant Soviet Pacific island of Sakahlin on the economic development of its timber resources. A consultancy in Riga is providing expert advice to the Siberian peninsula of Kamchutka on how to develop its timber resources. The Korean "Same, Same" concept has found a home in the Baltics.

POSITIVE BUSINESS CLIMATE

Although it is difficult to prove, and can only be described with less than scientific accuracy, the Baltics, as a result of their history and proximity to the West, offer the most positive and energetic business climate in the Soviet landscape. They constitute an aspiring Boston–New York–Washington corridor for the Soviet Union. There is a dynamism present in the Baltics that is otherwise absent or hard to find. Enthusiasm for things Western is widespread.

Economic experimentation has been the hallmark of the Baltics ever since their forced annexation by the Soviet Union. The Communist reasoning was quite simple. If "new" economic thinking could not work in the Baltics, with their pronounced Western orientation, it could not work anywhere in the Soviet Union. Thus, it is not surprising that the first joint venture in the Soviet Union was operating in Estonia even before the final touches of the Soviet joint venture law were in place. There are more individual farms in the Baltics than in any republic of the Soviet Union other than Georgia. More cooperatives—the Soviet answer to private business—on a per-capita basis, have been formed in the Baltics than in any part of the Soviet Union. The first cooperative bank in the Soviet Union was formed in Tartu, Estonia. Moreover, during the first few months after the enactment of a Soviet law on cooperatives, more than half of all cooperatives in the Soviet Union were located in the Baltics. This typifies the spirit of self-reliance evident throughout the Baltics (and a fortunate lack of a psychological dependence on the state as the depository of all answers). Entrepreneurship, notwithstanding half a century of efforts at creating a "Soviet man," who simply follows dictated instructions from cradle to grave, appears alive and well in the Baltics. Even high-school administrators have demonstrated such energy by organizing, already in 1988, the first school-to-school nongovernmental exchange program. It even provided for student home stays, which was a revolutionary concept in the Soviet Union as late as 1988. This exchange between the Tallinn Secondary School No. 21 and the Dalton School in New York set the pace for similar privately organized exchanges throughout the Soviet Union.

Latvia has announced that it will privatize 25 to 30 percent of state properties within the next few years and has already embarked on this process. Estonia is pursuing a comparable fast pace. Commercial laws dealing with foreign investment, joint stock companies, contracts, and stock markets are being considered and rapidly enacted. The necessary legal infrastructure for the transformation of the economy is steadily taking place.

Although chamber of commerce–type advertising can expand the list of advantages of the Baltics, there are no more forceful recommendations than those of businesses themselves. William E. LaMothe, chairman and chief executive officer of Kellogg Co., the world's largest maker of ready-to-eat cereals, stated that Kellogg sees its prospective joint venture in the Baltics "as a way to serve the Baltics and as an entry to the USSR."[4] He continued that Kellogg "found that the best people to work with turned out to be a Baltic partner."[5] The U.S. Chamber of Commerce, in a forthcoming report on the Soviet Union, states that the Baltics have a strong Western orientation and the best chances to catch up with the West after an initial transition period.

The Europeans have, as indicated, already acted on such opinions by establishing a considerable number of joint ventures in the Baltics. But with the publication of a recent report by Deutsche Bank, it is likely that more Western companies will look at the Baltics for their own sake as well as an entry point to the Soviet Union. Deutsche Bank, in an analysis of the Soviet Republics that

4. *Wall Street Journal*, November 1, 1990.
5. Id.

includes the Baltics, has given the Baltic countries a perfect "10" for "business mindedness."[6]   No other republic was so honored, though Georgia and Armenia were awarded a "9" and "8," respectively.[7]   The Ukraine and Russia received only a "3" and "2," respectively.[8]   In the vernacular of business development professionals, the Baltics have a positive business climate.   That is the hallmark of such diverse, but dynamic, business centers or gateways as Hong Kong and New York, where the "beat goes on."

BALTIC PLAN OF ACTION

If the Baltic nations indeed wish to capitalize on their unique gateway possibilities, they must rapidly and continuously pursue a strategy competitive with other potential gateways for the changing Soviet landscape.   Business mindedness must be actively encouraged and promoted (if not enshrined in law) by the governments of the Baltics.   Specifically:

1. The Baltics must maintain a sufficiently open economic or customs border with the Soviet Union providing for a rapid transhipment and re-export of goods, as well as communications and air links; contacts with all parts of the Soviet market must be expanded.
2. Companies incorporated in a Baltic nation must be able to do business in the Soviet Union without having to comply with burdensome administrative requirements, other than registration.
3. Rapid construction of suitable office, warehouse, and other commercial space must be encouraged through tax incentives and an absence of the type of bureaucratic red tape that handicaps major construction projects in Western Europe.
4. The corporate tax structure must be competitive with that of the Russian Republic and other parts of the Soviet Union as well as the Scandinavian countries and the nations of Eastern Europe.

6. "The Soviet Union at the Crossroads: Facts and Figures on the Soviet Republics," Deutsche Bank, 1990, 11.
7. Id.
8. Id.

5. English-language fluency must be even more actively supported.
6. International consultancies, accountants, trade intermediaries, financial institutions and other service businesses, both large and small, must be encouraged, through tax incentives and a Hong Kong–type pro-business environment, to locate in the Baltics.
7. The creation of new businesses for Baltic citizens as well as foreign investors must be made as easy as in Hong Kong or the United States.
8. The establishment of a world standard international communications system, particularly in such cities as Riga, Tallinn, and Vilnius, must be the top infrastructure investment priority.
9. A reliable and independent legal and judicial system must be established—a legal system that should draw on the established and internationally accepted legal systems of Germany and other members of the European Community for persuasive guiding authority.
10. The Baltics must become a major meeting place for East and West, where companies and enterprises from both areas establish offices.

In short, the Baltics, as Hong Kong, Korea, Singapore, and Taiwan have already done in the Far East, must demonstrate that they are the tigers of the "Emerging East," the Soviet landscape.

Part I V

Working Group Reports

11

Working Group 1: Strategies for Attracting Western Investment

Jeremy Ingpen and Robert L. Krattli
Liana Eglitis, Assistant

This working group report presents recommendations to the republics of the Soviet Union on how Western businesses view trade and investment with the Soviet Union, and what the republics should be doing to foster an attractive business climate.

This report may also be useful to Western companies considering the Soviet marketplace for the first time in developing strategies for doing business there and for understanding the issues associated with doing business in this difficult market. We have addressed two related but distinct elements: What has to be in place for the Soviet Union and the republics to attract foreign investment and trade? And what are the factors that a Western company considers before moving into the Soviet market?

With so many pieces of the legal and financial systems unresolved, with unclear progress toward a market economy, and with the collapse of the Soviet economy that is now occurring, the Soviet Union is a market that Western investors approach cautiously. This report addresses actions the republics and the union should take to alleviate some of the concerns of potential business investors and the capital markets.

The Soviet Union and the republics, which up to this point have been part of the Soviet Union, are a market of abundant resources, tremendous potential, and very high risks. This market can only be approached with a well-thought-out strategy and a realistic appraisal of the risks and the potential paybacks.

Initially, this working group approached its task with the ques-

tion of whether the "gateway" concept is one that is helpful to potential investors in evaluating a location in the Soviet Union. The
group concluded that with the exception of certain infrastructure
characteristics—port and airport facilities, telecommunications facilities—the gateway concept has little value as an organizing principle for considering a republic's investment potential.

WHAT THE REPUBLICS MUST DO
TO ATTRACT FOREIGN INVESTMENT

Certain actions must be taken to establish the environment for sustained Western investment in the Soviet Union and its republics.

1. The relations between the center and the republics have to be
   resolved. No foreign venture wants to be involved in inter-au-
   thority conflict or the "war of laws." Resolution of these disputes is an absolute priority to attract foreign investment.
2. There have to be basic laws on property ownership and on in-
   tellectual property.
3. A workable financial system must be in place: Currency convertibility and access to financing credits must be established
   within a reasonable timeframe.
4. There must be a clear commitment by each republic to introduce economic reform with a coherent program and timeframe.

These four items are fundamental and absolute requirements for
significant foreign investment or trade to occur. Additionally, infrastructure development—transportation, telecommunications—is
critical to the successful economic development strategy of each republic. We strongly recommend that the republics develop concrete and well-articulated plans for investment requirements for
infrastructure development.

   With such a plan, the republic will be able to approach the major international financing authorities—the European Bank for
Reconstruction and Development and the World Bank, for example—for financing as well as to show private investors specific investment opportunities.

HOW WESTERN COMPANIES EVALUATE
THE SOVIET MARKET

This section describes the rationale for considering the Soviet market, challenges associated with doing business there, and the need to define objectives clearly in considering this volatile region.

With a population of 290 million, the Soviet Union is potentially the third largest national consumer market after China and India. Its attributes include an educated and skilled population, a large base of natural resources and agricultural capability, and an infrastructure that needs very substantial investment to bring it up to adequate standards for transportation, communication, and distribution.

Despite this potential, the Soviet Union suffers from an uncertain political and economic situation, low per-capita GNP, and a host of structural and practical difficulties for the Western businessperson. As a consequence, Western companies should be very clear in their objectives in considering this difficult market in transition.

Objectives

Western companies must carefully establish their objectives for considering doing business in the Soviet Union today. Consideration of the Soviet market should be consistent with a company's global strategy and undertaken as part of the annual strategic planning process. The business objectives and the associated risks should be carefully defined and quantifiable.

Given the opportunity cost of capital and the current worldwide capital shortage, the Soviet Union will be considered by Western companies in the context of other worldwide business opportunities. The timeframe and length of commitment must also be determined. It should also be determined whether the company wants to assist the Soviets in selling for export markets or just focus on the Soviet domestic market.

Due to the difficulties currently involved in doing business in the Soviet Union, the size of the potential market, and the multiple geographic regions involved, Western companies must take a long-term perspective. This working group feels that a five- to ten-year period is the minimum realistic planning timeframe. Major Western corporations active in the Soviet marketplace are looking at a twenty- to thirty-year planning horizon. For the reasons listed above, in addition to the high cost of conducting business in the Soviet Union, small and medium-sized companies, or those without the resources to take this medium-term horizon, are not well equipped to consider the Soviet market at this juncture. An exception should be made for companies planning direct product sales through a Western or Soviet agent based in the Soviet Union. This is not the market for those who want to make a quick killing.

MARKET ASSESSMENT

This section describes how Western companies assess a potential market for trade or investment.

Issues Common to Companies

In assessing the opportunities and risks associated with the Soviet market, Western companies, whether involved in sales, investment, or services, will take into account the following common issues.

Assessment of Market Potential

Companies assessing the Soviet market consider the same issues as for Western markets: what products or services to sell, where to sell them, and how to get them to the potential customer.

In the Soviet marketplace, however, secondary market information is largely unavailable, unreliable, or unobtainable. Furthermore, primary market research is also difficult due to the lack of awareness of basic Western marketing concepts and the lack of established mechanisms for conducting market research. Western companies also need to assess which region or republic to consider as the base for their operations. At the present time, market assessment is complex and will involve a combination of local information, gut feeling, or just "blue sky" perception about future potential. Soviet partners and republic representatives can assist in this process by developing systematic databases of available resources, demographics, and market potential.

Barriers to Entry

Western companies are affected by significant barriers to entry into the Soviet market. These include the lack of currency convertibility; the absence of financing and loan guarantees for projects either from international agencies or from local sources; the lack of infrastructure; the lack of banking services and financial markets; and the absence of intellectual-property protection.

Western companies must also consider the practical problems of conducting business in the Soviet Union. These include uncertainty as to which level of government has the proper authority to regulate industry; the decline in creditworthiness of the Soviet Union and the associated problems of receiving payment from Soviet customers; the difficulty in finding office space; the lack of access to reliable telephone and communications systems; and the lack of appropriate accounting systems.

Western companies investing in the Soviet Union for production facilities also need to consider the problems of obtaining raw materials. State monopolies on raw materials and the disintegration of the central planning and supply system make access to raw materials difficult at best.

Additionally, Western companies that intend to export from the Soviet Union are affected by problems of licensing and tariff barriers, particularly for the U.S. market. All companies investing in the Soviet Union are affected by delays and bureaucracy.

ENTRY STRATEGIES TO OVERCOME BARRIERS

To overcome the barriers, Western companies need to develop a clear strategy for entering the Soviet market. We have identified the major steps that a Western company will consider for two categories of investment-selling goods or services and capital investment.

Entry Strategies for Selling Goods or Services

1. Establish where the company wants to be on the "risk-return frontier." Are you in the market for a quick turnaround or for the long term? How much time/effort/capital do you wish to risk in the venture?
2. Determine whether the company will set up the Soviet venture itself or use an agent.
3. Specify the vehicle/set-up that the company will use. This can include a branch office, direct sales, or a joint venture. Western companies should establish majority control in any joint venture.
4. Identify a list of potential joint venture partners or agents and conditions they will be required to meet (for example, experience, capital, and reputation).
5. If a product is being imported, the Western company will need to determine the preferred source of the product. From which branch or country will the product come? Considerations here will include the availability of trade credits and guarantees from the potential sourcing countries.
6. How will the Western company be paid? Cash or barter? If by barter, is that a short-term or long-term preference? What provisions exist for the repatriation of capital and profits? What are the tax consequences of any profits on Soviet operations?
7. Establish the training requirements for the Soviet operators. Will training occur at home or abroad?
8. Specify the amount of technology transfer required—short- vs. long-term. Do CoCom restrictions affect short- or long-term plans?
9. Develop the marketing plan needed to support the product—short- vs. long-term.

Entry Strategies for Local Investment

When considering investing for local production, many of the factors mentioned above will apply. Other factors that need to be addressed are:

1. Which of the raw materials and production inputs required can be supplied from within the market, and which will need to come from abroad?
2. How will the company establish security and predictability of supplies from within the Soviet market? It is essential to guarantee supply lines. These may be enhanced by getting key suppliers on board as minority joint venture parties.
3. To guarantee supplies and ensure standards, how much will the Soviet suppliers have to invest to meet the required standards?
4. How much will the company need to give them in terms of capital or technology transfer to make it possible for Soviet suppliers to meet the required standards? This question must be evaluated in relation to the project's expected life span and risk/return criteria.

Entry Strategies for Providing Services

In addition to the points outlined above, companies involved in the supply of services will also need to consider:

1. How to get exclusivity with its Soviet partners. Western companies do not like to be involved in joint ventures where the Soviet partner is signing a multitude of agreements at the same time with other foreign parties, possibly including direct competitors.
2. What telecommunications and business facilities will the company need to provide? Can these be reliably supplied by others? Location in the Soviet Union may require establishing a direct satellite link or other communications technologies.

IMPLEMENTATION: STEPPING STONES FOR GETTING
A PROJECT UP AND RUNNING

The following section lays out a checklist for how a Western company proceeds to establish a Soviet venture.

Find out what is out there.
- Establish contacts in the marketplace.

With whom are you going to work?
- If a partner is needed, find out some background: length
  of experience, exclusivity of ideas/product/technology,
  talent of the staff, etc.
- Determine the partners' objectives. Are they in mutual
  agreement, or are you going to run into disagreements
  some time down the line? This means addressing issues such as short- vs. long-term commitment, domestic
  vs. foreign markets, rubles vs. hard currency, who has
  control, etc.
- Conduct the basic negotiations with your partners your-
  self. Early on, resolve the main issues face to face and
  establish the protocols. This not only helps build confidence that the local partners are genuinely committed to
  what is being done but also enhances trust between the
  parties involved. Although some legal advice will be required at the outset, the final legal technicalities can be
  left until last. Once the protocols have been worked out,
  lawyers can take these and turn them into the appropriate legal documents.

Keep in touch with what is happening.
- Keep track of changes in local laws—what you might be
  aiming for may quite easily be a moving target if new
  laws are suddenly introduced or responsibilities for au-
  thorizations or approvals change (for example, between
  individuals or regions).
- Maintain contacts with as many responsible parties as
  possible—from the industry and regional level to officials in Moscow (or wherever the final decisions are be-

ing made). This also includes keeping an eye on what potential competitors (both local and foreign) might be doing in the market—their actions might give off useful signals.

Find out what special incentives are available.
- Identify the playing field as far as tax breaks or subsidies are concerned. What is being offered? Is your project or proposal of sufficient merit to warrant a special deal (for example, extended tax holidays)?

Operational requirements.
- Establish the financial plan that the project will be monitored against in both the short and long term. Establish appropriate financial controls and financial reporting standards.
- Will a financial controller be available locally or will an expatriate be required? How will you establish standard accounting procedures?
- Identify the means and ways of doing counter/barter trade if that will be a necessary part of the project. This will require additional planning and research and may potentially involve extending the joint venture to third-party suppliers.
- Will employee incentives be required? Will these come by way of an Employee Stock Ownership Plan, bonus payments (in rubles or hard currency), profit sharing, or "soft-dollars" (for example, goods and services such as products, health care, and trips abroad).

Maintain flexibility in the business plan.
- Make sure that your investment plan is flexible. Identify potential "escape routes" if something goes wrong (for example, product fails to come up to standard, joint venture partners cannot deliver, the legal environment changes, or the market for your product/service grows too slowly or too rapidly). Above all, do not commit more resources than you can afford to lose in a worst-case scenario.

APPENDIX 11-A. THE BALTICS CAN BE A GATEWAY

The Soviet Union is politically, socially, and economically not a homogeneous territory. In the near future, the differences among the regions that are a part of the Soviet Union today will deepen. This will be a concentric process with concentric configurations. As one such concentric region, the Baltic states can be clearly differentiated. In addition to the geographical argument (closeness to the large Russian markets), there exist a number of other factors that might point the interest of Western investors toward the Baltic states, especially if we compare the environment for investments in the Baltic states with the Soviet republics east of this region.

A transition to a market economy has started in the Baltic states. The psychological climate for it is rather favorable (market mentality, European way of thinking, level of education). The economics legislation, based on European examples, has been or is being drafted. Entrepreneurial ventures are booming, and privatization of the economy has begun.

Viable and efficient joint ventures can be established in the Baltic states. For example, every tenth joint venture established in the Soviet Union is in Estonia, which covers only 0.2% of the area of the Soviet Union. Only a few joint ventures established in Estonia have gone bankrupt.

Although the status of the Baltic states has not been determined yet, these states are entering a new stage of political stabilization in their internal relations and in their relations with the Soviet Union. Most other regions of the Soviet Union are entering the stage of destabilization.

The Baltic states have a much better infrastructure than the neighboring Eastern regions. By air, Helsinki can be reached from Tallinn in thirty minutes and Stockholm in fifty minutes. The Baltic states have worldwide connections via the telecommunications capabilities of the Scandinavian countries. There are representative offices of many Russian firms in the Baltic states, as well as those of Baltic-Western and Baltic-Western-Soviet joint ventures, international joint-stock companies, and consulting firms.

Proceeding from the above-mentioned circumstances, it may be stated that what will be possible in Russia tomorrow might be feasible in the Baltic states today. The Baltic states are a favorable starting position for the Western investor to move toward the Eastern markets.

Erik Terk
Deputy Minister for Economic Affairs
Estonia

APPENDIX 11-B. ADVANTAGES OF LATVIA AS A GATEWAY TO THE SOVIET UNION

1. Ice-free ports.
2. Good infrastructure.
3. Easy access by air and sea; proximity to countries bordering the Baltic Sea.
4. Skilled labor, well-educated, open to learning from the West.
5. Good work ethic.
6. Bicultural understanding of East and West.
7. Knowledge of foreign languages.
8. Availability of office space and support services.
9. Access to advice from American Latvians.
10. Historical center of trade.

The Latvian Delegation

12

Working Group 2: Horizontal Economic Relations

Gertrude E. Schroeder
Elena Glebova, Assistant

For many decades, the Soviet Union as a whole and each of its present constituent republics have developed economically within the framework of a tightly controlled political federation and development strategies dictated by central planners in Moscow. As a consequence, large economic interdependencies have arisen among the republics. Each one relies in substantial degree and in critical ways on all of the others to supply essential raw materials and final manufactures for use within the republic and also to provide outlets for its own surplus production. In addition, each republic obtains goods through imports from foreign countries and supplies goods for export to them. But for every republic, inter-republic trade is overwhelmingly dominant. These are economic facts of life—facets of the legacy of the past with which both the central government and each republic must conjure as they move to create a market economy and shape new political relationships.

The republics now exchange their products and resources (capital and labor) more within a large internal market. But trade and resource flows have been the result of central diktat. The present patterns reflect that diktat and not that of the free choices of consumers and producers. The basic problem is how to preserve the economic advantages of a large unfettered internal market while redirecting trade and resource flows in response to market forces. A related problem is how to maximize the contribution of foreign trade and foreign direct investment in this process.

Nobody knows what form the future relations among the republics in the present Soviet Union will take. One can envisage three outcomes of the present ferment: (1) a voluntary federation of all or most republics with a decentralized economy, but with a central government having sufficient power at least to regulate the macroeconomy and manage defense and foreign policy; (2) a confederation of sovereign republics with a largely symbolic central body; and (3) fully independent, nonaffiliated states. Given the shared economic inheritance of the past, the republics (or new states) will need each others' markets sorely for a long time, while they try to overcome that inheritance and to orient their economies more toward international markets.

While there are many related issues, we focus on the measures that are essential or at least advisable in order to optimize inter-republican trade flows and promote international trade.

SCENARIO 1: A RENEWED FEDERATION

The federation would be shaped by a new union treaty and Constitution. Under this scenario, the federal government must be a democratically elected government of trust with functions given to it by consensus. These probably should include:

1. overseeing the prosperity of a nationwide communications and transportation infrastructure. A modernized communications system should be of highest priority and Western assistance sought. Means of mass communication should be privatized, with federal government licensing of individual facilities;
2. management of agreed upon national and social programs;
3. the conduct of monetary policy and promotion of rapid convertibility of the ruble. The objective should be to curtail the rate of inflation and promote economic growth. A strong central bank would be required;
4. maintenance of an independent budget and sources of tax revenue with the need to achieve a balanced budget; and
5. establishment of a credible Western statistical system.

To foster and optimize internal and external trade within such a federation, the federal government should:

1. remove price controls quickly so that trade and other decisions can reflect supply and demand. Liberalization of foreign trade should be done concurrently with the introduction of a uniform system of tariffs and customs. The government might wish to adopt the GATT (General Agreement on Tariffs and Trade) rules for trade;
2. abolish the system of mandatory state orders;
3. remove all of the present union enterprises from central control. They should be transformed into independent corporations with freedom to make trade and other decisions on their own;
4. adopt foreign investment laws that conform to international standards; and
5. adopt legislation to create free trade and free movement of capital and labor within the federation.

The republican governments should:

1. have their own budgets and taxing authority and should operate within a balanced-budget regime;
2. abolish the system of mandatory republican state orders;
3. vigorously push forward the process of privatization, so that firms will have the powerful incentives of ownership;
4. adopt legislation allowing individuals or groups to form new firms so as to foster competition; especially needed are those that can provide information and trade-facilitating services; and
5. to promote foreign trade and investment, the republics might:
   a. provide incentives to attract foreign investors, including joint ventures; and
   b. conduct a vigorous export-promotion policy via providing information.

SCENARIO 2: CONFEDERATION

In this scenario, the individual member republics will have to take upon themselves the functions suggested for delegation to the fed-

eral government under Scenario 1. The difficult task of redistribut-
ing the present property and personnel among republics will have
to be carried out. The confederation members would delegate
agreed-upon functions to a central body and establish a formula for
sharing its cost. To promote trade flows, given the existing inter-
republic and international ties, the members should capitalize on
what now exists—an internal common market and a common external tariff.

1. To speed up and facilitate their integration into the world
   market, the confederation would be well advised to adopt the
   legal codes of the European Common Market and the international trading rules of GATT.
2. Each member will have its own currency. Members should
   move quickly to make their currencies convertible.
3. There should be no internal tariffs.
4. Members will need to move quickly to base their economies
   and trade flows on decisions made by fully autonomous business
   firms in response to market signals (prices).
5. Within this general framework, members might pursue
   trade-facilitating policies such as those suggested for the republics under Scenario 1.

TRANSITION STRATEGY FOR REPUBLICS
NOT WISHING TO JOIN A RENEWED FEDERATION

1. The new federal government should immediately enter into
   state-to-state negotiations with each such republic to effect an
   orderly separation. Myriad complex matters would need to be
   settled.
2. It is in the strong interest of both federation members and the
   republic nonmembers that the process of separation should proceed speedily and amicably, so that each party can become a
   functioning member of the international community of nations.

13

Working Group 3: The Emerging Legal Environment

Peter J. Pettibone
Nicola Bradley, Assistant

Both the Soviet Union and most if not all of the republics have publicly announced that they wish to move from the administrative-command economy to a market economy. The working group examined the legal prerequisites for a market economy and the legal issues of transition to a market economy.

The working group agreed that a fundamental premise of a market economy is the private right to own and dispose of property. For the optimum operation of a market economy, the law should allow full private ownership of all forms of property, including land. Realizing, however, the political controversy connected with private land ownership in the Soviet Union, the working group believes that long-term land leases under an appropriate legal regime could provide a workable basis for a market economy, even without private ownership of land. Such a legal regime must include the right freely to sell and mortgage all types of property, including land leases.

Rights of owners and secured lenders must be protected by a system of public registration of titles, mortgages, and security interests. In the case of immovables (land and things attached to land), the place of registration may be local, but in the case of moveables (for example, ships and aircraft) and intangibles (for example, patents and copyrights), the registry should be centrally located.

Privatization is the process of moving to a market economy. It must begin with a public, political commitment to providing a suitable legal environment. Much of this legislation is in place or is in the process of enactment. Already adopted are constitutional amendments and laws equalizing the different forms of ownership; an enterprise law; some company and small-business legislation; legislation on stocks, bonds and exchanges; and laws on entrepreneurship. The Soviet Union and the republics have enacted new tax legislation; however, conflicts, instability, and, in some cases, excessive tax rates make this legislation inhospitable to a market economy. New USSR banking and foreign currency legislation clarifies many issues, but it is suitable only for the preliminary stages of privatization, because it envisions heavy centralized control of financial transactions. USSR and republic legislation has, for the first time, recognized trade secrets, and draft legislation would substantially strengthen patent and copyright protection so as to provide a package of intellectual-property protection suitable for a market economy. Drafts of privatization legislation have appeared at both the USSR and republic levels. Below we explain refinements that we believe are necessary in this privatization legislation, as well as other areas in which further legislation is needed.

The "war of laws" threatens to undo this encouraging progress. At present, all levels of government assert and attempt to exercise conflicting legislation and authority. There are no clear legal rules or mechanisms for resolving these conflicts. The resulting environment prevents business planning by prospective investors, foreign and local. The working group takes no position on the appropriate distribution of powers between different levels of government, but we believe that it is urgent that those concerned resolve their differences, harmonize their legislation, and create an effective mechanism for handling future conflicts. On the other hand, differences in laws from republic to republic may actually facilitate the operation of a market economy. Experience in federal systems with market economies demonstrates that member states will compete to establish a favorable environment for business by adopting appropriate legislation and regulations.

In addition to the substantive legal prerequisites for privatization, there are two important procedural prerequisites. First, the participants in the market must be subject only to published laws and regulations. Second, there must be a fair and effective system for protection of the participants' rights, not only as against one another, but also as against government regulatory agencies.

Despite the lack of the complete package of market legislation, the current legal situation represents significant progress toward a market economy and is already permitting encouraging beginnings of privatization and attracting some foreign investment. The working group believes that in order for the privatization process to become widespread, it is necessary that additional legislation be enacted, including laws on title registration, mortgages, securities, and secured transactions. There should be bankruptcy legislation, including a law at the countrywide level, containing mechanisms for dealing with bankruptcies involving debtors and creditors in different republics.

The working group distinguished five forms of industries, four of which should be privatized. These four are: (1) farms and small businesses; (2) industries where there are multiple enterprises that provide the possibility for competition; (3) industries where state planning has created an artificial monopoly; and (4) industries with a natural monopoly. The fifth category is that of strategic industries, such as nuclear weapons plants, which should remain under state ownership.

Privatization of small business should be conducted rapidly and in an open or transparent manner, such as by public auctions. Valuation of small businesses is unnecessary because potential buyers can easily evaluate these businesses themselves so that auction prices would reflect market values. In some cases, it may be politically appropriate to provide employees of small businesses with the preferential right to purchase them. Because small businesses will not have monopoly power, they should be freed immediately from price regulation.

The second category is that where the existence of multiple enterprises makes rapid transfer to competition possible. Here we recommend that the government try a number of pilot projects, picking areas where successful privatization seems likely. On the basis of these pilot projects, the government should move rapidly to develop one or several privatization mechanisms. Once a number of competing privatized businesses exist in an industry, that industry should be freed from price regulation.

The third category is that of monopolies created by state plan ning. Here, demonopolization should accompany or precede privatization. Otherwise, experience shows that the privatized monopolies will remain inefficient and exploitative. While we realize that the demonopolization process will be difficult, the working group thinks it is better to face these difficulties than to continue a scheme of government ownership or regulation.

The fourth group is natural monopolies. Experience with deregulation in other countries and recent changes in technology leads to the conclusion that the sphere of natural monopolies is more restricted than had been thought. For instance, neither airline transportation nor telecommunications is now considered to be a natural monopoly. Thus, the first step is to remove from the natural monopoly category those areas of the economy that are not, in fact, natural monopolies. The remaining natural monopoly areas should be privatized and converted into regulated monopolies. However, creation of appropriate regulatory systems should precede privatization.

The category of strategic industries, like that of natural monopolies, should be severely limited. For instance, if a factory produces missiles and passenger airplanes, the passenger airplane portion of its business should be privatized.

Privatization does not ensure the permanence of a competitive economy. It is important that the government take an active role through antitrust enforcement in preventing privatized industry from establishing or reestablishing monopolies or engaging in anti-competitive practices.

The road to a market economy will not be an easy one. Public understanding and participation will be essential, particularly under current conditions of greater democratization. Successful marketization will enable the domestic economy to realize its potential and attract foreign investment.

Index

Abalkin, Leonid, 43
Accounting firms, need for, 84, 92
Agricultural enterprises, communal
  property and, 143
Agriculture
  Baltics and, 220, 228
  effects of radical reform on, 44
  Finland and, 187
  Lithuania and, 226
  local governments and, 144
  suggestions for reforms in, 48
Agroprombank, 124
Airlines, privatization of
  in Hungary, 82
  in Philippines, 85
Akayev, A., 138
Albania, 75
Alcoholic beverages
  generating hard-currency revenues
    with, 188
  inter-republic import/export data
    for, 25–26
  laws restricting production of, 126
  regaining revenues from, 42
Allocations of land. *See* Land
Allocations of revenues. *See* Revenues
All-union
  jurisdiction, 102
    land allocation and, 147
  law, 133
  market, 20, 33, 37, 51
  monetary system, 48

trade associations, local
  government and, 144
Amendments, March 14, USSR
  Constitution and, 140
Aquino, Corazon, 85
Armenia, 32, 51, 102, 130, 136, 224,
  230
  inter-republic trade, import/export
    data for, 21–24
  consumer goods, 25–26
  energy and raw materials, 27–30
  local vs. republic authority in, 142
  trade data for, 53
Arms manufacture
  laws forbidding, 126
  privatization of, 82
Asia, Central. *See* Central Asia
Attorneys, need for, 92
Auctions
  acquisition of state-owned property
    through, 115
  foreign exchange, 69
  procedures for, 116, 117
Austria, 209, 226
  East-West trade and, 173–203
    mechanisms for, 181–84
    role of government in, 180–81
  economic profile of, 179
  export/import data for, Soviet
    Union and, 177–80
  geopolitical background of, 176–77
  neutrality of, 210

255

About the Contributors

JOSEF C. BRADA is Professor of Economics, Arizona State University.

KAJ HOBÉR is Partner, White & Case, Stockholm.

JEREMY INGPEN is Vice President, Geonomics Institute, Middlebury, Vt.

ROBERT L. KRATTLI is President, Scott-European Corporation, Montpelier, Vt.

ALI M. KUTAN is Assistant Professor of Economics, Southern Illinois University–Edwardsville.

ROGER S. LEEDS is Executive Director, International Privatization Group, Washington, D.C.

PETER B. MAGGS is Professor of Law, University of Illinois.

PETER J. PETTIBONE is Partner, Lord Day & Lord, Barrett Smith.

VLADIMIR POPOV is Senior Fellow in Residence, Geonomics Institute; and Senior Fellow, Institute for the Study of the USA and Canada, Moscow.

JENIK RADON is Partner, Radon & Ishizumi, New York.

GERTRUDE E. SCHROEDER is Professor of Economics, University of Virginia.

EMILY SILLIMAN is Consultant on Soviet Law and Trade, Mountain View, Ca.

EUGENE ULJANOV is Executive Vice President, Vnesheconombank, New York.

NORBERT WALTER is Chief Economist, Deutsche Bank AG, Frankfurt.

About the Editors

MICHAEL P. CLAUDON is President and Managing Director of the Geonomics Institute and Professor of Economics at Middlebury College, Middlebury, Vermont. He has published numerous articles and books and is co-editor of three other volumes in, and serves as Series Editor for, the Geonomics Institute for International Economic Advancement Series. Claudon is a frequent commentator on topics concerning the emerging economies of the Soviet Union and Eastern Europe.

TAMAR L. GUTNER is Research Director at the Geonomics Institute. Previously, as a financial reporter for A.P.–Dow Jones and as a freelance writer, she wrote extensively on issues of economic reform in Eastern Europe and on international trade, finance, and markets. She is the author of *The Story of SAIS*, a history of the Johns Hopkins University School of Advanced International Studies, where she obtained her M.A. in International Relations.

List of Seminar Participants

Donna Bahry
Professor of Political Science
University of California–Davis

Stuart Bensley
Manager of Corporate Business
    Development
Brown & Root, Inc.

Josef C. Brada
Professor of Economics
Arizona State University

Charles Brophy
Senior Consultant
Hill and Knowlton, Inc.;
Trustee
Geonomics Institute

Andris Bunka
Assistant to the Prime Minister
Latvia

Susan E. Burns
Economist
U.S. Government

Michael P. Claudon
President and Managing Director
Geonomics Institute

Galen Cobb
Director–Energy Services Group
Halliburton Logging Services, Inc.

Joseph Condon
Senior Vice President
Asea Brown Boveri

Arthur Macy Cox
Secretary
American Committee on U.S.–
    Soviet Relations

Steven R. Cunningham
Professor of Economics
University of Connecticut

Daris G. Delins
Chief Economist
County NatWest Australia Ltd.

Barbara Rudolph Drake
Associate Director
International Trade Associates

Ivars Godmanis
Prime Minister
Latvia

Tamar L. Gutner
Research Director
Geonomics Institute

Amory Hall
Vice President
Hill and Knowlton, Inc.

Robert L. Happeny
General Director
International Trade Associates

Kaj Hobér
Partner
White & Case, Stockholm

Paul Hoffman
Partner
Arthur Andersen & Company

Jeremy Ingpen
Vice President
Geonomics Institute

Willard T. Jackson
Trustee
Geonomics Institute

B. S. Jaffray
Chairman
Sheffield Group, Ltd.

Robert A. Jones
Chairman of the Board
Geonomics Institute;
Chairman Emeritus
MMS International, Inc.

Arvi Jürviste
Counsellor
Estonian Ministry of Foreign
    Affairs

Ojars Kalnins
Public Affairs Liaison
Legation of Latvia

Robert L. Krattli
President
Scott-European Corporation

Andres Kurrik
Vice President
AM-RE Managers, Inc.

Aristids Lambergs
President
World Federation of Free Latvians
    Task Force on Economics

Marju Lauristin
Deputy Speaker
Estonian Parliament

Roger S. Leeds
Executive Director
International Privatization Group

Timothy Light
President
Middlebury College

Peter B. Maggs
Professor of Law
University of Illinois

Girt Mergins
Manager–Eastern Europe
Babson Brothers Company

Thomas Palm
Professor of Economics
Portland State University, Oregon

Scott Pardee
Chairman
Yamaichi International (America),
    Inc.

Peter J. Pettibone
Partner
Lord Day & Lord, Barrett Smith

Vladimir Popov
Senior Fellow in Residence
Geonomics Institute;
Senior Fellow
Institute for the Study of the USA
  and Canada, Moscow

Jenik Radon
Partner
Radon & Ishizumi

Stephan-Götz Richter
President
TransAtlantic Futures, Inc.

Donald A. Roach
Retired President and Chief
  Executive Officer
Brown & Sharpe Manufacturing
  Company;
Active Chairman
Brown & Sharpe-Precizika,
  Lithuania

Lance Roulic
Business Analyst
Polaroid Corporation

Leonard Santow
Managing Director
Griggs & Santow, Inc.;
Trustee
Geonomics Institute

Edgar Savisaar
Prime Minister
Estonia

Gertrude E. Schroeder
Professor of Economics
University of Virginia

Desmond Shaw
Senior Manager
Price Waterhouse

Emily Silliman
Consultant on Soviet Law and
  Trade

Chris Speirs
Trader
E. D. & F. Man (Sugar) Ltd.,
  London

Gail Stevenson
Adjunct Professor
The American University

Michael P. Tavis
Director–USSR and Eastern
  European Policy
Joseph E. Seagram & Sons, Inc.

Erik Terk
Deputy Minister for Economic
  Affairs
Estonia

W. Paul Tippett
Former Chairman and Chief
  Executive Officer
American Motors Corporation;
Ann Arbor Partners;
Trustee
Geonomics Institute

Eugene Uljanov
Executive Vice President
Vnesheconombank, New York

Norbert Walter
Chief Economist
Deutsche Bank AG, Frankfurt